Goa
with Mumbai

Victoria McCulloch & David Stott

Credits

Footprint credits

Managing Editor: Felicity Laughton
Production and layout: Emma Bryers
Maps and cover: Kevin Feeney

Publisher: Patrick Dawson
Advertising: Elizabeth Taylor
Sales and marketing: Kirsty Holmes

Photography credits
Front cover: Dreamstime.com/Styf22
Back cover: Shutterstock/Anatoli Styf

Printed in Great Britain by Alphaset,
Surbiton, Surrey

Every effort has been made to ensure that
the facts in this guidebook are accurate.
However, travellers should still obtain advice
from consulates, airlines, etc, about travel
and visa requirements before travelling.
The authors and publishers cannot accept
responsibility for any loss, injury or
inconvenience however caused.

The content of Footprint *Focus Goa
with Mumbai* has been taken directly
from Footprint's *India Handbook*,
which was researched and written
by David Stott, Vanessa Betts and
Victoria McCulloch.

Publishing information
Footprint *Focus Goa with Mumbai*
2nd edition
© Footprint Handbooks Ltd
November 2013

ISBN: 978 1 909268 42 5
CIP DATA: A catalogue record for this book
is available from the British Library

® Footprint Handbooks and the Footprint
mark are a registered trademark of
Footprint Handbooks Ltd

Published by Footprint
6 Riverside Court
Lower Bristol Road
Bath BA2 3DZ, UK
T +44 (0)1225 469141
F +44 (0)1225 469461
footprinttravelguides.com

Distributed in the USA by Globe Pequot
Press, Guilford, Connecticut

Contents

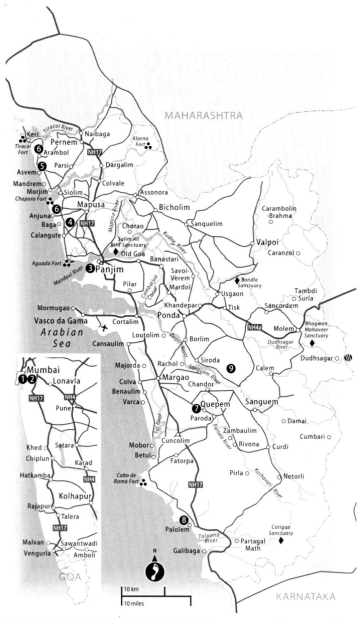

MAHARASHTRA

Tiracol River
Keri
Pernem
Tiracol
Fort
Arambol
Asvem
Mandrem
Morjim
Chapora Fort
Anjuna
Baga
Calangute
Aguada Fort
Naibaga
Alorna
Fort
Parsi
Dargalim
Colvale
Assonora
Siolim
Mapusa
Chorao
Salim Ali
Bird Sanctuary
Old Goa
Banastari
Pilar
Cambarjua
Canal
Savoi-
Verem
Mardol
Khandepar
Bicholim
Sanquelim
Carambolin
-Brahma
Valpoi
Caranzol
Bondla
Sanctuary
Usgaon
Tisk
Tambdi
Surla
Sancordem
Molem
Bhagwan
Mahaveer
Sanctuary
Dudhsagar
River
Dudhsagar

Panjim
Mormugao
Vasco da Gama
Arabian
Sea
Cortalim
Cansaulim
Loutolim
Ponda
Borlim
Zuari River
Calem

NH4a

Mumbai
Lonavla
NH17   NH4
Pune
Khed
Satara
Chiplun
Karad
Hatkamba
NH4
Rajapur
Kolhapur
Talera
NH17
Malvan
Vengurla
Sawantwadi
Amboli
GOA

Majorda
Colva
Benaulim
Varca
Mobor
Betul
Cabo de
Rama Fort
Rachol
Margao
Chandor
Quepem
Paroda
Cuncolim
Fatorpa
NH17
Siroda
Sanguem River
Sanguem
Zambaulim
Rivona
Curdi
Pirla
Damai
Cumbari
Netorli
Kushavati River
Paroda River

Palolem
Galibaga
Talpona River
Partagal
Math
Cotigao
Sanctuary

Arabian
Sea

KARNATAKA

N

10 km
10 miles

4 • Goa with Mumbai

Mumbai is the gateway city to southern India and Goa. Once upon a time you would have arrived through the Gateway to India from the Arabian Sea; now it's a drive from the airport that shows you the sights and sounds of a thriving energetic city with the odd traffic jam. Or you might be welcomed by the beautiful Gothic train terminal and the many beautiful museums, art galleries, hotels and restaurants. Away from this hub you will find the elegant sweep of Marine Drive leading to the atmospheric Chowpatty Beach – great for an evening stroll.

Goa, India's smallest state, was embraced by the travellers of the late 1960s and 1970s and became a haven for alternative living. Although it is still renowned for its trance parties and hedonism, it also offers much more.

Head north to the beaches of Anjuna and Arambol for yoga, meditation and a whole smorgasbord of complementary therapies, as well as a thriving live music scene. Central Goa, around Baga and Calangute and further south around Colva and Majorda, appeals more to the package tourists, but there are some great restaurants and sparkly shops. Southern Goa has more beautiful beaches, particularly Agonda and the busy strip of Palolem and Patnem. Benaulim too has an alternative arty scene.

Inland Goa is often overlooked but, just a short drive from the beach resorts, there are cashew and spice plantations, rolling hills, beautiful waterfalls and interesting wildlife; it's a little like walking back in time when you happen upon and the fading Portuguese-style mansions in villages such as Loutolim and Quepem.

So if it's beach life and sundowners, meditation and navel-gazing, or paragliding and kitesurfing, Goa has it all. There is a laid-back beauty that is inviting and intoxicating. And we didn't discover it. The Goans have had a word for it all along – *susegad* – a relaxed attitude and enjoyment of life to the fullest.

Planning your trip

Best time to visit Goa and Mumbai

Goa and Mumbai are always warm, but their coastal position means it never becomes unbearably hot. Nonetheless, from mid-April until the beginning of the monsoon in mid-June, both the temperature and humidity rise sharply, making for steamy hot days and balmy nights. The six weeks of the monsoon in June/July often come as torrential storms, while the warm dry weather of its tropical winter (October-March) is the best time to visit (although weather patterns have been fluctuating in recent years).

Getting to Goa and Mumbai

Air

India is accessible by air from virtually every continent. Most international flights arrive in Delhi, Mumbai, Chennai, Bangalore or Kolkata but Qatar Airways (and many charter flights) fly direct into Goa from Doha, which is making them very popular. Qatar Airways then have connections from Doha all over the globe. If you do fly into Mumbai then it is just a short one-hour flight to Dabolim airport in Goa.

From Europe Despite the increases to Air Passenger Duty, Britain remains the cheapest place in Europe for flights to India. **Virgin Atlantic** and **British Airways** fly from London to Delhi in 8½ hours or Mumbai in 9½ hours. From mainland Europe, **Jet Airways** flies to India from Brussels and Milan, while major European flag carriers including **KLM** and **Lufthansa** fly to Delhi and/or Mumbai from their respective hub airports. In most cases the cheapest flights are with Middle Eastern or Central Asian airlines, transiting via airports in the Gulf. Several airlines from the Middle East (eg **Emirates, Gulf Air, Kuwait Airways, Royal Jordanian, Qatar Airways, Oman Air**) offer good discounts to Mumbai and other Indian regional capitals from London, but fly via their hub cities, adding to the journey time. Consolidators in the UK such as **Flightbookers** ① *T0871-223 5000, www.ebookers.com*, **North South Travel** ① *T01245-608291, www.northsouthtravel.co.uk (profits to charity)*, and the very popular **Southall Travel** ① *T0844-855 8001, www.southalltravel.co.uk*, can quote some competitive prices.

   In 2013 the cheapest return flights to Mumbai from London started at around £450, but leapt to £900+ as you approached the high season of Christmas, New Year and Easter. Flights from London through Doha to Goa with Qatar Airways are around £750, but then you do not need to book any domestic flights or trains.

From North America From the east coast, several airlines including **Air India, Jet Airways, Continental** and **Delta** fly direct from New York to Delhi and Mumbai. **American** flies to both cities from Chicago. Discounted tickets on **British Airways, KLM, Lufthansa, Gulf Air** and **Kuwait Airways** are sold through agents although they will invariably fly via their country's capital cities. From the west coast, **Air India** flies from Los Angeles to Delhi and Mumbai, and **Jet Airways** from San Francisco to Mumbai via Shanghai. Alternatively, fly via Hong Kong, Singapore or Bangkok using one of those countries' national carriers. **Air Canada** operates between Vancouver and Delhi. **Air Brokers International** ① *www.*

Don't miss...

1 Haggling for all you're worth in Crawford Market and the Chor Bazar, page 36.
2 A sunset stroll along Marine Drive to Chowpatty Beach, page 37.
3 Panjim's Latin quarters, Fontainhas and San Thome, page 56.
4 All the fun of the fair at the Saturday Night Market, Arpora, page 75.
5 A walk along the beach from Arambol towards Morjim, page 77.
6 Perfecting your downward dog pose in Anjuna or Arambol, pages 96 and 97.
7 An Indo-Portuguese lunch at Palacio do Deao, Quepem, page 105.
8 A dolphin-watching or fishing trip from Palolem, page 108.
9 A motorbike trip into inland Goa, page 123.

Numbers relate to the map on page 4.

airbrokers.com, is competitive and reputable. **STA** ⓘ *www.statravel.co.uk*, has offices in many US cities, Toronto and Ontario. Student fares are also available from **Travel Cuts** ⓘ *www.travelcuts.com*, in Canada.

From Australasia Qantas, Singapore Airlines, Thai Airways, Malaysian Airlines, Cathay Pacific and Air India are the principal airlines connecting the continents, although Qantas is the only one that flies direct, with services from Sydney to Mumbai. **Tiger Airways** run a no-frills service from Darwin to Kochi via Singapore, and **AirAsia X** operates from Melbourne and the Gold Coast to several South Indian cities via Kuala Lumpur; these flights can be much cheaper than standard airlines, at the cost of extended layovers and the usual extra charges for checked luggage, food, etc. **STA** and **Flight Centre** offer discounted tickets from their branches in major cities in Australia and New Zealand. **Abercrombie & Kent** ⓘ *www.abercrombiekent.co.uk*, **Adventure World** ⓘ *www.adventure world.net.au*, **Peregrine** ⓘ *www.peregrineadventures.com*, and **Travel Corporation of India** ⓘ *www.tcindia.com*, organize tours.

Airport information The formalities on arrival in India have been increasingly streamlined during the last few years and the facilities at the major international airports greatly improved. However, arrival can still be a slow process and you may well find that there are delays of over an hour at immigration.

Mumbai's **Chhatrapati Shivaji International Airport** has had a recent facelift and is a large airport 30 km north of the city. **Dabolim Airport**, on the other hand, is small and old fashioned, although a shiny new terminal is sceduled to open in December 2013 (delays expected). There are no convenient public transport connections, so you have to rely on the pre-paid taxi booth to ferry you to your destination.

Departure tax Rs 500 is payable for all international departures other than those to neighbouring SAARC countries, when the tax is Rs 250. This is normally included in your international ticket; check when buying.

Transport in Goa and Mumbai

Air

India has a comprehensive network linking the major cities of the different states. Deregulation of the airline industry has had a transformative effect on travel within India, with a host of low-budget private carriers offering sometimes unbelievably cheap fares on an ever-expanding network of routes in a bid to woo the train-travelling middle class. Promotional fares as low as Rs 9 (US$0.20) are not unknown, though such numbers are rendered somewhat meaningless by additional taxes and fuel charges – an extra US$30-50 on most flights. On any given day, booking a few days in advance, you can expect to fly between Delhi and Mumbai for around US$100 one way including taxes, while a month's notice and flying with a no-frills airline can reduce the price to US$70-80. Typical fares for the Mumbai to Goa route are Rs 2000 (US$40).

Although flying is comparatively expensive, for covering vast distances or awkward links on a route it is an option worth considering, though delays and re-routing can be irritating.

The best way to get an idea of the current routes, carriers and fares is to use a third-party booking website such as **www.cheapairticketsindia.com** (toll-free numbers: UK T0800-101 0928, USA T1-888 825 8680), **www.cleartrip.com**, **www.makemytrip.co.in**, or **www.travelocity.com**. All accept international credit cards, while some of the other travel websites might not. Tickets booked on these sites are typically issued as an e-ticket which will need to be printed out. These services will also often send an SMS text if you have an an Indian mobile phone. You have to show your ticket to enter the terminal building at the airport.

Rail

If you don't want to take a connecting flight down to Goa, the Konkan railway makes a pretty, and increasingly speedy, alternative.

Trains can still be the cheapest and most comfortable means of travelling long distances saving you hotel expenses on overnight journeys. It gives access to booking station Retiring Rooms, which can be useful from time to time. Above all, you have an ideal opportunity to meet local travellers and catch a glimpse of life on the ground. Remember the dark glass on air-conditioned coaches does restrict vision. See also www.indianrail.gov.in. To investigate trains, timings and fares one of the best sites is www.cleartrip.com (on the government site you need to know the train number, whereas on Cleartrip you can just put starting city and destination).

High-speed trains There are several air-conditioned 'high-speed' **Shatabdi** (or 'Century') **Express** for day travel, and **Rajdhani Express** ('Capital City') for overnight journeys. These cover large sections of the network but due to high demand you need to book them well in advance (up to 90 days). Meals and drinks are usually included. For Mumbai to Goa, one of the best trains is the Konkan Kanya Express 10111 which is a night train so leaves Mumbai CST 2305 and arrives in Pernem (north Goa) 0852 and Madgaon (south Goa) 0700. For a day train take Mandovi Express 10103 0655 arriving 1845. You can expect to pay Rs 2000 for first-class sleeper, Rs 1200 for two-tier a/c, Rs 900 for three-tier a/c and Rs 330 for sleeper class. Fares are based on distance. Delhi trains only go into Madgaon and leave from Nizamuddin station. From Delhi to Goa, Mngla Lksdp Express 12618 goes every day leaving Nizamuddin station 0920 arriving Madgaon 1935 the following day (33 hours). Expect to pay Rs 2600 for two-tier a/c, Rs 1700 for three-tier a/c and Rs 700 for sleeper class. Check the transport section for more train info.

Royal trains You can travel like a maharaja on the **Deccan Odyssey** ① *www.indiarail.co.uk/do.htm*, a train running in Maharashtra, and the **Golden Chariot** ① *www.indiarail.co.uk/gt.htm*, a relatively new option running in Karnataka covering Belur, Halebid, Shravanabelagola and then Hampi and Badami/Aihole/Pattadakal, which make a nice side trip from Goa.

Classes **A/c First Class**, available only on main routes, is very comfortable (bedding provided). It will also be possible for tourists to reserve special coaches (some air conditioning) which are normally allocated to senior railway officials only. **A/c Sleeper**, two- and three-tier configurations (known as 2AC and 3AC) are clean and comfortable and popular with middle-class families; these are the safest carriages for women travelling alone. **A/c Executive Class**, with wide reclining seats, is available on many Shatabdi trains at double the price of the ordinary **a/c Chair Car** which is equally comfortable. **First Class (non-a/c)** is gradually being phased out, and is now restricted to a handful of routes in the south, but the run-down old carriages still provide a pleasant experience if you like open windows. **Second Class (non-a/c)** two- and three-tier (commonly called **Sleeper**), provides exceptionally cheap and atmospheric travel, with basic padded vinyl seats and open windows that allow the sights and sounds of India (not to mention dust, insects and flecks of spittle expelled by passengers up front) to drift into the carriage. On long journeys Sleeper can be crowded and uncomfortable, and toilet facilities can be unpleasant; it is nearly always better to use the Indian-style squat loos rather than the Western-style ones as they are better maintained. At the bottom rung is **Unreserved Second Class**, with hard wooden benches. You can travel long distances for a trivial amount of money, but unreserved carriages are often ridiculously crowded, and getting off at your station may involve a battle of will and strength against the hordes trying to shove their way on.

Indrail passes These allow travel across the network without having to pay extra reservation fees and sleeper charges but you have to spend a high proportion of your time on the train to make it worthwhile. However, the advantages of pre-arranged reservations and automatic access to 'Tourist Quotas' can tip the balance in favour of the pass for some travellers.

Tourists (foreigners and Indians resident abroad) may buy these passes from the tourist sections of principal railway booking offices and pay in foreign currency, major credit cards, traveller's cheques or rupees with encashment certificates. Fares range from US$57 to US$1060 for adults or half that for children. Rail-cum-air tickets are also to be made available.

Indrail passes can also conveniently be bought abroad from special agents. For people contemplating a single long journey soon after arriving in India, the Half- or One-day Pass with a confirmed reservation is worth the peace of mind; two- or four-day passes are also sold. The UK agent is **SDEL** ① *103 Wembley Park Dr, Wembley, Middlesex HA9 8HG, UK, T020-8903 3411, www.indiarail.co.uk*. They make all necessary reservations and offer excellent advice. They can also book **Indian Airlines** and **Jet Airways** internal flights.

A **White Pass** allows first-class air-conditioned travel (the top rung); a **Green**, a/c two-tier Sleepers and Chair Cars; and the **Yellow**, only second-class travel. Passes for up to four days' duration are only sold abroad.

Cost A/c First Class costs about double the rate for two-tier shown below, and non-a/c Second Class about half. Children (aged five to 12) travel at half the adult fare. The young (12-30 years) and senior citizens (65 years and over) are allowed a 30% discount on journeys over 500 km (just show your passport).

Period	US$ A/c 2-tier	Period	US$ A/c 2-tier
½ day	26	21 days	198
1 day	43	30 days	248
7 days	135	60 days	400
15 days	185	90 days	530

Fares for individual journeys are based on distance covered and reflect both the class and the type of train. Higher rates apply on the Mail and Express trains and the air-conditioned Shatabdi and Rajdhani Expresses.

Internet services Much information is available online at www.railtourismindia.com, www.indianrail.gov.in and www.trainenquiry.com, where you can check timetables (which change frequently), numbers, seat availability and even the running status of your train. E-tickets can be bought and printed at www.irctc.in, although the credit card process can be complicated, and at time of writing does not accept credit cards issued outside India. The best option is to use a third-party agent, such as www.makemytrip.com or www.cleartrip.com. An alternative is to seek a local agent who can sell e-tickets, and can save hours of hassle; simply present the printout to the ticket collector.

   Note All train numbers now have five digits; in most cases, adding a '1' to the start of an old four-figure number will produce the new number. Otherwise, try your luck with the 'train number enquiry' search at www.indianrail.gov.in/inet_trnno_enq.html.

Tickets and reservations It is now possible to reserve tickets for virtually any train on the network from one of the 1000 computerized reservation centres across India. It is always best to book as far in advance as possible (usually up to 60 days). To reserve a seat on a particular train, note down the train's name, number and departure time and fill in a reservation form while you line up at the ticket window; you can use one form for up to four passengers. At busy stations the wait can take an hour or more. You can save a lot of time and effort by asking a travel agent to get your tickets for a fee of Rs 50-100. If the class you want is full, ask if special 'quotas' are available (see above). If not, consider buying a 'wait list' ticket, as seats often become available close to the train's departure time; phone the station on the day of departure to check your ticket's status. If you don't have a reservation for a particular train but carry an Indrail Pass, you may get one by arriving three hours early. Be wary of touts at the station offering tickets, hotels or exchange.

Timetables Regional timetables are available cheaply from station bookstalls; the monthly *Indian Bradshaw* is sold in principal stations. The handy *Trains at a Glance* (Rs 30) lists popular trains likely to be used by most foreign travellers and is available at stalls at Indian railway stations and in the UK from SDEL (see page 9).

Road

For the uninitiated, travel by road can be a worrying experience because of the apparent absence of conventional traffic regulations. Vehicles drive on the left – in theory. Routes around the major cities are usually crowded with lorry traffic, especially at night, and the main roads are often poor and slow. There are a few motorway-style expressways in India, but in Goa most main roads are single track.

Bus Buses now reach virtually every part of India, offering a cheap, if often uncomfortable, means of visiting places off the rail network. Very few villages are now more than 2-3 km from a bus stop. Services are run by the State Corporation from the State Bus Stand (and private companies, which often have offices nearby). The private companies allow advance reservations, including e-tickets (check www.redbus.in and www.viaworld.in) and, although tickets prices are a little higher, the buses make fewer stops and are a bit more comfortable. There are many 'sleeper' buses running Mumbai–Goa, Bengaluru–Goa and Goa–Hampi. Naturally there are buses running Mumbai–Ahmedabad, Mumbai–Aurangabad and to many other destinations. If you take a sleeper bus, choose a lower berth near the front of the bus. The upper berths are almost always really uncomfortable.

Bus categories Though comfortable for sightseeing trips, apart from the very best 'sleeper coaches' even **air-conditioned luxury coaches** can be very uncomfortable for really long journeys. Often the air conditioning is very cold so wrap up. Journeys over 10 hours can be extremely tiring so it is better to go by train if there is a choice. **Express buses** run over long distances (frequently overnight), and are often called 'video coaches'. They can be an appalling experience unless you appreciate loud film music blasting through the night. Ear plugs and eye masks may ease the pain. They rarely average more than 45 kph. **Local buses** are often very crowded, quite bumpy, slow and usually poorly maintained. However, over short distances, they can be a very cheap, friendly and easy way of getting about and are easy in Goa as the distances are so short.

Bus travel tips Book in advance where possible for sleeper buses and avoid the back of the bus where it can be very bumpy. If your destination is only served by a local bus you may do better to take the Express bus and 'persuade' the driver, with a tip in advance, to stop where you want to get off. You will have to pay the full fare to the first stop beyond your destination but you will get there faster and more comfortably. When an unreserved bus pulls into a bus station, there is usually an unholy scramble for seats, whilst those arriving have to struggle to get off! In many areas there is an unwritten 'rule of reservation' using handkerchiefs or bags thrust through the windows to reserve seats. Some visitors may feel a more justified right to a seat having fought their way through the crowd, but it is generally best to do as local people do and be prepared with a handkerchief or 'sarong'. As soon as it touches the seat, it is yours. The main Kadamba bus stations in Goa are in Mapusa, Panjim and Margao.

Car A car provides a chance to travel off the beaten track, and gives unrivalled opportunities for seeing something of India's great variety of villages and small towns. If your trip is just within Goa it is unlikely you would ever need to get a car and driver, but it is easy to get taxis for short journeys – even one end of Goa to the other is really only 3½ hours by car. In Mumbai, expect heavy traffic and frequent jams. For a similar price, Maruti cars and vans (Omni) are much more reliable and are now the preferred choice in many areas. Maruti Esteems and Toyota Qualis are comfortable and have optional reliable air-conditioning. A specialist operator can be very helpful in arranging itineraries and car hire in advance.

Car hire With a driver, car hire is cheaper than in the West. A car shared by three or four can be very good value and might be a good idea if you plan to go to Hampi from Goa or perhaps Mumbai to Goa. Be sure to check carefully the mileage at the beginning and end of the trip. Two- or three-day trips from main towns can also give excellent opportunities for sightseeing off the beaten track and in reasonable comfort.

Cars can be hired through private companies. International companies such as **Hertz**, **Europcar** and **Budget** operate in some major cities and offer reliable cars; their rates are generally higher than those of local firms in Goa (eg **Wheels**).

Car with driver	Economy	Regular a/c	Premium a/c	Luxury a/c
	Maruti Swift	Maruti 800 Dzire	Maruti 1000 Qualis	Esteem Innova
8 hrs/80 km	Rs 2000	Rs 2000	Rs 200	Rs 2500
Extra km	Rs 20	Rs 20	Rs20	Rs 25

There are also additional charges for out-of-town trips of Rs 200 and night charges vary between Rs 250-500 depending on car.

Taxi There are no meter taxis in Goa but most have set fares for destinations around the state, the night market or the spice plantations. While in Mumbai or other major cities you find metered taxis, although tariffs change frequently. Increased night-time rates apply in some cities, and there is a small charge for luggage. Insist on the taxi meter being flagged in your presence. If the driver refuses, the official advice is to contact the police. This may not work, but it is worth trying. When a taxi doesn't have a meter, you will need to fix the fare before starting the journey. Ask at your hotel desk for a guide price. As a foreigner, it is rare to get a taxi in the big cities to use the meter – if they are eager to, watch out as sometimes the meter is rigged and they have a fake rate card. Also, watch out for the David Blaine-style note shuffle: you pay with a Rs 500 note, but they have a Rs 100 note in their hand.

Rickshaw **Auto-rickshaws** (autos) are almost universally available in towns across India and are the cheapest and most convenient way of getting about. In Goa, rickshaws plough the streets around Mapusa, Panjim, Margao and Canacona/Palolem, but there are no rickshaws that ply the northern beaches Arambol to Morjim, you will have to use a taxi or bike taxi instead. In addition to using them for short journeys it is often possible to hire them by the hour, or for a half or full day's sightseeing in Panjim. In major Indian cities and other tourist spots in India, rickshaw drivers are often paid a commission by hotels, restaurants and gift shops so advice is not always impartial. Drivers generally refuse to use a meter, often quote a ridiculous price or may sometimes stop short of your destination. If you have real problems it can help to note down the vehicle licence number and threaten to go to the police. Beware of some rickshaw drivers who show the fare chart for taxis, especially in Mumbai.

Where to stay in Goa and Mumbai

Goa has a wide range of accommodation from upmarket resorts to simple beach huts, while Mumbai has uber-luxe to youth hostels. You can stay safely and very cheaply by Western standards right across the country. In all the major cities there are also high-quality hotels, offering a full range of facilities; in small towns, such as Mapusa, hotels are much more variable. In the peak season (October to April for most of India) bookings can be extremely heavy in popular destinations. It is sometimes possible to book in advance by phone, fax or email, but double check your reservation, and always try to arrive as early as possible in the day. For the last couple of years in Arambol beach, for example, there have been no free rooms over the Christmas and New Year period. And book well ahead for Diwali time in Mumbai.

Hotels
Price categories The category codes used in this book are based on prices of double rooms excluding taxes. They are **not** star ratings and individual facilities vary considerably. The most expensive hotels charge in US dollars only. Some hotels operate a 24-hour checkout system. Goa is becoming increasingly expensive for mid-range to upmarket properties, but you can still get cheap rooms near the beach in the less developed beaches of Palolem and Patnem in the south and Arambol and Mandrem in the north. Expect to pay more in Delhi, Mumbai and, to a lesser extent, in Bengaluru (Bangalore), Chennai and Kolkata for all categories; also Mumbai seems to be the most expensive of all these cities and it does not have the backpacker enclave like Paharganj in Delhi.

Off-season rates Large discounts are made by hotels in all categories out of season in many resorts. Always ask if any is available. You may also request the 10-15% agent's commission to be deducted from your bill if you book direct. Clarify whether the agreed figure includes all taxes.

Taxes In general most hotel rooms rated at Rs 1200 or above are subject to a tax of 10%. Many states levy an additional luxury tax of 10-25%, and some hotels add a service charge of 10% on top of this. Taxes are not necessarily payable on meals, so it is worth settling your meals bill separately. Most hotels in the **$$** category and above accept payment by credit card. Check your final bill carefully. Visitors have complained of incorrect bills, even in the most expensive hotels. The problem particularly afflicts groups, when last-minute extras appear mysteriously on some guests' bills. Check the evening before departure, and keep all receipts.

Hotel facilities You have to be prepared for difficulties which are uncommon in the West. It is best to inspect the room and check that all equipment (air conditioning, TV, water heater, flush) works before checking in at a modest hotel. Many hotels try to wring too many years' service out of their linen, and it's quite common to find sheets that are stained, frayed or riddled with holes. Don't expect any but the most expensive or tourist-savvy hotels to fit a top sheet to the bed.

In Goa **power cuts** are common, or hot water may be restricted to certain times of day. The largest hotels have their own generators but it is best to carry a good torch.

Price codes

Where to stay
$$$$ over US$150   **$$$** US$66-150
$$ US$30-65   **$** under US$30
For a double room in high season, excluding taxes.

Restaurants
$$$ over US$12   **$$** US$6-12   **$** under US$6
For a two-course meal for one person, excluding drinks and service charge.

Food and drink in Goa and Mumbai

Food
You find just as much variety in dishes and presentation crossing South India as you would on an equivalent journey across Europe. Combinations of spices give each region its distinctive flavour. Traditional Goan food is one of the spiciest on offer in the country, it is the home of the *vindaloo*, although not nearly as spicy as the version on offer in curry houses in Birmingham where it is usually eaten as a bet. Calamari *vindaloo* is a real treat. Other Goan specialities include *chicken xacuti* and *pork sorpotel*, and it is also not uncommon to see beef on the menu as Goa is a Catholic state. You will also see North Indian dishes and South Indian *dosas* on many menus. In fact, the average menu in Goa takes in tastes from all over the world, although executed with varying degrees of success. With a large ex-pat community, though, there are some exceptional French, Burmese and fusion restaurants offering up amazing food at a fraction of the cost you would pay in the West. In Mumbai there is a wide variety of dining with international-style Sunday buffets in the big hotels, South Indian *dosas*, North Indian kebabs and the local *bhel puri* stands.

The larger hotels, open to non-residents, often offer **buffet** lunches with Indian, Western and sometimes Chinese dishes. These can be good value (Rs 250-300; but Rs 450 in the top grades), however, there can be considerable health risks if food is kept warm for long periods, especially if turnover at the buffet is slow. We have received several complaints of stomach trouble following a buffet meal, even in five-star hotels.

Hygiene standards in Goa are pretty good compared to the rest of India but it is essential to be very careful since flies abound and refrigeration in the hot weather may be inadequate and intermittent because of power cuts. It is best to eat only freshly prepared food by ordering from the menu (especially meat and fish dishes). There is so much fresh fruit on offer in Goa and most good establishments will say on the menu that their salads are cleaned in drinking water.

If you are unused to spicy food, go slow. Stick to Western or mild Chinese meals in good restaurants and try the odd Indian dish to test your reaction. Food is often spicier when you eat with families or at local places. Popular local restaurants are obvious from the number of people eating in them. Try a traditional *thali*, which is a complete meal served on a large stainless steel plate. Several preparations, placed in small bowls, surround the central serving of wholewheat chapati and rice. A vegetarian *thali* would include *dhal* (lentils), two or three curries (which can be quite hot) and crisp poppadums, although there are regional variations. A variety of pickles are offered – mango and lime are two of the most popular. These can be exceptionally hot, and are designed to be taken in minute quantities alongside the main dishes. Plain *dahi* (yoghurt) in the south, or *raita* in the north, usually acts as a bland 'cooler'. Simple *dhabas* (rustic roadside eateries) are an alternative experience for sampling authentic local dishes.

Many city restaurants offer a choice of so-called **European options** such as toasted sandwiches, stuffed pancakes, apple pies, fruit crumbles and cheesecakes. Italian favourites (pizzas, pastas) can be very different from what you are used to. Western confectionery, in general, is disappointing, although **ice creams** can be exceptionally good; there are excellent Indian ones as well as some international brands.

India has many delicious tropical **fruits**. Some are seasonal (eg mangoes, pineapples and lychees), while others (eg bananas, grapes and oranges) are available throughout the year. It is safe to eat the ones you can wash and peel.

Drink

Drinking water used to be regarded as one of India's biggest hazards. It is still true that water from the tap or a well should never be considered safe to drink since public water supplies are often polluted. Bottled water is now widely available although not all bottled water is mineral water; most are simply purified water from an urban supply. Buy from a shop or stall, check the seal carefully (some companies now add a second clear plastic seal around the bottle top) and avoid street hawkers. When disposing of bottles puncture the neck to prevent misuse but allow recycling.

There is growing concern over the mountains of plastic bottles that are collecting, so travellers are being encouraged to use alternative methods of getting safe drinking water. You can buy five- and 20-litre bottles and refill a smaller one. You may wish to purify water yourself. A portable water filter is a good idea, carrying the drinking water in a plastic bottle in an insulated carrier. Always carry enough drinking water with you when travelling. It is important to use pure water for cleaning teeth.

Tea and **coffee** are safe and widely available. Both are normally served sweet, and with milk. If you wish, say 'no sugar' (*chini nahin*), 'no milk' (*dudh nahin*) when ordering. Alternatively, ask for a pot of tea and milk and sugar to be brought separately. Even in aspiring smart cafés, espresso or cappuccino may not turn out quite as you'd expect in the West.

Bottled **soft drinks** such as Coke, Pepsi, Teem, Limca, Thums Up and Gold Spot are universally available; always check the seal when you buy from a street stall. There are also several brands of fruit juice sold in cartons, including mango, pineapple and apple – Indian brands are very sweet. Don't add ice cubes as the water source may be contaminated. Take care with fresh fruit juices or *lassis* as ice is often added. Again in good Goan establishments and Western-run joints ice is made from drinking water.

In Goa, alcohol is a lot cheaper than the rest of India due to different taxation. In the past wines and spirits were generally either imported and extremely expensive, or local and of poor quality. Now, the best Indian whisky, rum and brandy (IMFL or 'Indian Made Foreign Liquor') are widely accepted, as are good Champagnoise and other wines from Maharashtra. If you hanker after a bottle of imported wine, you will only find it in the top restaurants for at least Rs 10-20.

In Goa, you will find beach shacks to upmarket hotels all sell a range of cocktails, beers and wines. Then there is also the local hooch, coconut and cashew *feni* and *arak,* which is deceptively potent.

Goa and Mumbai have occasional alcohol-free days or enforce degrees of Prohibition when there are elections. Other states in India, such as Gujarat, are dry states. Even in Kerala you often have to order your beer in a teapot.

Festivals in Goa and Mumbai → *For public holidays, see page 23.*

India has a wealth of festivals with many celebrated nationwide, while others are specific to a particular state or community or even a particular temple. Many fall on different dates each year depending on the Hindu lunar calendar, so check with the tourist office. Goa also has a range of local and Catholic festivals and its carnival season in February/March. Around festivals like Diwali especially, hotels can get very full as people embark on their holidays. ▸▸ *Local festivals are listed throughout the book.*

The Hindu calendar
Hindus follow two distinct eras: The *Vikrama Samvat* which began in 57 BC and the *Salivahan Saka* which dates from AD 78 and has been the official Indian calendar since 1957. The *Saka* new year starts on 22 March and has the same length as the Gregorian calendar. The 29½-day lunar month with its 'dark' and 'bright' halves based on the new and full moons, are named after 12 constellations, and total a 354-day year. The calendar cleverly has an extra month (*adhik maas*) every 2½ to three years, to bring it in line with the solar year of 365 days coinciding with the Gregorian calendar of the West.

Major festivals and fairs
Jan New Year's Day (1 Jan) is accepted officially when following the Gregorian calendar but there are regional variations which fall on different dates, often coinciding with spring/harvest time in Mar and Apr.

Feb Vasant Panchami, the spring festival when people wear bright yellow clothes to mark the advent of the season with singing, dancing and feasting.

Feb-Mar Maha Sivaratri marks the night when Siva danced his celestial dance of destruction (*Tandava*), which is celebrated with feasting and fairs at Siva temples, but preceded by a night of devotional readings and hymn singing. Many people travel to Gokarna south of Goa for this. **Carnival** in Goa. Spectacular costumes, music and dance, float processions and feasting mark the 3-day event.

Mar Holi, the festival of colours, marks the climax of spring. The previous night bonfires are lit symbolizing the end of winter (and conquering of evil). People have fun throwing coloured powder and water at each other and in the evening some gamble with friends. If you don't mind getting covered in colours, you can risk going out but celebrations can sometimes get very

rowdy (and unpleasant). Some worship Krishna who defeated the demon Putana.

Apr/May Buddha Jayanti, the 1st full moon night in Apr/May marks the birth of the Buddha.

Jul/Aug Raksha (or Rakhi) Bandhan symbolizes the bond between brother and sister, celebrated at full moon. A sister says special prayers for her brother and ties coloured threads around his wrist to remind him of the special bond. He in turn gives a gift and promises to protect and care for her. Sometimes *rakshas* are exchanged as a mark of friendship. Narial Purnima on the same full moon. Hindus make offerings of *narial* (coconuts) to the Vedic god Varuna (Lord of the waters) by throwing them into the sea.

15 Aug is Independence Day, a national secular holiday is marked by special events. Ganesh Chaturthi was established just over 100 years ago by the Indian nationalist leader Tilak. The elephant-headed God of good omen is shown special reverence. On the last of the 5-day festival after harvest, clay images of Ganesh are taken in procession with dancers and musicians, and are immersed in the sea, river or pond. This is very popular in Goa, Mumbai and Maharastra.

Sep/Oct Dasara has many local variations. Celebrations for the 9 nights (*navaratri*) are marked with **Ramlila**, various episodes of the Ramayana story are enacted with particular reference to the battle between the forces of good and evil. In some parts of India it celebrates *Rama*'s victory over the Demon king *Ravana* of Lanka with the help of loyal *Hanuman* (Monkey). Huge effigies of *Ravana* made of bamboo and paper are burnt on the 10th day (*Vijaya dasami*) of Dasara in public open spaces. In some regions the focus is on Durga's victory over the demon *Mahishasura*.

Oct/Nov Gandhi Jayanti (2 Oct), Mahatma Gandhi's birthday, is remembered with prayer meetings and devotional singing.

Diwali/Deepavali (*Sanskrit ideepa* lamp), the festival of lights. Some Hindus celebrate Krishna's victory over the demon *Narakasura*, some Rama's return after his 14 years' exile in the forest when citizens lit his way with oil lamps. The festival falls on the dark *chaturdasi* (14th) night (the one preceding the new moon), when rows of lamps or candles are lit in remembrance, and *rangolis* are painted on the floor as a sign of welcome. Fireworks have become an integral part of the celebration which are often set off days before Diwali. Equally, Lakshmi, the Goddess of Wealth (as well as Ganesh) is worshipped by merchants and the business community who open the new financial year's account on the day. Most people wear new clothes; some play games of chance.

Guru Nanak Jayanti commemorates the birth of Guru Nanak. **Akhand Path** (unbroken reading of the holy book) takes place and the book itself (*Guru Granth Sahib*) is taken out in procession.

Dec Christmas Day (25 Dec) sees Indian Christians celebrate the birth of Christ in much the same way as in the West; many churches hold services/Mass at midnight. There is an air of festivity in city markets which are specially decorated and illuminated. Over **New Year's Eve** (31 Dec) hotel prices peak and large supplements are added for meals and entertainment in the more upmarket hotels. Some churches mark the night with a Midnight Mass. Naturally this is very popular in Goa.

Muslim holy days

These are fixed according to the lunar calendar. According to the Gregorian calendar, they tend to fall 11 days earlier each year, dependent on the sighting of the new moon.

Ramadan is the start of the month of fasting when all Muslims (except young children, the very elderly, the sick, pregnant women and travellers) must abstain from food and drink, from sunrise to sunset.

Id ul Fitr is the 3-day festival that marks the end of Ramadan.

Id-ul-Zuha/Bakr-Id is when Muslims commemorate Ibrahim's sacrifice of his son according to God's commandment; the main time of pilgrimage to Mecca (the Hajj). It is marked by the sacrifice of a goat, feasting and alms giving.

Muharram is when the killing of the Prophet's grandson, Hussain, is commemorated by Shi'a Muslims. Decorated *tazias* (replicas of the martyr's tomb) are carried in procession by devout wailing followers who beat their chests to express their grief. Hyderabad and Lucknow are famous for their grand *tazias*. Shi'as fast for the 10 days.

Responsible travel in Goa and Mumbai

As well as respecting local cultural sensitivities, travellers can take a number of simple steps to reduce, or even improve, their impact on the local environment. Environmental concern is relatively new in India. Don't be afraid to pressurize businesses by asking about their policies.

Spending your money carefully can have a positive impact. Sleeping, eating and shopping at small, locally owned businesses directly supports communities, while specific community tourism concerns, such as those operated by **Green Goa Works** in Benaulim, are trying to come up with conscious solutions to the rubbish problem.

Bucket baths or showers The biggest issue relating to responsible and sustainable tourism is water. The traditional Indian 'bucket bath', in which you wet, soap then rinse off using a small hand-held plastic jug dipped into a large bucket, uses on average around 15 litres of water, as compared to 30-45 litres for a shower. These are commonly offered except in four- and five-star hotels.

Litter Many travellers think that there is little point in disposing of rubbish properly when the tossing of water bottles, plastic cups and other non-biodegradable items out of train or car windows is already so widespread. Don't follow an example you feel to be wrong. You can immediately reduce your impact by refusing plastic bags and other excess packaging when shopping – use a small backpack or cloth bag instead – and if you do collect a few, keep them with you to store other rubbish until you get to a litter bin.

Plastic mineral water bottles, an inevitable corollary to poor water hygiene standards, are a major contributor to India's litter mountain. However, many hotels, including nearly all of the upmarket ones, most restaurants and bus and train stations, provide drinking water purified using a combination of ceramic and carbon filters, chlorine and UV irradiation. Ask for '*filter paani*'; if the water tastes like a swimming pool it is probably quite safe to drink, though it's best to introduce your body gradually to the new water. If purifying water yourself, bringing it to a boil at sea level will make it safe, but at altitude you have to boil it for longer to ensure that all the microbes are killed. Various sterilizing methods containing chlorine or iodine can be used and there are a number of mechanical or chemical water filters available on the market.

Nudity Although nudity and topless bathing are illegal in Goa, the law is often flouted. Be aware of local customs and dress appropriately both on and off the beach.

Transport Choose walking, cycling or public transport over fuel-guzzling cars and motorbikes.

Essentials A-Z

Accident and emergency

Contact the relevant emergency service (police T100, fire T101, ambulance T102) and your embassy. Make sure you obtain police/medical reports required for insurance claims.

Customs and duty free
Duty free

Tourists are allowed to bring in all personal effects 'which may reasonably be required', without charge. The official customs allowance includes 200 cigarettes or 50 cigars, 0.95 litres of alcohol, a camera and a pair of binoculars. Valuable personal effects and professional equipment including jewellery, special camera equipment and lenses, laptop computers and sound and video recorders must be declared on a Tourist Baggage Re-Export Form (TBRE) in order for them to be taken out of the country. These forms require the equipment's serial numbers. It saves considerable frustration if you know the numbers in advance and are ready to show them on the equipment. In addition to the forms, details of imported equipment may be entered into your passport. Save time by completing the formalities while waiting for your baggage. It is essential to keep these forms for showing to the customs when leaving India, otherwise considerable delays are very likely at the time of departure.

Prohibited items

The import of live plants, gold coins, gold and silver bullion and silver coins not in current use are either banned or subject to strict regulation. Enquire at consular offices abroad for details.

Drugs

Certain areas, such as Goa's beaches, Gokarna and Hampi, have become associated with foreigners who take drugs. These are likely to attract local and foreign drug dealers but be aware that the government takes the misuse of drugs very seriously. Anyone charged with the illegal possession of drugs risks facing a fine of Rs 100,000 and a minimum 10 years' imprisonment. Several foreigners have been imprisoned for drugs-related offences in the last decade.

Electricity

Electricity supply is 220-240 volts AC. Some top hotels have transformers. There may be pronounced variations in the voltage, and power cuts are common. Power back-up by generator or inverter is becoming more widespread, even in humble hotels, though it may not cover a/c. Socket sizes vary so take a universal adaptor; low-quality versions are available locally. Many hotels, even in the higher categories, don't have electric razor sockets. Invest in a stabilizer for a laptop.

Embassies and consulates

For information on visas and immigration, see page 25. For details of Indian embassies and consulates around the world, go to embassy.goabroad.com.

Health

Local populations in India are exposed to a range of health risks not encountered in the Western world. Many of the diseases are major problems for the local poor and destitute and, although the risk to travellers is more remote, they cannot be ignored. Obviously 5-star travel is going to carry less risk than backpacking on a budget.

Health care in India is varied, but in Goa there are many excellent private and government clinics/hospitals. As with all medical care, first impressions count. If you do get ill, and you have the opportunity, you should also ask your medical insurer whether they are satisfied that the medical centre/hospital you have been referred to is of a suitable standard.

Before you go
Ideally, you should see your GP or travel clinic at least 6 weeks before your departure for general advice on travel risks, malaria and vaccinations. Make sure you have travel insurance, get a dental check (especially if you are going to be away for more than a month), know your own blood group and if you suffer a long-term condition such as diabetes or epilepsy make sure someone knows or that you have a Medic Alert bracelet/necklace with this information on it. Remember that it is risky to buy medicinal tablets abroad because the doses may differ and India has a huge trade in counterfeit drugs.

Vaccinations
If you need vaccinations, see your doctor well in advance of your travel. The following vaccinations are recommended: typhoid, polio, tetanus, infectious hepatitis and diptheria. For details of malaria prevention, contact your GP or local travel clinic. There is no malaria risk in Goa and Mumbai, although if you are travelling further afield you might want to look into medication.

The following vaccinations may also be considered: rabies, possibly BCG (since TB is still common in the region) and in some cases meningitis and diphtheria (if you're staying in the country for a long time). Yellow fever is not required in India but you may be asked to show a certificate if you have travelled from Africa or South America. Japanese encephalitis may be required for rural travel at certain times of the year (mainly rainy seasons). An effective oral cholera vaccine (Dukoral) is now available as 2 doses providing 3 months' protection.

Websites
British Travel Health Association (UK), www.btha.org This is the official website of an organization of travel health professionals.

Fit for Travel, www.fitfortravel.scot. nhs.uk This site from Scotland provides a quick A-Z of vaccine and travel health advice requirements for each country.
Foreign and Commonwealth Office (FCO) (UK), www.fco.gov.uk This is a key travel advice site, with useful information on the country, people, climate and lists the UK embassies/consulates. The site also promotes the concept of 'know before you go' and encourages travel insurance and appropriate travel health advice. It has links to Department of Health travel advice site.
The Health Protection Agency, www. hpa.org.uk Up-to-date malaria advice guidelines for travel around the world. It gives specific advice about the right drugs for each location. It also has useful information for those who are pregnant, suffering from epilepsy or planning to travel with children.
Medic Alert (UK), www.medicalalert.com This is the website of the foundation that produces bracelets and necklaces for those with existing medical problems. Once you have ordered your bracelet/necklace you write your key medical details on paper inside it, so that if you collapse, a medic can identify you as having epilepsy or a nut allergy, etc.
Travel Screening Services (UK), www.travelscreening.co.uk A private clinic dedicated to integrated travel health. The clinic gives vaccine, travel health advice, email and SMS text vaccine reminders and screens returned travellers for tropical diseases.
World Health Organisation, www.who. int The WHO site has links to the *WHO Blue Book* on travel advice. This lists the diseases in different regions of the world. It describes vaccination schedules and makes clear which countries have yellow fever vaccination certificate requirements and malarial risk.

Language

Hindi, spoken as a mother tongue by over 400 million people, is India's official language. The use of English is also enshrined in the Constitution for a wide range of official purposes, notably communication between Hindi and non-Hindi speaking states. In Mumbai, you will hear Hindi and Marathi, while in Goa, Konkani and Marathi are the most common languages, but unless you are really off the beaten track you will find someone who speaks English.

English now plays an important role across India. It is widely spoken in towns and cities and even in quite remote villages it is usually not difficult to find someone who speaks at least a little English. Outside major tourist sites, other European languages are almost completely unknown although Goans are increasingly learning Russian due to the influx of Russian tourists. The accent in which English is spoken is often affected strongly by the mother tongue of the speaker and there have been changes in common grammar which sometimes make it sound unusual. Many of these changes have become standard Indian English usage, as valid as any other varieties of English used around the world. It is possible to study a number of Indian languages at language centres.

Money → *UK £1 = Rs 98.3, €1 = Rs 83.4, US$1 = Rs 61.5 (Nov 2013).*

Indian currency is the Indian rupee (Re/Rs). It is **not** possible to purchase these before you arrive. If you want cash on arrival it is best to get it at the airport bank, although see if an ATM is available as airport rates are not very generous. Rupee notes are printed in denominations of Rs 1000, 500, 100, 50, 20, 10. The rupee is divided into 100 paise. Coins are minted in denominations of Rs 10, Rs 5, Rs 2, and Rs 1. **Note** Carry money in a money belt worn under clothing. Have a small amount in an easily accessible place. ATMs are now so widely found in Goa and even in the rest of India, you rarely have to carry excessive amounts of cash on you.

ATMs

By far the most convenient method of accessing money, ATMs are all over India, usually attended by security guards, with most banks offering some services to holders of overseas cards. Banks whose ATMs will issue cash against Cirrus and Maestro cards, as well as Visa and MasterCard, include **Bank of Baroda**, **Citibank**, **HDFC**, **HSBC**, **ICICI**, **Axis**, **Punjab National Bank**, **State Bank of India (SBI)**, **Standard Chartered** and UTI. Some of the smaller or regional banks do not take International cards. A withdrawal fee is usually charged by the issuing bank on top of the conversion charges applied by your own bank. Fraud prevention measures quite often result in travellers having their cards blocked by the bank when unexpected overseas transactions occur; advise your bank of your travel plans before leaving.

Currency cards

If you don't want to carry lots of cash, pre-paid currency cards allow you to preload money from your bank account, fixed at the day's exchange rate. They look like a credit or debit card and are issued by specialist money changing companies, such as **Travelex** and **Caxton FX**. You can top up and check your balance by phone, online and sometimes by text.

Credit cards

Major credit cards are increasingly acceptable in the main centres, though in smaller cities and towns it is still rare to be able to pay by credit card. Payment by credit card can sometimes be more expensive than payment by cash, whilst some credit card companies charge a premium on cash withdrawals. **Visa** and **MasterCard** have a growing number of ATMs in major cities and several banks offer withdrawal facilities for **Cirrus** and **Maestro** cardholders. It is however easy to obtain a cash advance against a credit card. Railway reservation centres in major cities take payment for train tickets by Visa card which can be very quick as the queue is short, although they cannot be used for Tourist Quota tickets.

Traveller's cheques (TCs)

TCs issued by reputable companies (eg Thomas Cook, American Express) are widely accepted. They can be easily exchanged at small local travel agents and tourist internet cafés but are rarely used directly for payment. Try to avoid changing at banks, where the process can be time consuming; opt for hotels and agents instead, take large denomination cheques and change enough to last for some days. Most banks, but not all, will accept US dollars, pounds sterling and euro TCs.

Changing money

The State Bank of India and several others in major towns are authorized to deal in foreign exchange. Some give cash against Visa/MasterCard (eg ANZ, Bank of Baroda who print a list of their participating branches, Andhra Bank). American Express cardholders can use their cards to get either cash or TCs in Mumbai and Chennai. They also have offices in Coimbatore, Goa, Hyderabad, and Thiruvananthapuram. The larger cities have licensed money changers with offices usually in the commercial sector. Changing money through unauthorized dealers is illegal. Premiums on the currency black market are very small and highly risky. Large hotels change money 24 hrs a day for guests, but banks often give a substantially better rate of exchange. It is best to exchange money on arrival at the airport bank or the Thomas Cook counter. Many international flights arrive during the night and it is generally far easier and less time consuming to change money at the airport than in the city. You should be given a foreign currency encashment certificate when you change money through a bank

or authorized dealer; ask for one if it is not automatically given. It allows you to change Indian rupees back to your own currency on departure. It also enables you to use rupees to pay hotel bills or buy air tickets for which payment in foreign exchange may be required. The certificates are only valid for 3 months.

Cost of travelling

Most food, accommodation and public transport, especially rail and bus, is still cheap compared to Western standards. There is a widening range of moderately priced but clean hotels and restaurants outside the big cities, making it possible to get a great deal for your money. Budget travellers sharing a room, taking public transport, avoiding souvenir stalls, and eating nothing but rice and dhal can get away with a budget of Rs 500-800 a day. This sum leaps up if you drink alcohol (still cheap by European standards at about Rs 80 for a pint), smoke foreign-brand cigarettes or want to have your own wheels (you can expect to spend between Rs 150 and 250 to hire a scooter or motorbike per day). Those planning to stay in fairly comfortable hotels and use taxis sightseeing should budget at US$70-100 (£50-80) a day. Then again you could always check into Ananda Spa or the Taj Falaknuma for Christmas and notch up an impressive US$600 (£350) bill on your B&B alone. India can be a great place to pick and choose, save a little on basic accommodation and then treat yourself to the type of meal you could only dream of affording back home. Also, be prepared to spend a fair amount more in Mumbai, Bengaluru (Bangalore) and many of the resorts in Goa, where not only is the cost of living significantly higher but where it's worth coughing up extra for a half-decent room; you can penny-pinch by the beach when you'll be spending precious little time indoors anyway. A newspaper costs Rs 5 and breakfast for 2 with coffee can come to as little as Rs 50 if you eat the local Goan staple of bhaji beans and local bread, but if you intend to eat banana pancakes with a cappuccino or pasta and fish beside the beach, you can expect to pay more like Rs 100-350 a plate.

Opening hours
Banks are open Mon-Fri 1030-1430, Sat 1030-1230. Top hotels sometimes have a 24-hr money-changing service. **Post offices** open Mon-Fri 1000-1700, often shutting for lunch, and Sat mornings. **Government offices** Mon-Fri 0930-1700, Sat 0930-1300 (some open on alternate Sat only). **Shops** open Mon-Sat 0930-1800. Beach street markets stay open late often until midnight. The Sat Night Market stays open until around 0200.

Public holidays
26 Jan Republic Day; **15 Aug** Independence Day; **2 Oct** Mahatma Gandhi's Birthday; **25 Dec** Christmas Day.

Safety
Personal security
In general the threats to personal security for travellers in India are remarkably small. However, incidents of petty theft and violence directed specifically at tourists have been on the increase so care is necessary in some places, and basic common sense needs to be used with respect to looking after valuables. Follow the same precautions you would when at home. There have been incidents of sexual assault in and around the main tourist beach centres, particularly after full moon parties. Avoid wandering alone outdoors late at night in these places. During daylight hours be careful in remote places, especially when alone. If you are under threat, scream loudly. Be very cautious before accepting food or drink from casual acquaintances, as it may be drugged. There have been some recent reports of people trying to grab bags off scooters and motorbikes in the Baga and Calangute areas.

In Mumbai, the UK's Foreign and Commonwealth Office warns of a risk of armed robbers holding up taxis travelling along the main highway from the airport to the city in the early hours of the morning (0200-0600) when there is little traffic on the roads. If you are using the route during these times, you should, if possible, arrange to travel by coach or seek advice at the airport on arrival.

That said, in the great majority of places visited by tourists, violent crime and personal attacks are extremely rare.

Travel advice
It is better to seek advice from your consulate than from travel agencies. Before you travel you can contact: **British Foreign & Commonwealth Office Travel Advice Unit**, T0845-850 2829 (Pakistan desk T020-7270 2385), www.fco.gov.uk. **US State Department's Bureau of Consular Affairs**, Overseas Citizens Services, Room 4800, Department of State, Washington, DC 20520-4818, USA, T202-647 1488, http://travel.state.gov. **Australian Department of Foreign Affairs Canberra**, Australia, T02-6261 3305, www.smartraveller.gov.au. **Canadian** official advice is on www.voyage.gc.ca.

Theft
Theft is not uncommon. It is best to keep TCs, passports and valuables with you at all times. Don't regard hotel rooms as being automatically safe; even hotel safes don't guarantee secure storage. Avoid leaving valuables near open windows even when you are in the room – as items are sometimes hooked out. Use your own padlock in a budget hotel when you go out. Pickpockets and other thieves operate in the big cities. Crowded areas are particularly high risk. Take special care of your belongings when getting on or off public transport.

If you have items stolen, they should be reported to the police as soon as possible. Keep a separate record of vital documents, including passport details and numbers of TCs. Larger hotels will be able to assist in contacting and dealing with the police. Dealings with the police can be challenging. The paperwork involved in reporting losses can be time consuming and irritating and your own documentation (eg passport and visas) may be demanded.

In some states the police occasionally demand bribes, though you should not assume that if procedures move slowly you are automatically being expected to offer a bribe. Traffic police have the right to make on-the-spot fines for speeding and illegal parking. If you face a fine, insist on a receipt. If you have to go to a police station, try to take someone with you. In Goa, it is common to be stopped for licence, bike documents, etc, which is normally an excuse for a bribe.

Confidence tricksters are particularly common where people are on the move, notably around railway stations or places where budget tourists gather, more common in Mumbai than Goa.

Telephone
The international code for India is +91. International Direct Dialling is widely available in privately run call booths, usually labelled on yellow boards with the letters 'PCO-STD-ISD'. You dial the call yourself, and the time and cost are displayed on a computer screen. Telephone calls from hotels are usually more expensive (check price before calling), though some will allow local calls free of charge. Internet phone booths, usually associated with cybercafés, are the cheapest way of calling overseas and cheap SIM cards are now available (see below).

Directory enquiries, T197, can be helpful but works only for the local area code.

Mobile phones are for sale everywhere, as are local SIM cards that allow you to make calls within India and overseas at much lower rates than using a 'roaming' service from your normal provider at home – sometimes for as little as Rs 0.5 per min. **Univercell**, www.univercell.in, and **The Mobile Store**, www.themobilestore.in,

are 2 widespread and efficient chains selling phones and SIM cards.

India is divided into a number of 'calling circles' or regions, and if you travel outside the region where your connection is based, eg from Goa into Karnataka, you will pay higher charges for making and receiving calls. Goa and Maharastra, however, are the same region.

Time
India doesn't change its clocks, so from the last Sun in Oct to the last Sun in Mar the time is GMT +5½ hrs, and the rest of the year it's +4½ hrs (USA, EST +10½ and +9½ hrs; Australia, EST -5½ and -4½ hrs).

Tipping
A tip of Rs 10 to a bellboy carrying luggage in a modest hotel (Rs 20 in a higher category) would be appropriate. In upmarket restaurants, a 10% tip is acceptable when service is not already included, while in places serving very cheap meals, round off the bill with small change. Indians don't normally tip taxi drivers but a small extra is welcomed. Porters at airports and railway stations often have a fixed rate displayed but will usually press for more. Ask fellow passengers what a fair rate is.

Tourist information
There are **Government of India** tourist offices in the state capitals, as well as state tourist offices (sometimes **Tourism Development Corporations**) in the major cities and a few important sites. They produce their own tourist literature, either free or sold at a nominal price, and some also have lists of city hotels and paying guest options. The quality of material is improving though maps are often poor. Many offer tours of the city, neighbouring sights and overnight and regional packages. Some run modest hotels and midway motels with restaurants and may also arrange car hire and guides. The staff in the regional and local offices are usually helpful.

Visas and immigration

Virtually all foreign nationals, including children, require a visa to enter India. The rules regarding visas change frequently and arrangements for application and collection also vary from town to town so it is essential to check details and costs with the relevant embassy or consulate. These remain closed on Indian national holidays. Many consulates and embassies are currently outsourcing the visa process; it's best to find out in advance how long it will take. Note that visas are valid from the date granted, not from the date of entry.

Recently, the Indian government has decided to issue 'visas on arrival' for some 40 countries (including the UK, the USA, France and Germany), as well as for citizens of all countries who are over the age of 60. The exact time frame for the change is not yet clear, so check the latest situation online before travelling.

For up-to-date information on visa requirements visit www.india-visa.com.

No foreigner needs to register within the 180-day period of their tourist visa. If you have a 1-year visa or as a US citizen a 10-year visa and wish to stay longer than 180 days you will need to register with the Foreign Registration Office (in Panjim if you are in Goa). Applications for visa extensions should be made to the Foreigners' Regional Registration Offices at Panjim and Mumbai.

Weights and measures

Metric is in universal use in the cities. In remote areas local measures are sometimes used. One lakh is 100,000 and 1 crore is 10 million.

Contents

Mumbai

Mumbai (Bombay)

Maximum City, the City of Dreams, India's economic capital and melting pot. You can throw epithets and superlatives at Mumbai until the cows come home, but it refuses to be understood on a merely intellectual level. Like London and New York, it's a restless human tapestry of cultures, religions, races, ways of surviving and thriving, and one that evokes palpable emotion; whether you love it or hate it, you can't stay unaffected.

From the cluster of fishing villages first linked together by the British East India Company in 1668, Mumbai has swelled to sprawl across seven islands, which now groan under the needs of 19 million stomachs, souls and egos. Its problems – creaking infrastructure, endemic corruption coupled with bureaucratic incompetence, and an ever-expanding population of whom more than two thirds live in slums – are only matched by the enormous drive that makes it the centre of business, fashion and film-making in modern India, and both a magnet and icon for the country's dreams, and nightmares.

The taxi ride from the airport shows you both sides of the city: slum dwellers selling balloons under billboards of fair-skinned models dripping in gold and reclining on the roof of a Mercedes; the septic stench as you cross Mahim Creek, where bikers park on the soaring bridge to shoot the breeze amid fumes that could drop an elephant; the feeling of diesel permeating your bloodstream and the manically reverberating mantra of *Horn OK Please* as you ooze through traffic past Worli's glitzy shopping malls and the fairytale island mosque of Haji Ali. And finally the magic moment as you swing out on to Chowpatty Beach and the city throws off her cloak of chaos to reveal a neon-painted skyscape that makes you feel like you've arrived at the centre of all things.

Arriving in Mumbai

Getting there
Chhatrapati Shivaji International Airport is 30 km from Nariman Point, the business heart of the city. The domestic terminals at Santa Cruz are 5 km closer. Pre-paid taxis to the city centre are good value and take 40-90 minutes; buses are cheaper but significantly slower. If you arrive at night without a hotel booking it is best to stay at one of the hotels near the airports. If you're travelling light (and feeling brave), local trains head into the city from Vile Parle (International) and Santa Cruz (Domestic) stations, but these are daunting at any time (passengers leap off while the train is still moving and will 'help' you if you're in their way) and become impossibly crowded during the morning and evening rush hours.

Getting around
The sights are spread out and you need transport. Taxis are metered and good value. Older taxis carry a rate card to convert the meter reading to the correct fare. You can download the rate card in advance from www.hindustantimes.com/farelist, and various fare conversion apps are available for smartphones. There are frequent buses on major routes, and the two suburban railway lines are useful out of peak hours, but get horrendously crowded. Auto-rickshaws are only allowed in the suburbs north of Mahim Creek.

Tourist information
Government of India ① *123 M Karve Rd, opposite Churchgate, T022-2207 4333, Mon-Sat 0830-1730 (closed 2nd Sat of month from 1230); counters open 24 hrs at both airports; Taj Mahal Hotel, Mon-Sat 0830-1530 (closed 2nd Sat from 1230).* **Maharashtra Tourist Development Corporation (MTDC)** ① *CDO Hutments, Madam Cama Rd, T022-2204 4040, www.maharashtratourism.gov.in; Koh-i-Noor Rd, near Pritam Hotel, Dadar T022-2414 3200; Gateway of India, T022-2284 1877.* Information and booking counters at international and domestic terminals and online.

Background

Hinduism made its mark on Mumbai long before the Portuguese and British transformed it into one of India's great cities. The caves on the island of Elephanta were excavated under the Kalachuris (AD 500-600). Yet, only 350 years ago, the area occupied by this great metropolis comprised seven islands inhabited by Koli fishermen. The British acquired these marshy and malarial islands as part of the marriage dowry paid by the Portuguese when Catherine of Braganza married Charles II in 1661. Four years later, they took possession of the remaining islands and neighbouring mainland area and in 1668 the East India Company leased the whole area from the crown for £10 a year, which was paid for nearly 50 years. The East India Company shifted its headquarters to Mumbai in 1672.

Isolated by the sharp face of the Western Ghats and the constantly hostile Marathas, Mumbai's early fortunes rested on the shipbuilding yards established by progressive Parsis. It thrived entirely on overseas trade and, in the cosmopolitan city this created, Parsis, Sephardic Jews and the British shared common interests and responded to the same incentives.

After a devastating fire on 17 February 1803, a new town with wider streets was built. Then, with the abolition of the Company's trade monopoly, the doors to rapid expansion were flung open and Mumbai flourished. Trade with England boomed, and under the governorship of Sir Bartle Frere (1862-1869) the city acquired a number of extravagant

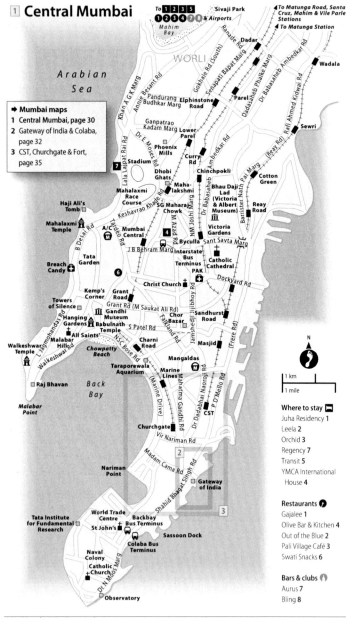

1 Central Mumbai

→ Mumbai maps
1 Central Mumbai, page 30
2 Gateway of India & Colaba, page 32
3 CST, Churchgate & Fort, page 35

Arabian Sea

To Matunga Road, Santa Cruz, Mahim & Vile Parle Stations

To Matunga Station

Sivaji Park & Airports

Mahim Bay

WORLI

Dadar

Wadala

Sewri

Ranade Rd
Gokhale Rd (South)
Senapati Bapat Marg
Dadasaheb Phalke Marg
Dr Babasaheb Ambedkar Rd
Rafi Ahmed Kidwai Rd
(Reay Rd)

Annie Besant Rd
Khan A GK Marg
Pandurang Budhkar Marg
Elphinstone Road
Parel

Ganpatrao Kadam Marg
Lower Parel
Dr E Moses Rd
Phoenix Mills
Curry Rd
Chinchpokli
Cotton Green

Stadium
Dhobi Ghats
Maha-lakshmi
Bhau Daji Lad (Victoria & Albert Museum)
Reay Road

Mahalaxmi Race Course
SG Maharaj Chowk
Keshavrao Khade Rd
M Azad Rd
NM Joshi Rd
Dr Babasaheb Ambedkar Rd
Barrister Nath Pai Marg
Victoria Gardens
Sant Savta Marg

Haji Ali's Tomb
Mahalaxmi Temple
B Desai Rd
A/C Market
Tardeo Rd
Mumbai Central
Byculla

Breach Candy
Tata Garden
J B Behram Marg
Interstate Bus Terminus
Catholic Cathedral
PAK
Dockyard Rd

Kemp's Corner
Grant Road
Christ Church
Sandhurst Road

Towers of Silence
Gandhi Museum
Grant Rd (M Saukat Ali Rd)
Chor Bazaar
Jamshedji Jijibhoy Rd
Falkland Rd

Hanging Gardens
Babulnath Temple
All Saints
S Patel Rd
Charni Road
Masjid
(Frere Rd)

Walkeshwar Temple
Malabar Hill
Walkeshwar
Chowpatty Beach
NSC Bose Rd
Mangaldas
Marine Lines
Dr Dadabhai Naoroji Rd
P D'Mello Rd

Raj Bhavan
Taraporewala Aquarium
Mahatma Gandhi Rd
CST

Back Bay

Malabar Point

Churchgate

Vir Nariman Rd

Nariman Point
Madam Cama Rd
Shahid Bhagat Singh Rd
Gateway of India

Tata Institute for Fundamental Research
World Trade Centre
St John's
Backbay Bus Terminus
Sassoon Dock
Colaba Bus Terminus

Naval Colony
Catholic Church
Dr N Moos Marg
Observatory

N

1 km
1 mile

Where to stay
Juha Residency 1
Leela 2
Orchid 3
Regency 7
Transit 5
YMCA International House 4

Restaurants
Gajalee 1
Olive Bar & Kitchen 4
Out of the Blue 2
Pali Village Café 3
Swati Snacks 6

Bars & clubs
Aurus 7
Bling 8

Indo-Gothic landmarks, most notably the station formerly known as the Victoria Terminus. The opening of the Suez Canal in 1870 gave Mumbai greater proximity to European markets and a decisive advantage over its eastern rival Kolkata. It has since become the headquarters for many national and international companies, and was a natural choice as home to India's stock exchange (BSE). With the sponsorship of the Tata family, Mumbai has also become the primary home of India's nuclear research programme, with its first plutonium extraction plant at Trombay in 1961 and the establishment of the Tata Institute for Fundamental Research, the most prestigious science research institute in the country.

Mumbai is still growing fast, and heavy demand for building space means property value is some of the highest on earth. As in Manhattan, buildings are going upward: residential skyscrapers have mushroomed in the upscale enclaves around Malabar Hill. Meanwhile, the old mill complexes of Lower Parel have been rapidly revived as shopping and luxury apartment complexes. An even more ambitious attempt to ease pressure on the isthmus is the newly minted city of Navi Mumbai, 90 minutes east of the city, which has malls, apartments and industrial parks, but little of the glamour that makes Mumbai such a magnet.

The latest project is the controversial redevelopment of Dharavi, a huge chunk of prime real estate that's currently occupied by Asia's biggest slum – home to one third of Mumbai's population, in desperately squalid makeshift hovels originally designed to house migrant mill workers. In addition, an uncounted number live precariously in unauthorized, hastily rigged and frequently demolished corrugated iron or bamboo-and-tarpaulin shacks beside railways and roads, while yet more sleep in doorways and on sheets across the pavement.

In recent decades, the pressure of supporting so many people has begun to tell on Mumbai. Communal riots between Hindus and Muslims have flared up several times since the destruction by militant Hindus of the Babri Masjid in 1992, and the disastrous 2005 monsoon, which dumped almost a metre of rainfall on the city overnight and left trains stranded with water up to their windows, laid bare the governmental neglect which had allowed drainage and other infrastructure to lag behind the needs of the populace.

The unprecedented attacks of 26 November 2008, when Lashkar-e-Taiba terrorists held staff and foreign guests hostage in the Taj Mahal and Oberoi hotels, have been widely read as a strike against the symbols of India's overseas business ambitions. They further served to illustrate that money cannot buy protection from the harsh realities of Indian life. Yet the citizens did not vent their anger on each other, but at the government that had failed to deal effectively with the attacks. Within weeks the front of the Taj had been scrubbed clean and tourists were packing out the Leopold Café, while CST station emerged from the bullets a cleaner, calmer, less chaotic place. Somehow, whether through economic imperative or a shared mentality of forward thinking, the city always finds a way to bounce back.

Gateway of India and Colaba → For listings, see pages 42-50.

The Indo-Saracenic-style Gateway of India (1927), designed by George Wittet to commemorate the visit of George V and Queen Mary in 1911, is modelled in honey-coloured basalt on 16th-century Gujarati work. The great gateway is an archway with halls on each side capable of seating 600 at important receptions. The arch was the point from which the last British regiment left on 28 February 1948, signalling the end of the empire. The whole area has a huge buzz at weekends. Scores of boats depart from here for **Elephanta Island**, creating a sea-swell which young boys delight in diving into. Hawkers, beggars and the general throng of people all add to the atmosphere. A short distance behind the Gateway is an impressive **statue of Shivaji**.

The original red-domed **Taj Mahal Hotel** was almost completely gutted by fire in the aftermath of the 26/11 terrorist attacks, which saw guests and staff of the hotel taken hostage and several killed, but the outside has been swiftly restored to normal and has fully reopened for business. It is worth popping into the Taj for a bite to eat or a drink, or

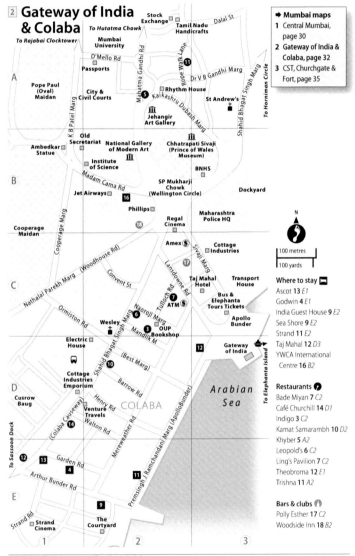

Gateway of India & Colaba

2

→ Mumbai maps
1 Central Mumbai, page 30
2 Gateway of India & Colaba, page 32
3 CST, Churchgate & Fort, page 35

To Hutatma Chowk
To Rajabai Clocktower
Stock Exchange
Tamil Nadu Handicrafts
Dalal St
Mumbai University
D'Mello Rd
Passports
Rope Walk Lane
Dr V B Gandhi Marg
Mahatma Gandhi Rd
Shahid Bhagat Singh Marg
To Horniman Circle

A
Pope Paul (Oval) Maidan
City & Civil Courts
Rhythm House
Kaikashru Dubash Marg
St Andrew's
K B Patel Marg
Jehangir Art Gallery
Old Secretariat
National Gallery of Modern Art
Ambedkar Statue
Institute of Science
Chhatrapati Sivaji (Prince of Wales) Museum
BNHS

B
Madam Cama Rd
SP Mukharji Chowk (Wellington Circle)
Dockyard
Jet Airways
Phillips
Cooperage Maidan
Cooperage Marg
Regal Cinema
Maharashtra Police HQ
Amex
Cottage Industries
N
100 metres
100 yards

C
Nathalal Parekh Marg
Convent St
Woodhouse Rd
Landsdowne Rd
Sivaji Marg
Taj Mahal Hotel
Transport House
Ormiston Rd
Naoroji Marg
Tulloch Rd
Bus & Elephanta Tours Tickets
ATM
Wesley
OUP Bookshop
Mandlik M
Apollo Bunder
Electric House
Shahid Bhagat Singh Marg
(Best Marg)
Gateway of India

D
Cottage Industries Emporium
Barrow Rd
COLABA
Arabian Sea
Cusrow Baug
Henry Rd
(Coloba Causeway)
Venture Travels
Walton Rd
Mereweather Rd
To Elephanta Island
To Sassoon Dock
Garden Rd
Premsingh J Ramchandani Marg (Apollo Bunder)

E
Arthur Bunder Rd
Strand Rd
Strand Cinema
The Courtyard

1　　**2**　　**3**

Where to stay 🛏
Ascot 13 *E1*
Godwin 4 *E1*
India Guest House 9 *E2*
Sea Shore 9 *E2*
Strand 11 *E2*
Taj Mahal 12 *D3*
YWCA International Centre 16 *B2*

Restaurants 🍴
Bade Miyan 7 *C2*
Café Churchill 14 *D1*
Indigo 3 *C2*
Kamat Samarambh 10 *D2*
Khyber 5 *A2*
Leopold's 6 *C2*
Ling's Pavilion 7 *C2*
Theobroma 12 *E1*
Trishna 11 *A2*

Bars & clubs 🍸
Polly Esther 17 *C2*
Woodside Inn 18 *B2*

to go to the nightclub with its clientele of well-heeled young Indians. Unfortunately, drug addicts, drunks and prostitutes frequent the area behind the hotel, but you can also find couples and young families taking in the sea air around the Gateway at night.

South of the Gateway of India is the crowded southern section of Shahid (literally 'martyr') Bhagat Singh Marg, or Colaba Causeway, a brilliantly bawdy bazar and the epicentre of Mumbai's tourist scene; you can buy everything from high-end jeans to cheaply made *kurtas* and knock-off leather wallets at the street stalls, and the colourful cast of characters includes Bollywood casting agents, would-be novelists plotting a successor to *Shantaram* in the **Leopold Café** (another bearer of bullet scars from 26/11), and any number of furtive hash sellers. The Afghan Memorial **Church of St John the Baptist** (1847-1858) is at the northern edge of Colaba itself. Early English in style, with a 58-m spire, it was built to commemorate the soldiers who died in the First Afghan War. Fishermen still unload their catch early in the morning at **Sassoon Dock**, the first wet dock in India; photography prohibited. Beyond the church near the tip of the Colaba promontory lie the **Observatory** and **Old European cemetery** in the naval colony (permission needed to enter). Frequent buses ply this route.

Fort → *For listings, see pages 42-50.*

The area stretching north from Colaba to CST (Victoria Terminus) is named after Fort St George, built by the British East India Company in the 1670s and torn down by Governor Bartle Frere in the 1860s. Anchored by the superb Chhatrapati Shivaji Museum to the south and the grassy parkland of Oval Maidan to the west, this area blossomed after 1862, when Sir Bartle Frere became governor (1862-1867). Under his enthusiastic guidance Mumbai became a great civic centre and an extravaganza of Victorian Gothic architecture, modified by Indo-Saracenic influences. This area is worth exploring at night, when many of the old buildings are floodlit.

Chhatrapati Shivaji (Prince of Wales) Museum ① *Oct-Feb Tue-Sun 1015-1800, last tickets 1645; foreigners Rs 300 (includes audio guide), Indians Rs 15, camera Rs 15 (no flash or tripods), students Rs 10, children Rs 5, avoid Tue as it is busy with school visits*, is housed in an impressive building designed by George Wittet to commemorate the visit of the Prince of Wales to India in 1905. The dome of glazed tiles has a very Persian and Central Asian flavour. The archaeological section has three main groups: Brahminical; Buddhist and Jain; Prehistoric and Foreign. The art section includes an excellent collection of Indian miniatures and well displayed *tankhas* along with a section on armour that is well worth seeing. There are also works by Gainsborough, Poussin and Titian as well as Indian silver, jade and tapestries. The Natural History section is based on the collection of the Bombay Natural History Society, founded in 1833. Good guidebooks, cards and reproductions on sale. **Jehangir Art Gallery** ① *within the museum complex, T022-2284 3989*, holds short-term exhibitions of contemporary art. The **Samovar café** is good for a snack and a chilled beer in a pleasant, if cramped, garden-side setting. Temporary members may use the library and attend lectures.

The **National Gallery of Modern Art** ① *Sir Cowasji Jehangir Hall, opposite the museum, T022-2285 2457, foreigners Rs 150, Indians Rs 10*, is a three-tiered gallery converted from an old public hall which gives a good introduction to India's contemporary art scene.

St Andrew's Kirk (1819) ① *just behind the museum, daily 1000-1700*, is a simple neoclassical church. At the south end of Mahatma Gandhi (MG) Road is the renaissance-style **Institute of Science** (1911) designed by George Wittet. The Institute, which includes a scientific library, a public hall and examination halls, was built with gifts from the Parsi and Jewish communities.

The **Oval Maidan** has been restored to a pleasant public garden and acts as the lungs and public cricket pitch of the southern business district. On the east side of the **Pope Paul Maidan** is the Venetian Gothic-style **old Secretariat** (1874), with a façade of arcaded verandas and porticos that are faced in buff-coloured porbander stone from Gujarat. Decorated with red and blue basalt, the carvings are in white *hemnagar* stone. The **University Convocation Hall** (1874) to its north was designed by Sir George Gilbert Scott in a 15th-century French decorated style. Scott also designed the adjacent **University Library** and the **Rajabai clock tower** (1870s) next door, based on Giotto's campanile in Florence. The sculpted figures in niches on the exterior walls of the tower were designed to represent the castes of India. Originally the clock could chime 12 tunes including *Rule Britannia*. The **High Court** (1871-1879), in early English Gothic style, has a 57-m-high central tower flanked by lower octagonal towers topped by the figures of Justice and Mercy. The Venetian Gothic **Public Works Office** (1869-1872) is to its north. Opposite, and with its main façade to Vir Nariman Road, is the gorgeously wrought former **General Post Office** (1869-1872). Now called the Telegraph Office, it stands next to the original Telegraph Office adding romanesque to the extraordinary mixture of European architectural styles.

From here you can walk east and delve into the dense back lanes of the Fort district, crossing the five-way junction of **Hutatma Chowk** ('Martyrs' Corner', in the centre of which stands the architecturally forgettable but useful landmark of the Flora Fountain (1869). This is an interesting area to explore although there are no particular sights

Vir Nariman Road cuts through to the elegant tree-shaded oval of **Horniman Circle**, laid out in 1860 and renamed in 1947 after Benjamin Horniman, editor of the pro-independence *Bombay Chronicle* – one of the few English names remaining on the Mumbai map. The park in the middle is used for dance and music performances during the **Kala Ghoda Arts Festival**, held in January. On the west edge are the Venetian Gothic **Elphinstone Buildings** (1870) in brown sandstone, while to the south is the **Cathedral Church of St Thomas** (1718), which contains a number of monuments amounting to a heroic 'Who's Who of India'.

South of Horniman Circle on Shahid Bhagat Singh Marg, the **Custom House** is one of the oldest buildings in the city, believed to incorporate a Portuguese barrack block from 1665. Over the entrance is the crest of the East India Company. Remnants of the old Portuguese fort's walls can be seen and many Malabar teak 'East Indiamen' ships were built here. Walk north from here and you'll reach the **Town Hall** (1820-1823), widely admired and much photographed as one of the best neoclassical buildings in India. The Corinthian interior houses the **Assembly Rooms** and the **Bombay Asiatic Society**. Immediately north again is the **Mint** (1824-1829) ① *visit by prior permission from the Mint Master, T022-2270 3184, www.mumbaimint.org*, built on the Fort rubbish dump, with Ionic columns and a water tank in front of it. The nearby **Ballard Estate** is also worth a poke around while you're in the area, with some good hotels and restaurants, as well as Hamilton Studios, the swanky offices of *Vogue* magazine, and the Mumbai Port Authority.

Around the CST (VT) → *For listings, see pages 42-50.*

Chhatrapati Shivaji Terminus (1878-1887), formerly Victoria Terminus and still known to many elder taxi drivers as 'VT', is far and away the most remarkable example of Victorian Gothic architecture in India. Opened during Queen Victoria's Golden Jubilee year (1887), over three million commuters now swarm through the station daily, though the bustling chaos of old has been reined in somewhat since November 2008's terror attacks, when at

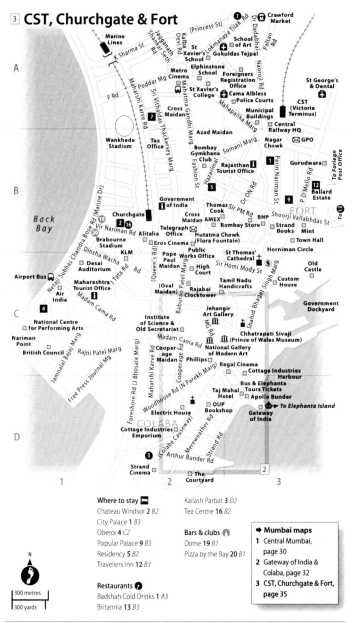

3 CST, Churchgate & Fort

Crawford Market

Marine Lines

(Princess St)

K Sharma St

School of Art

Gokuldas Tejpal

St Xavier's School

Elphinstone School

Metro Cinema

Foreigners Registration Office

St George's & Dental

St Xavier's College

Cama Albless

Police Courts

CST (Victoria Terminus)

Cross Maidan

Municipal Buildings

Central Railway HQ

Tax Office

Azad Maidan

Nagar Chowk

GPO

Wankhede Stadium

Bombay Gymkhana Club

Gurudwara

Rajasthan Tourist Office

To Foreign Post Office

Ballard Estate

Government of India

FORT

Back Bay

Churchgate

Cross Maidan

Thomas Cook

AMEX

BNP

Shoorji Vallabhdas St

Mint

Telegraph Office

Hutatma Chowk (Flora Fountain)

Bombay Store

Strand Books

Brabourne Stadium

Alitalia

Eros Cinema

Public Works Office

St Thomas' Cathedral

Horniman Circle

Town Hall

KLM

Pope Paul Maidan

High Court

Old Castle

Desai Auditorium

Airport Bus

Air India

(Oval Maidan)

Rajabai Clocktower

Tamil Nadu Handicrafts

Custom House

Government Dockyard

National Centre for Performing Arts

Institute of Science & Old Secretariat

Jehangir Art Gallery

Nariman Point

British Council

Cooper-age Maidan

National Gallery of Modern Art

Chhatrapati Sivaji (Prince of Wales Museum)

Phillips

Regal Cinema

Cottage Industries Harbour

Electric House

Woodhouse Rd (N Parekh Marg)

Taj Mahal Hotel

Bus & Elephanta Tours Tickets

Apollo Bunder

To Elephanta Island

OUP Bookshop

Gateway of India

COLABA

Cottage Industries Emporium

Strand Cinema

The Courtyard

N

300 metres

300 yards

least 50 people were shot dead here. Several scenes from *Slumdog Millionaire* were filmed on the suburban platforms at the west end of the station.

The station was built at a time when fierce debate was taking place among British architects working in India as to the most appropriate style to develop to meet the demands of the late 19th-century boom. One view held that the British should restrict themselves to models derived from the best in Western tradition. Others argued that architects should draw on Indian models, trying to bring out the best of Indian tradition and encourage its development. By and large, the former were dominant, but the introduction of Gothic elements allowed a blending of Western traditions with Indian (largely Islamic) motifs, which became known as the Indo-Saracenic style. The station that resulted, designed by FW Stevens, is its crowning glory: a huge, symmetrical, gargoyle-studded frontage capped by a large central dome and a 4-m-high statue of Progress, with arcaded booking halls, stained glass and glazed tiles inspired by St Pancras. The giant caterpillar-like walkway with perspex awnings looks truly incongruous against the huge Gothic structure.

There are many more Victorian buildings in the area around CST, particularly along Mahapalika Marg (Cruickshank Road), which runs northwest of the station past the grand **Municipal Buildings** (also by Stevens, 1893), and Lokmanya Tilak Marg (Camac Road), which joins Mahapalika Marg at the Metro Cinema traffic circle – a landmark known to every Mumbai cabbie.

Immediately to the north of CST lies **Crawford Market** (1865-1871), now renamed **Mahatma Jyotiba Phule Market** after a Maharashtran social reformer, designed by Emerson in 12th-century French Gothic style, with paving stones imported from Caithness and fountains carved by Lockwood Kipling. The market is divided into bustling sections for fruit, vegetables, fish, mutton and poultry, with a large central hall and clock tower.

Running northwest of Crawford Market towards Mumbai Central Railway Station is **Falkland Road**, the centre of Mumbai's red-light district. Prostitutes stand behind barred windows, giving the area its other name, 'The Cages' – many of the girls are sold or abducted from various parts of India and Nepal. AIDS is very widespread, and a lot of NGOs are at work in the area educating the women about prevention.

North of Crawford Market is **Masjid Station**, the heart of the Muslim quarter, where agate minarets mingle with the pollution-streaked upper storeys of 1960s residential towers. The atmosphere here is totally different from the crumbling colonial architectural glory of the Colaba and Fort area: balconies on faded apartment blocks are bedecked with fairy lights, laundry dries on the window grilles, and at sunset the ramshackle roads hum with taxis, boys wielding wooden carts through traffic and Muslim women at a stroll. One of the city's most interesting markets, the **Chor Bazar** (Thieves' Market) ① *Sat to Thu 1100-1900*, spreads through the streets between the station and Falkland Road. The bazar is a great place to poke around in with tonnes of dealers in old watches, film posters, Belgian- or Indian-made temple lamps, enamel tiles and door knobs. The area around Mutton Street is popular with film prop-buyers and foreign and domestic bric-a-brac hunters.

Marine Drive to Malabar Hill → *For listings, see pages 42-50.*

When the hustle of the city becomes too much, do as the Mumbaikars do and head for the water. The 3-km sweep of **Marine Drive** (known as the 'Queen's Necklace' for the lines of streetlights that run its length) skirts alongside the grey waters of the Arabian Sea from Nariman Point in the south to exclusive Malabar Hill in the north. This is where you'll see Mumbai at its most egalitarian: servants and *babus* alike take the air on the esplanades in the evening. For an interesting half-day trip, start downtown at Churchgate Station and follow the curving course of the Queen's Necklace to the Walkeshwar Temple out on the end of Malabar Hill; start at lunchtime and you can be strolling back down Marine Drive, ice cream in hand, among the atmospheric sunset crush of power-walking executives and festive families.

Churchgate Station (1894-1896), on Vir Nariman Road at the north end of the Oval Maidan, was the second great railway building designed by FW Stevens. With its domes and gables, Churchgate has an air of Byzantine simplicity that contrasts with CST's full-tilt Gothic overload, but the rush hour spectacle is no less striking: Sebastiao Salgado's famous photograph of commuters pouring out of suburban trains was taken here.

A block to the west is Netaji Subhash Road, better known as **Marine Drive**, which bends northwest past Wankhede cricket stadium, several luxury hotels and the run-down Taraporewala Aquarium. At the north end in the crook of Malabar Hill is **Chowpatty Beach**, a long stretch of grey-white sand that looks attractive from a distance, but is polluted. Swimming here is not recommended but there is a lot of interesting beach activity in the evening. Chowpatty was the scene of a number of important 'Quit India' rallies during the Independence Movement. During important festivals, like **Ganesh Chaturthi** and **Dussehra**, it is thronged with jubilant Hindu devotees.

Mahatma Gandhi Museum (**Mani Bhavan**) ① *west of Grant Rd station at 19 Laburnum Rd, www.gandhi-manibhavan.org, 0930-1800, Rs 10, allow 1 hr*, is north of Chowpatty on the road to Nana Chowk. This private house, where Mahatma Gandhi used to stay on visits to Mumbai, is now a memorial museum and research library with 20,000 volumes. There is a diorama depicting important scenes from Gandhi's life, but the display of photos and letters on the first floor is more interesting, and includes letters Gandhi wrote to Hitler in 1939 asking him not to go to war, and those to Roosevelt, Einstein and Tolstoy.

At the end of Chowpatty, Marine Drive becomes Walkeshwar Road and bends southwest to pass the **Jain Temple** (1904), built of marble and dedicated to the first Jain Tirthankar. Much of the colourful decoration depicts the lives of the Tirthankars. Visitors can watch various rituals being performed. Jains play a prominent part in Mumbai's banking and commerce and are one of the city's wealthiest communities. Beyond, on the tip of Malabar Point, is **Raj Bhavan**, now home to the Governor of Maharashtra.

Behind the Jain Temple, Gangadhar Kher Rd (Ridge Road) runs up Malabar Hill to the **Hanging Gardens** (**Pherozeshah Mehta Gardens**) so named since they are located on top of a series of tanks that supply water to Mumbai. The gardens are well kept with lots of topiary animals and offer an opportunity to hang out with Mumbai's elite, whose penthouse apartments peer down on the park from all sides; there are good views over the city and Marine Drive from the **Kamala Nehru Park** across the road. It's worth a visit after 1700 when it's a bit cooler, but it's reputed to be unsafe after nightfall. Immediately to the north are the Parsi **Towers of Silence**, set in secluded gardens donated by Parsi industrialist Sir Jamshetji Jeejeebhoy. This very private place is not accessible to tourists but it can be glimpsed from the road. Parsis believe that the elements of water, fire and earth must not be polluted by the dead, so they lay their 'vestments of flesh and bone' out on the top of the towers to be picked clean by vultures. The depletion in the number of vultures is a cause for concern, and more and more agiarys now opt for solar panels to speed up the process of decay.

At the end of the headland behind Raj Bhavan stands the **Walkeshwar Temple** ('Lord of Sand'), built about AD 1000 and one of the oldest buildings in Mumbai. In legend this was a resting point for Lord Rama on his journey from Ayodhya to Lanka to free Sita from the demon king Ravana. One day Rama's brother failed to return from Varanasi at the usual time with a *lingam* that he fetched daily for Rama's worship. Rama then made a *lingam* from the beach sand to worship Siva. You'd also do well to visit **Banganga**, a freshwater tank that's part of an 12th-century temple complex. Legend has it that when Rama got thirsty Lakshman raised his bow and shot a *baan* (arrow) into the ground, bringing forth fresh water from the Ganga in this ocean locked island. The site is being renovated and is regularly used as a venue for concerts, festivals and pilgrimages alike.

Central Mumbai → *For listings, see pages 42-50. See map on page 30.*

Other than to catch a train from Mumbai Central Station, relatively few visitors venture into the area north of Marine Drive, yet it contains some fascinating only-in-Mumbai sights which, with judicious use of taxis and the odd suburban train, can easily be combined into a day trip with the coastal sights described above.

On the coast, 1 km north of the Ghandi Museum on Bhulabhai Desai (Warden Road), are the **Mahalakshmi temples**, the oldest in Mumbai, dedicated to three goddesses whose images were found in the sea. Lakshmi, goddess of wealth, is the unofficial presiding deity of the city, and the temple is host to frenzied activity – pressing a coin into the wall of the main shrine is supposed to be a sign of riches to come. Just to the north, **Haji Ali's Mosque** sits on an islet 500 m offshore. The mosque, built in 1431, contains the tomb of Muslim saint Haji Ali, who drowned here while on pilgrimage to Mecca, and as a last request demanded that he be buried neither on land nor at sea. A long causeway, usable only at low tide, links the mosque and tomb to the land, and is lined by Muslim supplicants. The money changers are willing to exchange one-rupee coins into smaller coins, enabling pilgrims to make several individual gifts to beggars rather than one larger one, thereby reputedly increasing the merit of the gift.

From Haji Ali's Tomb go east along Keshavrao Khade Road, passing the **Mahalakshmi Race Course** ① *racing season Nov-Apr, www.rwitc.com*, to SG Maharaj Chowk (**Jacob's Circle**), and turn north to Mahalakshmi Bridge, reachable by local trains from Churchgate. From the bridge there is a view across the astonishing Municipal **dhobi ghats**, where Mumbai's dirty laundry is soaked, smacked in concrete tubs and aired in public by the *dhobis* (washerfolk); vistas unfold in blocks of primary colours, though you may have to fend off junior touts to enjoy them in peace. A short distance further north are the disused Victorian cotton mills of **Lower Parel**. Closed in 1980 after an all-out strike, some remain standing in a state of picturesque ruin (local residents may offer to show you round for Rs 50-100) while others, notably the Phoenix, Mathuradas and Bombay Dyeing mill compounds, have been converted into slick new malls, nightclubs and studio spaces popular with publishers and advertising agencies.

Southeast of Mahalakshmi station in Byculla are the **Veermata Jijibai Bhonsle Udyan** gardens, formerly Victoria Gardens. The attractive 48-acre park is home to Mumbai's **zoo** ① *Thu-Tue 0900-1800, Rs 5*, be warned though, the signboards are missing and while the birds are gorgeous – they have birds of paradise, white peacocks and pink pelicans among others – there's no indication of what you're looking at. The gardens share space with the newly renovated **Bhau Daji Lad Museum** (**Victoria and Albert Museum**) ① *www.bdl museum.org, Thu-Tue, 1000-1730, foreigners Rs 100, Indians Rs 10, children half price*. Inspired by the V&A in London and financed by public subscription, it was built in 1872 in a palladian style and is the second oldest museum in India. The collection covers the history of Mumbai and contains prints, maps and models that show how the seven disjointed islands came to form Mumbai.

Bandra, Juhu Beach and Andheri → *For listings, see pages 42-50.*

If you really want to get under the skin of the city, a jaunt into the far-flung northern suburbs is essential. Close to the airports and relatively relaxed compared to living in the city centre, Bandra and Juhu are popular with Mumbai's upper crust, and most Bollywood A-listers have at least one of their homes here. **Bandra** is a lively suburb, full of the young and wealthy, with some exciting places to eat and some of the coolest bars, coffee shops, gyms and lounges in the city. Linking Road is home to a long open-air shoe bazar where you can find cheap, colourful sandals and knock-offs of every brand of clothing. Bandra's two seaside promenades, one at Bandra Bandstand by the Taj Lands End Hotel and one at Carter Road, the next bay northwards, feature sea-facing coffee shops with spectacular sunset views.

Juhu Beach, 20 km north of the centre, used to be an attractive and relaxed seaside area, but one sniff of the toxic water oozing out of Mahim Creek is enough to dissuade anyone from dipping so much as a toe in the ocean. Hordes of people still visit every day to walk on the beach, eat *bhel puri* and other spicy street food that delicate stomachs had best avoid, while kids buy balloons and take rides on horse-driven chariots. Beyond the beach Juhu is primarily a residential area, full of luxurious apartments, elegant old bungalows (Bollywood megastar Amitabh Bachchan has a place here) and day spas.

Andheri, spreading north of the airports, is the biggest suburb in Mumbai: it covers 50 sq km, is home to between 1.5 million and four million people depending on who's counting, and has sprung up from villages and mangrove swamps in a mere 30 years. There are few sights of note, but as a city within a city, with its own social subdivisions (mega-trendy residential enclaves and malls to the west, business parks and down-at-heel slums to the east, and even a suburban monorail system in construction), Andheri may well come to represent Mumbai's second city centre. If you want to explore, the areas to know about are Lokhandwala, New Link Road and Seven Bungalows/Versova; all are in Andheri West.

Elephanta Caves → *For listings, see pages 42-50.*

Ten kilometres east of the Gateway of India, the heavily forested **Elephanta Island**, barely visible in the haze from Mumbai, rises out of the bay like a giant whale. The setting is symbolically significant; the sea is the ocean of life, a world of change (Samsara) in which is set an island of spiritual and physical refuge. The 'caves', excavated over 1000 years ago in the volcanic lava high up the slope of the hill, saw Hindu craftsmen express their view of spiritual truths in massive carvings of extraordinary grace. Sadly a large proportion have been severely damaged, but enough remains to illustrate something of their skill.

Background

The vast majority of India's 1200 **cave sites** were created as temples and monasteries between the third century BC and the 10th century AD. Jain, Buddhist and Hindu caves often stand side by side. The temple cave on Elephanta Island, dedicated to Siva, was probably excavated during the eighth century by the Rashtrakuta Dynasty which ruled the Deccan AD 757-973, though the caves may have had earlier Buddhist origins. An earlier name for the island was Garhapuri ('city of forts') but the Portuguese renamed it after the colossal sculpted elephants when they captured Mumbai from the Sultan of Gujarat in 1535, and stationed a battalion there. They reportedly used the main pillared cave as a shooting gallery causing some of the damage you see. Muslim and British rulers were not blameless either.

Arriving in Elephanta Caves

Boats to Elephanta Island leave every few minutes from 0900, from the jetty in front of the Gateway of India. The crossing takes about an hour. From the landing place, a 300-m unshaded path along the quayside and then about 110 rough steps lead to the caves at a height of 75 m. The walk along the quay can be avoided when the small train functions (Rs 10 return). The climb can be trying for some, especially if it is hot, though *doolies* (chairs carried by porters) are available for Rs 300 return, Rs 200 one-way. At the start of the climb there are stalls selling refreshments, knick-knacks and curios (including models of the Eiffel Tower), but if you're carrying food watch out for aggressive monkeys. **Maharashtra Tourism** normally organizes a festival of classical music and dance on the island in the third week of February. Early morning is the best time for light and also for avoiding large groups with guides which arrive from 1000. The caves tend to be quite dark so carry a powerful torch.

The site

ⓘ *Tue-Sun, sunrise to sunset; foreigners Rs 250, Indians Rs 10, plus Rs 5 passenger tax. Weekends are very busy.*

Entrance Originally there were three entrances and 28 pillars at the site. The entrances on the east and west have subsidiary shrines which may have been excavated and used for different ceremonies. The main entrance is now from the north. At dawn, the rising sun casts its rays on the approach to the *garbagriha* (main shrine), housed in a square structure at the west end of the main hall. On your right is a carving of Siva as Nataraj. On the left he appears as Lakulisa in a much damaged carving. Seated on a lotus, the Buddha-like figure is a symbol of the unconscious mind and enlightenment, found also in Orissan temples where Lakulisa played a prominent role in attempting to attract Buddhists back into Hinduism. From the steps at the entrance you can see the *yoni-lingam*, the symbol of the creative power of the deity.

Main Hall The ribbed columns in the main hall, 5- to 6-m high and in a cruciform layout, are topped by a capital. At the corner of each pillar is a dwarf signifying *gana* (the earth spirit), and sometimes the figure of Ganesh (Ganapati). To the right, the main **Linga Shrine** has four entrances, each corresponding to a cardinal point guarded by a *dvarpala*. The sanctum is bare, drawing attention to the *yonilingam* which the devotee must walk around clockwise.

Wall panels To the north of the main shrine is **Bhairava killing the demon Andhakasura**. This extraordinarily vivid carving shows Siva at his most fearsome, with a necklace of skulls, crushing the power of Andhaka, the Chief of Darkness. It was held that if he was wounded each drop of his blood would create a new demon. So Siva impaled him with his sword and collected his blood with a cup, which he then offered to his wife Shakti. In winter this panel is best seen in the early afternoon.

Opposite, on the south side of the main shrine is the damaged panel of **Kalyan Sundari**, in which Siva stands with Parvati on his right, just before their wedding (normally a Hindu wife stands on her husband's left). She looks down shyly, but her body is drawn to him. Behind Parvati is her father Himalaya and to his left Chandramas, the moon god carrying a gift – *soma*, the food of the gods. On Siva's left is Vishnu and below him Brahma.

At the extreme west end of the temple are **Nataraja** (left) and **Yogisvara Siva** (right). The former shows a beautiful figure of Ganesh above and Parvati on his left. All the other gods watch him. Above his right shoulder is the four-headed God of Creation, Brahma. Below Brahma is the elephant-headed Ganesh.

On the south wall, opposite the entrance are three panels. **Gangadhara** is on the west. The holy River Ganga (Bhagirathi) flowed only in heaven but was brought to earth by her father King Bhagiratha (kneeling at Siva's right foot). Here, Ganga is shown in the centre, flanked by her two tributaries, Yamuna and Saraswati. These three rivers are believed to meet at Allahabad.

To the left of these is the centre piece of the whole temple, the remarkable **Mahesvara**, the Lord of the Universe. Here Siva is five-headed, for the usual triple-headed figure has one face looking into the rock and another on top of his head. Nearly 6 m high, he unites all the functions of creation, preservation and destruction. Some see the head on the left (your right) as representing Vishnu, the Creator, while others suggest that it shows a more feminine aspect of Siva. To his right is Rudra or Bhairava, with snakes in his hair, a skull to represent ageing from which only Siva is free, and he has a look of anger. The central face is Siva as his true self, Siva Swarupa, balancing out creation and destruction. In this mode he is passive and serene, radiating peace and wisdom like the Buddha. His right hand is held up in a calming gesture and in his left hand is a lotus bud.

The panel to the left has the **Ardhanarisvara**. This depicts Siva as the embodiment of male and female, representing wholeness and the harmony of opposites. The female half is relaxed and gentle, the mirror in the hand symbolizing the woman reflecting the man. Siva has his 'vehicle', Nandi on the right.

To the east, opposite the *garbha-griha*, was probably the original entrance. On the south is Siva and Parvati **Playing chaupar on Mount Kailash**. Siva is the faceless figure. Parvati has lost and is sulking but her playful husband persuades her to return to the game. They are surrounded by Nandi, Siva's bull, celestial figures and an ascetic with his begging bowl.

On the north is **Ravana Shaking Mount Kailash** on which Siva is seated. Siva is calm and unperturbed by Ravana's show of brute strength and reassures the frightened Parvati. He pins down Ravana with his toe, who fails to move the mountain and begs Siva's forgiveness which is granted.

Kanheri Caves → *For listings, see pages 42-50.*

Sanjay Gandhi National Park, north of the city at Goregaon, is worth a visit in itself for its dense deciduous and semi-evergreen forest providing a beautiful habitat for several varieties of deer, antelope, butterflies, birds and the occasional leopard. However, the main reason for visiting is for the **Kanheri Caves** situated in the heart of the park.

Some 42 km north of Mumbai, the caves (also known as Mahakali Caves) are on a low hill midway between Borivli and Thane. The hills used to form the central part of Salsette Island, but the surrounding land has long since been extensively built on. Further up the ravine from the caves there are some fine views across the Bassein Fort and out to sea. Still shaded by trees, the entrance is from the south. There are 109 Buddhist caves, dating from the end of the second to the ninth century AD with flights of steps joining them. The most significant is the **Chaitya Cave** (cave 3) circa sixth century. The last Hinayana chaitya hall to be excavated is entered through a forecourt and veranda. The pillared entrance has well carved illustrations of the donors, and the cave itself comprises a 28 m x 13 m colonnaded hall of 34 pillars. At one end these encircle the 5-m-high *dagoba*. Some of the pillars have carvings of elephants and trees. Some 50 m up the ravine is **Darbar of the Maharajah Cave** (Cave 10). This was a *dharamshala* (resthouse) and has two stone benches running down the sides and some cells leading off the left and back walls. Above Cave 10 is **Cave 35** which was a *vihara* (monastery), which has reliefs of a Buddha seated on a lotus and of a disciple spreading his cloak for him to walk on. All the caves have an elaborate drainage and water storage system, fresh rainwater being led into underground storage tanks.

Above the cave complex is **Ashok Van**, a sacred grove of ancient trees, streams and springs. From there, a three-hour trek leads to 'View Point', the highest in Mumbai. There are breathtaking views. Photography is prohibited from the radar station on top of the hill; there are excellent opportunities just below it.

The park is also home to hyena and panther, though rarely seen, while three lakes have ducks, herons and crocodiles. Nature trails lead from Film City (reached by bus from Goregaon station). A lion safari leaves from **Hotel Sanjay** near Borivli station.

Mumbai listings

For hotel and restaurant price codes and other relevant information, see pages 13-15.

🛏 Where to stay

Room prices in Mumbai are stratospheric by Indian standards, and there's no such thing as low-season: if possible make reservations in advance or arrive as early in the day as you can. Most hotels are concentrated in the downtown area, between **Colaba** and **Marine Dr**, and around the airport in the suburbs of **Santa Cruz**, **Juhu**, **Bandra** and **Andheri**. There are also several options around Mumbai Central and Dadar stations – handy for a quick getaway or an un-touristy view of the city.

Backpackers usually head for the **Colaba** area, which has some of the cheapest rooms in the city. **Arthur Bunder Rd** is a hotspot, with several places hidden away on upper floors of apartment blocks, usually with shared facilities, cold water and sometimes windowless rooms; arrive early and inspect room first. For a more personal view of the city, consider staying in a private home: browse the listings on Airbnb (www.airbnb.com), or contact **India Tourism**, 123 M Karve Rd, Churchgate, T022-2203 3144.

Gateway of India and Colaba *p31, map p32*

$$$$ Ascot, 38 Garden Rd, Colaba, T022-6638 5566, www.ascothotel.com.

The tan-wood rooms, shoehorned into a graceful 1930s building, veer dangerously close to IKEA anonymity, but they're generously proportioned and new, with safe deposit boxes, work desks and granite shower stalls. Great views from the upper floors. Breakfast included.

$$$$ Taj Mahal, Apollo Bunder, T022-6665 3366, www.tajhotels.com. The grand dame of Mumbai lodging, over a century old. The glorious old wing has been fully restored and updated after the 26/11/08 attacks, joining the 306 rooms in the **Taj Mahal Intercontinental** tower. Several top-class restaurants and bars, plus fitness centre, superb pool and even a yacht on call.

$$$ Godwin, 41 Garden Rd, Colaba, T022-2287 2050, hotelgodwin@mail.com. 48 large, clean, renovated, a/c rooms with superb views from upper floors, mostly helpful management and a good rooftop restaurant – full of wealthy Mumbaikars on Fri and Sat night.

$$$ Strand, 25 PJ Ramchandani Marg, T022-2288 2222, www.hotelstrand.com. Friendly. Clean rooms, some with bath and sea view.

$$$ YWCA International Centre, 18 Madame Cama Rd, Colaba, T022-2202 0598, www.ywcaic.info. For both sexes, 34 clean and pleasant rooms with bath, and breakfast and buffet dinner included in the price. A reliable and sociable budget option, though the deposit required to hold your booking is a slight hassle.

$ India Guest House, 1/49 Kamal Mansion, Arthur Bunder Rd, T022-2283 3769. 20 rooms along long corridor, white partitions that you could, at a push, jump over. Fan, no toilet or shower. The corner room has a neat panorama over the bay. Sound will travel.

$ Sea Shore, top floor, 1/49 Kamal Mansion, Arthur Bunder Rd, T022-2287 4238. Kitsch as you like, 15 bright gloss-pink rooms and purple corridors with plastic flowers, shower in room but no sink, 7 with window and TV and fan, 8 without. Sea view room has 4 beds. 2 rooms comewith toilet, TV and hot water.

Fort *p33, map p35*

$$$ Residency, corner of Rustom Sidhwa Marg and DN Rd, T022-6667 0555, www. residencyhotel.com. Clean and modern rooms in an interesting 19th-century building halfway between Flora Fountain and CST. Great location and good value.

$$-$ Traveller's Inn, 26 Adi Murzban Path, Ballard Estate, Fort, T022-2264 4685, www. hoteltravellersinn.co.in. A relatively new addition to Mumbai's backpacker repertoire, with simple, clean rooms, a 3-bed dormitory, internet and Wi-Fi, and friendly staff.

$ Popular Palace, 104-106 Mint Rd, near GPO, Fort Market, T022-2269 5506. Small but clean rooms with bath (hot water), some a/c, helpful staff, good value.

Around the CST (VT) *p34, map p35*

$$ City Palace, 121 City Terrace (Nagar Chowk), opposite CST Main Gate, T022-2261 5515. Decrepit guesthouse with tiny but functional rooms bang opposite the station. An OK place to crash before catching an early train.

Marine Drive to Malabar Hill *p36, map p35*

$$$$-$$$ Regency, 73 Nepean Sea Rd, T022-66571234, www.regencymumbai.com. 80 modest but immaculate rooms in quiet spot close to the sea at the base of upmarket Malabar Hill. Personable, friendly staff and free breakfast.

$$$$ The Oberoi, Nariman Pt, T022-6632 5757, www.oberoimumbai.com. Newly renovated and reopened, with beautiful sea-view rooms, glass-walled bathrooms, and 3 top-class restaurants.

$$$ Chateau Windsor Guest House, 86 Vir Nariman Rd, T022-6622 4455, www. cwh.in. Friendly and helpful place in a great location. The rooms on the 1st and 3rd floors are the best, newly renovated with large spotless bathrooms, marble tiles and balconies. Some of the older rooms are small, poky and dark. Recommended.

Central Mumbai *p38, map p30*

$$ YMCA International House, 18 YMCA Rd, near Mumbai Central, T022-6154 0100. Decent rooms, shared bath, meals included, temp membership Rs 120, deposit Rs 1300, good value, book 3 months ahead.

Bandra, Juhu Beach and Andheri *p39, map p30*

$$$$ Leela, near International Terminal, T022-6000 2233, www.theleela.com. One of the best of the airport hotels, with 460 modern rooms, excellent restaurants, pricey but excellent bar (residents only after 2300), all-night coffee shop, happening nightclub.

$$$$ Orchid, 70C Nehru Rd, Vile Parle (east), 5 mins' walk from domestic terminal, T022-2616 4040, www.orchidhotel.com. Refurbished, attractive rooms, eco-friendly. Boulevard restaurant boasts a good midnight buffet and '15-min lightning' buffet. Recommended.

$$$ Juhu Residency, 148B Juhu Tara Rd, Juhu Beach, T022-6783 4949, www.juhuresidency.com. Across the road from Juhu Beach, with just 28 attractive refurbished rooms, free Wi-Fi, friendly efficient staff and 2 excellent restaurants. A decent deal by Mumbai standards.

$$$ Transit, off Nehru Rd, Vile Parle (east), T022-6693 0761, www.hoteltransit.in. Modern, 54 rooms, reasonable overnight halt for airport, excellent restaurant (draught beer), airport transfer. Special rates for day use (0800-1800).

🍽 Restaurants

Gateway of India and Colaba *p31, map p32*

$$$ Indigo, 4 Mandlik Rd, behind Taj Hotel, T022-6636 8999. Excellent Mediterranean in smart restaurant, good atmosphere and wine list, additional seating on rooftop.

$$$ Khyber, 145 MG Rd, Kala Ghoda, T022-4039 6666. North Indian. For an enjoyable evening in beautiful surroundings, outstanding food, especially lobster and *reshmi* chicken kebabs, try *paya* soup (goats' trotters).

$$$ Ling's Pavilion, 19/21 KC College Hostel Building, off Colaba Causeway (behind Taj and Regal Cinema), T022-2285 0023. Stylish decor, good atmosphere and delightful service, colourful menu, seafood specials, generous helpings. Recommended.

$$$ Trishna, Sai Baba Marg, next to Commerce House, T022-2270 3213. Good coastal cuisine, seafood, excellent butter garlic crab. Recommended.

$$ Café Churchill, 103-8, East West Court Building, opposite Cusrow Baug, Colaba Causeway, T022-2284 4689. Open 1000-2330. A tiny little café with 7 tables crammed with people basking in a/c, towered over by a cake counter and a Winston Churchill portrait. Great breakfasts, club sandwiches, seafood, fish and chips, lasagne and Irish stew.

$$ Leopold's, Colaba, T022-2282 8185. An institution among Colaba backpackers and Mumbai shoppers. The food, predominantly Western with a limited choice of Indian vegetarian, is average and pricey (similar cafés nearby are far better value) but Leo's gained cachet from its cameo role in the novel *Shantaram*, and was the first target of the terror attacks in Nov 2008.

$ Bade Miyan, Tullock Rd behind Ling's Pavilion. Streetside kebab corner, but very clean. Try *baida roti, shammi* and *boti* kebabs. The potato *kathi* rolls are excellent veg options.

$ Kailash Parbat, 1st Pasta La, Colaba. Excellent snacks and *chats*, in an old-style eatery also serving Punjabi *thalis*.

The milky-sweet *pedas* from the counter are a Mumbai institution.

$ Kamat Samarambh, opposite Electric House, Colaba Causeway. Very good and authentic South Indian food, *thalis* and snacks. Try the moist, fluffy *uttapam* and *upma*. Clean drinking water.

Cafés and snacks

Theobroma, Colaba Causeway, next to Cusrow Baug. Decent coffee and terrific egg breakfasts. The brownies here are to die for – try the millionaire brownie or the rum-and-raisin with coffee. Egg-free cakes available.

Fort *p33, map p35*

$$ Britannia, Wakefield House, Sprott Rd, opposite New Custom House, Ballard Estate, T022-22615264. Mon-Sat 1200-1600. Incredible Parsi/Iranian fare with a delicious berry *pullav* made from specially imported Bol berries (cranberries from Iran). Try the *dhansak* and the egg curry. Recommended.

Around the CST (VT) *p34, map p35*

$$ Badshah Cold Drinks & Snacks, opposite Crawford Market. Famous for its *kulfi* (hand-churned ice cream) and fresh fruit juices (drink without ice), it's a default stop for everyone shopping at Crawford Market. Good and fast *pav-bhaji* (mixed veggies with buttered rolls).

Marine Drive to Malabar Hill *p36, map p35*

$ Tea Centre, 78 Vir Nariman Rd, near Churchgate. A little old-fashioned and colonial, but dozens of refreshing tea options, and a menu of heavy Indian food. Good value and a/c.

Central Mumbai *p38, map p30*

$$$ Olive, Union Park, Pali Hill, Bandra, T022-2605 8228. 'Progressive Mediterranean' food, served in an upscale environment to a cast of Bollywood celebs. Packed on Thu, when there's live music, and for brunch on Sun. Also has a branch at Mahalaxmi racecourse, T022-4085 9595.

$$$ Pali Village Cafe, Ambedkar Rd, Bandra (W), T022-2605 0401. Super-trendy new restaurant done out in shabby-chic industrial style, cascading across different rooms and levels. Good desserts and tapas-style starters, though the wine list and general vibe outweigh the quality of food and service.

$ Swati Snacks, Tardeo Rd, opposite Bhatia Hospital, T022-6580 8405. Gujarati and Parsi snacks along with street foods made in a hygienic fashion: try *khichdi, sev puri, pav bhaji, dahi puri* here. Be prepared for a 20- to 40-min wait, but it's worth it.

Bandra, Juhu Beach and Andheri
p39, map p30

$$ Gajalee, Kadambari Complex, Hanuman Rd, Vile Parle (E), T022-6692 9592, www.gajalee.com; also in Phoenix Mills. Fine coastal cuisine, try fish tikka, stuffed bombay duck and shellfish with the traditional breads *ghawne* and *amboli*.

$$ Out of the Blue, 14 Union Park, off Carter Rd, Khar West, T022-2600 3000. Romantic candlelit restaurant with a Goan beach-shack vibe. Great sizzlers, and live music most nights.

🎵 Bars and clubs

Gateway of India and Colaba *p31, map p32*

Polly Esther, Gordon House Hotel. A reggae, pop, rock disco, retro-themed club, where anything goes. Open late, most people come here after they finish partying elsewhere.

Woodside Inn, opposite Regal Cinema Colaba. Cramped pub carved out of stone Gothic building, with decent retro music, good dining upstairs (pizzas and sandwiches are surprisingly decent) and good selection of whiskies. Free Wi-Fi too.

Marine Drive to Malabar Hill *p36, map p35*

Dome, Intercontinental Hotel, Marine Dr, T022-6639 9999. Rooftop restaurant and

lounge bar with a stunning view of the Queen's Necklace. Try the grilled prawns with your cocktails.

Pizza by the Bay, 143 Marine Dr, T022-2285 1876. Fun place near Churchgate, with live music, karaoke, good food menu (great starters and desserts), generous portions, wide selection of drinks. Loud and lively.

Bandra, Juhu Beach and Andheri
p39, map p30

Aurus, Juhu Tara Rd, Juhu. Trendy seaside patio bar where Bollywood stars rub shoulders with the glitterati. Avant garde DJs, some international, spin inside. Expensive appetizers, good signature drinks and ocean views. Free entry, easier for couples.

Bling, Leela Hotel (see Where to stay, page 43). Club that lives up to its name, stays open late so attracts the spillover from the other clubs. Entry Rs 700-2500 depending on the time, the night and the bouncers.

Toto's, 30th Rd, off Pali Naka, Bandra (W). Retro music, regular clients, and no attitude amid funky automotive decor.

✱ Festivals

Mumbai *p28, maps p30, p32 and p35*
In addition to the national Hindu and Muslim festivals (see pages 16 and 17) there are the following:

Feb Elephanta Cultural Festival at the caves. Great ambience. Contact MTDC, T022-2202 6713, for tickets Rs 150-200 including launch at 1800. **Kala Ghoda Arts Festival**, held in various locations around Colaba and Fort, T022-2284 2520, showcases of all forms of fine arts.

Mar Jamshed Navroz. This is New Year's Day for the Parsi followers of the Fasli calendar. The celebrations, which include offering prayers at temples, exchanging greetings, alms-giving and feasting at home, date back to Jamshed, the legendary King of Persia.

Jul-Aug Janmashtami celebrates the birth of Lord Krishna. Boys and young men form human pyramids and break pots of curd hung up high between buildings.

Aug Coconut Day. The angry monsoon seas are propitiated by devotees throwing coconuts into the ocean.

Aug-Sep Ganesh Chaturthi. Massive figures of Ganesh are towed through the streets to loud techno and storms of coloured powder, before a final *puja* at Chowpatty Beach where they're finally dragged out into the sea. The crowds making their way on foot to the beach cause immense traffic pile ups, and the scene at Chowpatty is chaotic, with priests giving *puja* to Ganesh and roaring crowds of men psyching themselves up for the final push into the ocean. A similar celebration happens shortly after at **Durga Pooja**, when the goddess Durga is worshipped and immersed.

Sep-Oct Dussehra. Group dances by Gujarati women in all the auditoria and residents have their own *garba* and *dandiya* dance nights in the courtyards of their apartment buildings. There are also **Ram leela** celebrations at Chowpatty Beach, where the story of the *Ramayana* is enacted in a dance drama. Diwali (The Festival of Lights) is particularly popular in mercantile Mumbai when the business community celebrate their New Year and open new account books. **Eid ul-Fitr**, the celebration when Ramzan with its 40 days of fasting is also observed. Since both the Hindu and Islamic calendar are lunar, there is often overlap between the holidays.

25 Dec Christmas. Christians across Mumbai celebrate the birth of Christ. A pontifical High Mass is held at midnight in the open air at the Cooperage Grounds, Colaba.

O Shopping

Mumbai *p28, maps p30, p32 and p35*
Most shops are open Mon-Sat 1000-1900, the bazars sometimes staying open as late as 2100. Mumbai prices are often higher than in other Indian cities, and hotel arcades tend to be very pricey but carry good-quality select items. Best buys are textiles, particularly tie-dye from Gujarat, hand-block printed cottons, Aurangabad and 'Patola' silks, gold-bordered saris from Surat and Khambat, handicrafts, jewellery and leather goods. It is illegal to take anything over 100 years old out of the country. CDs of contemporary Indian music in various genres make good souvenirs as well as gifts.

Bazars

Crawford Market, Ambedkar Rd (fun for bargain hunting) and **Mangaldas Market**. Other shopping streets are South Bhagat Singh Marg, M Karve Rd and Linking Rd, Bandra. For a different experience try **Chor (Thieves') Bazar**, on Maulana Shaukat Ali Rd in Central Mumbai, full of finds from Raj leftovers to precious jewellery. Make time to stop at the **Mini Market**, 33-31Mutton St, T022-2347 2425, minimarket@rediffmail.com, nose through the Bollywood posters, lobby cards, and photo-stills. On Fri, 'junk' carts sell less expensive 'antiques' and fakes.

Books

There are lines of second-hand stalls along Churchgate St and near the University. An annual book fair takes place at the Cross Maidan near Churchgate each Dec.
Crossword, under the flyover at Kemps Corner bridge (east of Malabar Hill). Smart, spacious, good selection.
Nalanda, Taj Mahal Hotel. Excellent art books, Western newspapers/magazines.
Strand Books, off Sir PM Rd near HMV, T022-2206 1994. Excellent selection, best deals, reliable shipping.

Clothes

Benzer, B Desai Rd, Breach Candy. Open daily. Good saris and Indian garments.
The Courtyard, 41/44 Minoo Desai Marg, Colaba. Very elite and fashionable mini-mall includes boutiques full of stunning heavy deluxe designs (Swarovski crystal-studded saris, anyone?) by Rohit Bal and **Rabani & Rakha** (Rs 17,000 for a sari) but probably

most suitable to the Western eye is textile designer **Neeru Kumar's Tulsi**, a cotton textiles designer from Delhi. Beautiful linen/silk stoles and fine *kantha* thread work. There's also a store from top menswear designer **Rajesh Pratap Singh**.
Ensemble, 130-132 South Bhagat Singh Marg, T022-2287 2882. Superb craftsmanship and service for women's clothes – Indian and 'East meets West'.
Fabindia, Jeroo Building, 137MG Rd, Kala Ghoda, and 66 Pali Hill, Bandra, www.fabindia.com. Fair-trade handloom Western and Indian wear including *kurtas*, pants, etc, for men, women and children (also bamboo, earthenware and jute home furnishings, *khadi* and *mulmul* cloth).

Crafts and textiles

Government emporia from many states sell good handicrafts and textiles; several at **World Trade Centre**, Cuffe Parade. In Colaba, a street **Craft Market** is held on Sun (Nov-Jan) in K Dubash Marg.
Anokhi, 4B August Kranti Marg, opposite Kumbala Hill Hospital. Gifts and handicrafts.
Bombay Electric, 1 Reay House, BEST Marg, Colaba, T022-2287 6276, www.bombayelectric.in. Pricey, chic, trendsetter art and couture.
Bombay Store, Western India House, 1st floor, PM Rd, Fort, www.bombaystore.com. Open daily. Ethnic lifestyle supplies, from home decor and fancy paper to clothing, gifts; best one-stop shop, value for money.
Cottage Industries Emporium, Apollo Bunder, Colaba. A nationwide selection, especially Kashmiri embroidery, South Indian handicrafts and Rajasthani textiles. Colaba Causeway, next to BEST, for ethnicware, handicrafts and fabrics.
Curio Cottage, 19 Mahakavi Bhushan Rd, near the Regal Cinema, Colaba, T022-2202 2607. Silver jewellery and antiques. Natesan in Jehangir Gallery basement; also in Taj Hotel. For fine antiques and copies.
Phillips, Madame Cama Rd, Colaba. A pricey Aladdin's cave of bric-a-brac and curios.

Sadak Ali, behind Taj Hotel, Colaba. Good range of carpets, but bargain hard.

Jewellery

The **Cottage Industries Emporium**, near Radio Club, Colaba Causeway, has affordable silver and antique jewellery from across India.
Popli Suleman Chambers, Battery St, Apollo Bunder, Colaba, T022-2285 4757. Semi-precious stones, gems, garnets and pearls.

Music

Musical instruments on VB Patel Rd, RS Mayeka at No 386, **Haribhai Vishwanath** at No 419 and Ram Singh at Bharati Sadan.
Planet M, opposite CST station; smaller branches in most malls. Also has book/poetry readings, gigs.
Rhythm House, next to Jehangir Gallery. Excellent selection of jazz and classical CDs. Also sells tickets for classical concerts.

Silks and saris

Biba, next to Crossword, Kemp's Corner, Phoenix Mills, Lower Parel, Bandra (W). Affordable designer wear for ladies, alterations possible.
Nalli, Shop No 7, Thirupathi Apartments, Bhulabhai Desai Rd, T022-23535577. Something for every budget.

☉ What to do

Mumbai *p28, maps p30, p32 and p35*
Adventure tourism
Maharashtra Tourism, www.maharashtra tourism.gov.in. Actively encourages adventure tourism (including jungle safaris and water sports) by introducing 'rent-a-tent', hiring out trekking gear and organizing overnight trips; some accommodation included. Prices range from US$35-150 per day/weekend depending on season and activity. It has also set up 27 holiday resorts around the state providing cheap accommodation at hill stations, beaches, archaeological sites and scenic spots. Details from tourist offices.

Odati Adventures, T(0)9820-079802, www. odati.com. Camping, weekend hiking, bike rides, rock climbing and waterfall rappelling around the Mumbai area. If you go rappelling in Maljesh Ghat during the monsoon, you'll glimpse thousands of flamingos. Bikes can be hired. Call or book online. Weekend cycle tours are Rs 2000-3000.

Body and soul

Aquarium, Marine Dr, T022-2281 8417. Good therapeutic yoga classes.
Iyengar Yogashraya, Elmac House, 126 Senapati Bapat Marg (off Tulsi Pipe Rd opposite Kamla Mills), Lower Parel, T022-2494 8416, www.bksiyengar.com. Iyengar drop-in centre. Call before dropping in.
Kerala Ayurvedic Health Spa, Prabhadevi, next to Subway and Birdy's, T022-6520 7445. Very reasonable rates for massage, Rs 900 for 45 mins. Call for an appointment.

Tour operators

If you wish to sightsee independently with a guide, ask at the tourist office. See page 29.
Be the Local, T(0)9930-027370, www.bethe localtoursandtravels.com. Fascinating walking tours of Dharavi, which take you through some of the cottage industries – from traditional Gujarati pottery to plastic – which sustain Mumbai from within Asia's largest slum. Owned and run by local students, the tours are neither voyeuristic nor intrusive, and photography is prohibited. Rs 400 per person includes transport from Colaba; private tours Rs 3500 for up to 5 people.
Bombay Heritage Walks, T022-2369 0992, www.bombayheritagewalks.com. Informative walking tours specializing in Mumbai's built history, founded by a pair of local architects.
City sightseeing Approved guides from the India tourist office, T022-2203 6854. City tour usually includes visits to The Gateway of India, the Chhatrapati Shivaji (Prince of Wales) Museum, Jain temple, Hanging Gardens, Kamla Nehru Park and Mani Bhavan (Gandhi Museum). Suburban tour includes Juhu Beach, Kanheri Caves and Lion Safari Park.

MTDC, Madam Cama Rd, opposite LIC Building, T022-2202 6713. City tour Tue-Sun 0900-1300 and 1400-1800, Rs 100. Evening open-top bus tour of Colaba, Marine Drive and Fort, runs Sat and Sun at 1900 and 2015; Rs 150 (lower deck Rs 50). Elephanta tours from Gateway of India. Boat 0900-1415, Rs 130 return; reserve at Apollo Bunder, T022-2284 1877.
Mumbai Magic, T(0)98677-07414, www.mumbaimagic.com. A vast range of tours covering every inch of the city from Colaba to Bandra and beyond. Highlights include South Indian cuisine tours of Matunga, a walk through the Chor Bazaar, and the Mumbai Local tour which hops you around the city by taxi, local train and bus. Personalized itineraries available. Professional and highly recommended.

⊖ Transport

Mumbai *p28, maps p30, p32 and p35*
Mumbai is one of the 2 main entry points to India, with daily international flights from Europe, North America, the Middle East, Asia, Australia and Africa, and frequent domestic connections with every major city in India, and most minor ones. All touch down at **Chhatrapati Shivaji International Airport**, enquiries T022-6685 0222, www.csia.in. The recently smartened-up international terminal is 30 km north of the city. There are exchange counters, ATMs, tourist offices, domestic airline and railway reservation counters, and a cloakroom for left luggage.

The domestic airport, recently renovated with 2 separate terminals – 1A for **Air India** (enquiries T022-6685 1351), 1B for **Jet Airways** and all budget airlines (enquiries T022-2626 1149), is 4 km closer to the city in Santa Cruz and has most of the same facilities. Free shuttle buses link the domestic and international terminals every few mins.
Transport to and from the airport
Pre-paid taxis, from counters at the exits, are the simplest way of getting downtown. Give the exact area or hotel and the number of

pieces of luggage, and pay at the booth. On the receipt will be scribbled the number of your taxi: ask the drivers outside to help you find it, and hand the receipt to the driver at the end of the journey. There is no need to tip, though drivers will certainly drop heavy hints. To **Nariman Point** or **Gateway of India**, about Rs 430, 1-2 hrs depending on traffic. To **Juhu Beach** Rs 290. Metered taxis picked up outside the terminal should be marginally cheaper than a pre-paid, but make sure the driver starts the meter when you get in. The cheaper alternatives – crowded and slow BEST buses that connect both terminals with the city, and even more crowded local trains – have only economy in their favour. The closest railway stations are **Vile Parle** (for international) and **Santa Cruz** (domestic), both on the Western line to Mumbai Central and Churchgate.

Airline offices
The easiest way to comparison shop for domestic fares is online, though not all sites accept international credit cards. One that does is www.cleartrip.com.

Air India (Indian Airlines) and Jet Airways are full-service airlines and have the most comprehensive networks; budget carriers such as Go Air, Indigo and Spicejet serve major routes and charge for extras. During the winter, prepare for a 'congestion charge' on certain domestic routes, including Mumbai–Delhi.

Bus
Local Red BEST (Brihanmumbai Electrical Supply Co) buses are available in most parts of Greater Mumbai. There's a handy route finder at http://bestundertaking. com/transport/index.htm. Fares are cheap, but finding the correct bus is tricky as the numbers and destinations on the front are only in Marathi. English signs are displayed beside the back doors. Ask locals to help point out a bus going your way.
Long distance Maharashtra SRTC operates from the Mumbai Central Bus Stand,

T022-2307 4272, http://msrtconline.in/timetable.aspx, to most major centres in the state as well as several destinations in Goa.

Private buses also serve long-distance destinations: most leave from the streets surrounding Mumbai Central, where there are ticket agents, while others leave from Dadar; information and tickets from **Dadar Tourist Centre**, outside Dadar station, T022-2411 3398. The most popular company is **Neeta Volvo**, T022-2890-2666. Some private buses can be booked in advance on www.redbus.in.

Car
Costs for hiring a car are (for 8 hrs or 80 km): luxury a/c cars Rs 1500; Indica/Indigo, a/c Rs 1000, non-a/c Rs 800. Companies include: **Auto Hirers**, 7 Commerce Centre, Tardeo, T022-2494 2006. **Blaze**, Colaba, T022-2202 0073. **Budget**, T022-2494 2644, and **Sai**, PhoenixMill Compound, Senapati Bapat Marg, Lower Parel, T022-2494 2644. Recommended. **NRI Services**, Chowpatty, T(0)9821-252287, www.nriservicesindia.com. **Wheels**, T022-2282 2874.

Auto-rickshaw
Not available in Central Mumbai (south of Mahim). Metered; about Rs 9 per km, revised tariff card held by the driver, 25% extra at night (2400-0500). Some rickshaw drivers show the revised tariff card for taxis!

Taxi
Metered yellow-top cabs and more expensive a/c Cool Cabs are easily available. Meter rates are Rs 16 for the 1st km and Rs 10 for each extra km. Drivers should carry tariff cards that convert the meter fee into current prices; a new fleet of yellow-top Indica cars have digital meters that show the correct price. Always get a pre-paid taxi at the airport.

A/c radio taxis can be pre-booked. They charge Rs 15 per km and provide metered receipts at the end of your journey. Tip the driver about 10% if you feel they had to do a lot of waiting. **Megacab**, T022-4242 4242. **Meru Cab**, T022-4422 4422.

Train

Local Suburban electric trains are economical. They start from Churchgate for the western suburbs and from CST (VT) for the east but are often desperately crowded; stay near the door or you may miss your stop. There are 'ladies' cars' in the middle and ends. Avoid peak hours (southbound 0700-1100, northbound 1700-2000), and keep a tight hold on valuables. The difference between 1st and 2nd class is not always obvious although 1st class is 10 times more expensive. Inspectors fine people for travelling in the wrong class or without a ticket. If you're travelling frequently, invest in a smart card that lets you avoid queues at the ticket counter by printing tickets from a machine.

Long distance Many daily trains travel down the coast from Mumbai to **Madgaon**, the main jumping-off point for Goa; some stop at intermediate stations (such as **Pernem** and **Thivim**) closer to the northern beaches. The most convenient departures are the *Mandovi Exp 10103*, 0710, 11½ hrs; *Konkan Kanya Exp 10111*, 2305, 11½ hrs; and *Mangalore Exp 12133*, 2210, 9 hrs. These all depart from CST (enquiries T134/135; reservations T022-2265 9512, 0800-1230, 1300-1630), while all other trains leave from far flung suburban stations in the suburbs: **Lokmanya Tilak** terminus, 13 km northeast of the centre, has the *Netravati Exp 16345*, 1140, 12 hrs. **Dadar**, 6 km north, has the *Madgaon Jan Shatabdi Exp*, *12051*, 0525, 8¾ hrs.

Mumbai–Goa is one of India's busiest train routes and advance bookings are imperative, especially during holiday season. Night trains tend to fill up faster than daytime departures.

There's a useful **Foreign Tourist** counter at CST (opens 0900 – arrive early) for Indrail Passes and ticket bookings under Foreign Tourist Quota; bring your passport and an ATM receipt or currency encashment certificate.

Mumbai *p28, maps p30, p32 and p35*
Banks ATMs are now ubiquitous in all parts of the city, including at the airports and stations, and most take foreign cards. For other services, branches open Mon-Fri 1000-1400, Sat 1000-1200. It's more efficient to change money at the airport, or at specialist agents, eg **Bureau de Change**, upstairs in Air India Building, Nariman Pt; **Thomas Cook**, 324 Dr DN Rd, T022-2204 8556; also at 102B Maker Tower, 10th floor, F Block, Cuffe Pde, Colaba. **Credit cards** American Express, Oriental Bldg, 364 Dr DN Rd; **Diners Club**, Raheja Chambers, 213 Nariman Pt; **MasterCard**, C Wing, Mittal Tower, Nariman Pt; **Visa**, Standard Chartered Grindlays Bank, 90 MG Rd, Fort. **Embassies and consultes** For up-to-date details of foreign embassies and consulates in India, go to embassy.goabroad.com. **Emergencies** Ambulance T102. Fire T101. Police T100. **Internet** Internet cafés are increasingly strict about demanding photo ID. There are several on the back streets of Colaba near Leopold Café. **Medical services** The larger hotels usually have a house doctor, the others invariably have a doctor on call. Ask hotel staff for prompt action. The telephone directory lists hospitals and GPs. Admission to private hospitals may not be allowed without a large cash advance (eg Rs 50,000). Insurers' guarantees may not be sufficient. **Prince Aly Khan Hospital**, Nesbit Rd near the harbour, T022-2377 7800/900, **Jaslok Hospital**, Peddar Rd, T022-6657 3333; **Hinduja Hospital**, T022-2444-0431; **Lilavati Hospital**, in Bandra (W), T022-2642 1111 are recommended. **Chemists**: several open day/night, especially opposite **Bombay Hospital**. **Wordell**, Stadium House, Churchgate; **New Royal Chemist**, New Marine Lines. **Useful contacts** Commissioner's Office, Dr DN Rd, near Phule Market. **Foreigners' Regional Registration Office**, 3rd floor, Special Branch Building, Badruddin Tayabji Lane, Behind St Xaviers College, T022-2262 1169. **Passport office**, T022-2493 1731.

Contents

Footprint features

Goa

Panjim (Panaji) and Old Goa

Sleepy, dusty Panjim was adopted as the Portuguese capital when the European empire was already on the wane, and the colonizers left little in the way of lofty architecture. A tiny city with a Riviera-style promenade along the Mandovi, it's also splendidly uncommercial: the biggest business seems to be in the sale of *kaju* (cashews), gentlemen-shaves in the *barbieris* and *feni*-quaffing in the booths of pokey bars – and city folk still insist on sloping off for a siesta at lunch. The 18th- and 19th-century bungalows clustered in the neighbouring quarters of San Thome and Fontainhas stand as the victims of elegant architectural neglect. Further upriver, a thick swathe of jungle – wide fanning raintrees, the twists of banyan branches and coconut palms – has drawn a heavy, dusty blanket over the relics of the doomed Portuguese capital of Old Goa, a ghost town of splendid rococo and baroque ecclesiastical edifices.

Arriving in Panjim and Old Goa

Getting there Panjim is the transport hub of Central Goa. Pre-paid taxis or buses run the short distance from Dabolim airport across Mormugao Bay to Panjim. The closest station on the Konkan Railway is at Karmali, 10 km east, with trains from Mumbai to the north and coastal Karnataka and Kerala to the south; taxis and buses run from Karmali to Panjim. The state-run Kadamba buses and private coach terminals are in Patto to the east of town. From there it is a 10-minute walk across the footbridge over the Ourem Creek to reach the city's guesthouses. ▸▸ *See Transport, page 66.*

Getting around Panjim is laid out on a grid and the main roads run parallel with the seafront. The area is very easy to negotiate on foot, but autos are readily available. Motorcycle rickshaws are cheaper but slightly more risky. Local buses run along the waterfront from the City Bus Stand past the market and on to Miramar.

Tourist information Goa Tourism Development Corporation (GTDC) ① *east bank of the Ourem Creek, beside the bus stand at Patto, T0832-243 8750, www.goa-tourism. com, Mon-Sat 0900-1130, 1330-1700, Sun 0930-1400.* Also has an information counter at Dabolim airport, and runs a moderately helpful information line, T0832-241 2121. **India Tourism** ① *Church Sq, T0832-222 3412, www.incredibleindia.com.*

There are some great themed walks around Panjim with **Cholta Cholta** ① *www.cholta cholta.com* (which means 'whilst walking' in Konkani) and their popular tours offer real insight into the city and its history. Many of the walks focus on the areas of San Thome and Fontainhas and their beautiful architecture.

Goa ins and outs

Vasco da Gama is the passenger railway terminus of the Central Goa branch line, and is the capital of the industrial heart of modern Goa. Dabolim Airport is 3 km away and was developed by the Navy. It is currently shared between the needs of the military and the escalating demands of tourism. Vasco is 30 km from Panjim, the main arrival point for long-distance buses. Trains via Londa bring visitors from the north and east (Delhi and Agra, Hospet and Bengaluru) while trains from Mumbai, Kerala and coastal points in between arrive via the Konkan Railway, which offers several jumping-off points in Goa besides the main station at Margao (Madgaon). For rail reservations, call T0832-251 2833.

Charter companies fly direct to Dabolim Airport between October and April from the UK, the Netherlands, Switzerland and Russia. There are several flights daily from various cities in India (including Mumbai, Thiruvananthapuram, Bengaluru, Delhi and Chennai) with Air India, Indian Airlines, Indigo and Spice Jet. Package tour companies and luxury hotels usually arrange courtesy buses for hotel transfer, but even if you're coming independently the Arrivals terminal is relatively relaxed. A pre-paid taxi counter immediately outside has rates clearly displayed (such as Panjim Rs 700, 40 minutes; north Goa beaches from Rs 700; Tiracol Rs 1600; Arambol Rs 1400; south Goa beaches from Rs 500; Palolem Rs 1200). State your destination at the counter, pay and obtain a receipt that will give the registration number of your taxi. Keep hold of this receipt until you reach your destination. The public bus stop on the far side of the roundabout outside the airport gates has buses to Vasco da Gama, from where there are connections to all the major destinations in Goa.

A popular way to get around is by hiring a scooter, available in all towns and villages. However, make sure the bike has yellow and black number plates, which signal that the vehicle is for hire; plain black-and-white plates could result in a fine from the police.

See also pages 6-12.

Panaji is the official spelling of the capital city, replacing the older Portuguese spelling Panjim. It is still most commonly referred to as Panjim, so we have followed usage.

Background

The Portuguese first settled Panjim as a suburb of Old Goa, the original Indian capital of the sea-faring *conquistadores*, but its position on the left bank of the Mandovi River had already attracted Bijapur's Muslim king Yusuf Adil Shah in 1500, shortly before the Europeans arrived. He built and fortified what the Portuguese later renamed the Idalcao Palace, now the oldest and most impressive of downtown Panjim's official buildings. The palace's service to the sultan was short-lived: Alfonso de Albuquerque seized it, and Old Goa upstream – which the Islamic rulers had been using as both a trading port and their main starting point for pilgrimages to Mecca – in March 1510. Albuquerque, like his Muslim predecessors, built his headquarters in Old Goa, and proceeded to station a garrison at Panjim and made it the customs clearing point for all traffic entering the Mandovi.

The town remained little more than a military outpost and a staging post for incoming and outgoing viceroys on their way to Old Goa. The first Portuguese buildings, after the construction of a church on the site of the present Church of Our Lady of Immaculate

Conception in 1541, were noblemen's houses built on the flat land bordering the sea. Panjim had to wait over two centuries – when the Portuguese Viceroy decided to move from Old Goa in 1759 – for settlement to begin in earnest. It then took the best part of a century for enough numbers to relocate from Old Goa to make Panjim the biggest settlement in the colony and to warrant its status as official capital in 1833.

Places in Panjim → *For listings, see pages 62-67.*

The waterfront
The leafy boulevard of Devanand Bandodkar (DB) Marg runs along the Mandovi from near the New Patto Bridge in the east to the Campal to the southwest. When Panjim's transport and communication system depended on boats, this was its busiest highway and it still holds the city's main administrative buildings and its colourful market.

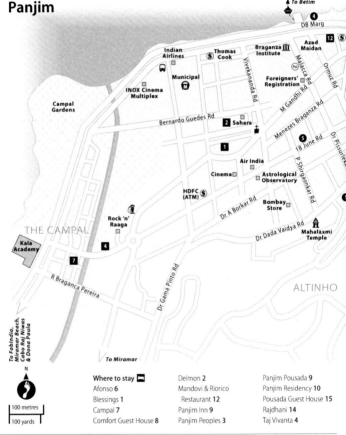

Panjim

Where to stay 🛏	Delmon **2**	Panjim Pousada **9**
Afonso **6**	Mandovi & Riorico	Panjim Residency **10**
Blessings **1**	Restaurant **12**	Pousada Guest House **15**
Campal **7**	Panjim Inn **9**	Rajdhani **14**
Comfort Guest House **8**	Panjim Peoples **3**	Taj Vivanta **4**

Walking from the east, you first hit **Idalcao Palace** ① *behind the main boat terminal, DB Marg.* Once the castle of the Adil Shahs, the palace was seized by the Portuguese when they first toppled the Muslim kings in 1510 and was rebuilt in 1615 to serve as the Europeans' Viceregal Palace. It was the official residence to Viceroys from 1759 right up until 1918 when the governor-general (the viceroy's 20th-century title) decided to move to the Cabo headland to the southwest – today's Cabo Raj Niwas – leaving the old palace to become government offices. After Independence it became Goa's secretariat building (the seat of the then Union Territory's parliament) until that in turn shifted across the river to Porvorim. It now houses the bureaucracy of the state passport office. Next to it is a striking dark statue of the **Abbé Faria** (1756-1819) looming over the prone figure of a woman. José Custodio de Faria, who went on to become a worldwide authority on hypnotism, was born into a Colvale Brahmin family in Candolim. The character in Dumas' Count of Monte Cristo may have been based on this Abbé.

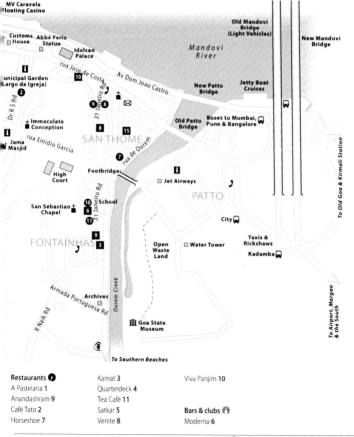

Restaurants 🍴
A Pastelaria **1**
Anandashram **9**
Café Tato **2**
Horseshoe **7**

Kamat **3**
Quarterdeck **4**
Tea Café **11**
Satkar **5**
Venite **8**

Viva Panjim **10**

Bars & clubs 🍸
Moderna **6**

Further west, on Malacca Road, almost opposite the wharf, are the central library and public rooms of the **Braganza Institute** ① *Mon-Fri 0930-1300, 1400-1745*. It was established as the Instituto Vasco da Gama in 1871 (the anniversary of the date that the Portuguese explorer da Gama sailed round the Cape of Good Hope), to stimulate an interest in culture, science and the arts. It was renamed for Luis Menezes de Braganza (1878-1938), an outstanding figure of social and political reform in early 20th-century Goa. The blue tile frieze in the entrance, hand painted by Jorge Colaco in 1935, is a mythical representation of the Portuguese colonization of Goa. An art gallery upstairs has paintings by European artists of the late 19th and early 20th centuries and Goan artists of the 20th century. The **central library** ① *0930-1300, 1200-1700*, dating from 1832, has a rare collection of religious and other texts.

City centre

The giant whitewashed 16th-century **Church of the Immaculate Conception** ① *Church Sq, Emidio Gracia Rd, Mon-Sat 0900-1230, 1530-1730, Sun 1100-1230, 1530-1700, free, English Mass Mon-Fri 0800, Sun 0830*, looms pristine and large up a broad sweep of steps off the main square, Largo Da Igreja, blue and white flags fluttering at its fringes. Its dimensions were unwarranted for the population of what was at the time of its construction in 1541, in Panjim, little more than a marshy fishing village; its tall, Portuguese baroque twin towers were instead built both to act as a landmark for and to tend to the spiritual needs of arriving Portuguese sailors, for whom the customs post just below the hill at Panjim marked their first step on Indian soil. The church was enlarged in 1600 to reflect its status as parish church of the capital and in 1619 was rebuilt to its present design. Inside is an ornate jewel in Goan Catholicism's trademark blue, white and gold, wood carved into gilt corkscrews, heavy chandeliers and chintz. The classic baroque main altar *reredos* (screens) are sandwiched between altars to Jesus the Crucified and to Our Lady of the Rosary, in turn flanked by marble statues of St Peter and St Paul. The panels in the Chapel of St Francis, in the south transept, came from the chapel in the Idalcao Palace in 1918. Parishioners bought the statue of Our Lady of Fatima her crown of gold and diamonds in 1950 (candlelight procession every 13 October). The church's feast day is on 8 December.

The Hindu **Mahalaxmi Temple** ① *Dr Dada Vaidya Rd, free* (originally 1818, but rebuilt and enlarged in 1983) is now hidden behind a newer building. It was the first Hindu place of worship to be allowed in the Old Conquests after the close of the Inquisition. The **Boca de Vaca** ('Cow's Mouth') spring is nearby.

San Thome and Fontainhas

On Panjim's eastern promontory, at the foot of the Altinho and on the left bank of the Ourem Creek, sit first the San Thome and then, further south, Fontainhas districts filled with modest 18th- and 19th-century houses. The cumulative prettiness of the well-preserved buildings' colour-washed walls, trimmed with white borders, sloping tiled roofs and decorative wrought-iron balconies make it an ideal area to explore on foot. You can reach the area via any of the narrow lanes that riddle San Thome or take the footbridge across the Ourem Creek from the New Bus Stand and tourist office that feeds you straight into the heart of the district. A narrow road that runs east past the Church of the Immaculate Conception and main town square also ends up here. But probably the best way in is over the Altinho from the Mahalaxmi Temple: this route gives great views over the estuary from the steep eastern flank of the hill, a vantage point that was once used for defensive purposes. A footpath drops down between the Altinho's 19th- and 20th-century buildings just south of San Sebastian Chapel to leave you slap bang in middle of Fontainhas.

The chief landmark here is the small **San Sebastian Chapel** ① *St Sebastian Rd, open only during Mass held in Konkani Mon-Tue, Thu-Sat 0715-0800, Wed 1800-1900, Sun 0645-0730, English Mass Sun 0830-0930, free* (built 1818, rebuilt 1888) which houses the large wooden crucifix that until 1812 stood in the Palace of the Inquisition in Old Goa where the eyes of Christ watched over the proceedings of the tribunal. Before being moved here, it was in Idalcao Palace's chapel in Panjim for 100 years.

The **Goa State Museum** ① *Patto, 0930-1730, free, head south of Kadamba Bus Stand, across the Ourem Creek footbridge, right across the waste ground and past the State Bank staff training building*, is an impressive building that contains a disappointingly small collection of religious art and antiquities. Most interesting are the original Provedoria lottery machines built in Lisbon that are on the first floor landing. A few old photos show how the machines were used.

Old Goa and around → *For listings, see pages 62-67.*

The white spires of Old Goa's glorious ecclesiastical buildings burst into the Indian sky from the depths of overgrown jungle that has sprawled where admirals and administrators of the Portuguese Empire once tended the oriental interests of their 16th-century King Manuel. The canopies of a hundred raintrees cast their shade across the desolate streets, adding to the romantic melancholy beauty of the deserted capital. Tourists and pilgrims continue to flock to the remains of St Francis Xavier in the giddying baroque Basilica of Bom Jesus, where hawkers thrust spindly votive candles into their hands and compete to slake thirsts with fresh coconut, lime or sugarcane juice.

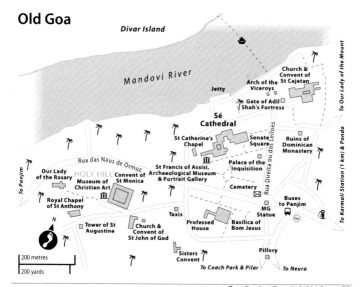

Old Goa

Arriving in Old Goa

Getting there Old Goa lies on the south bank of the Mandovi on the crest of a low hill 8 km from Panjim. The frequent bus service takes 15-20 minutes. Buses drop you off opposite the Basilica of Bom Jesus; pick up the return bus near the police station. Karmali station on the Konkan Railway, just east of the centre, has taxis for transfers.

Getting around The major monuments are within easy walking distance of the bus stop. All monuments are open daily year-round 0830-1730.

Background

Old Goa is to Christians the spiritual heart of the territory. It owes its origin as a Portuguese capital to Afonso de Albuquerque and some of its early ecclesiastical development to St Francis Xavier who was here, albeit for only five months, in the mid-16th century. Before the Portuguese arrived it was the second capital of the Muslim Bijapur Kingdom. Today, all the mosques and fortifications of that period have disappeared and only a fragment of the Sultan's palace walls remain.

Under the Portuguese, Old Goa was grand enough to be dubbed the 'Rome of the East', but it was a flourishing port with an enviable trade even before the Portuguese arrived. The bustling walled city was peopled by merchants of many nationalities who came to buy and sell horses from Arabia and Hormuz, to trade silk, muslin, calico, rice, spices and areca nuts from the interior and other ports along the west coast. It was a centre of shipbuilding and boasted fine residences and public buildings.

After the arrival of the Portuguese, Old Goa swelled still further in size and significance. In the west lay barracks, mint, foundry and arsenal, hospital and prison. The banks of the Mandovi held the shipyards of Ribeira des Gales and next door lay the administrative and commercial centre. Streets and areas of the city were set aside for different activities and merchandise, each with its own character. The most important, Rua Direita ou dos Leiloes (Straight Street), was lined with jewellers, bankers and artisans. It was also the venue for auctions of precious goods, held every morning except Sunday. To the east was the market and the old fortress of Adil Shah, while the true centre of the town was filled with magnificent churches built by the Franciscans, themselves joined by waves of successive religious orders: first the Dominicans in 1548, the Augustinians from 1572, the Carmelites from 1612 and finally the Theatines from 1655. By the mid-17th century, the city, plagued by cholera and malaria and crippled economically, was abandoned for Panjim.

Basilica of Bom Jesus

The Renaissance façade of Goa's most famous church, the Basilica of Bom (the Good) Jesus, a UNESCO World Heritage Site, reflects the architectural transition to baroque then taking place in Europe. Apart from the elaborate gilded altars, wooden pulpit and the candy-twist Bernini columns, the interior is very simple.

The church has held the treasured remains of **St Francis Xavier**, a former pupil of soldier-turned-saint Ignatius Loyola, the founder of the Order of Jesuits since the 17th century. Francis's canonization was in 1622.

The tomb, which lies to the right of the main chancel (1698), was the gift of one of the last of the Medicis, Cosimo III, Grand Duke of Tuscany, and took the Florentine sculptor Giovanni Batista Foggini 10 years to complete. It is made of three tiers of marble and jasper; the upper tier holds scenes from the saint's life. The casket is silver and has three locks, the keys being held by the Governor, the Archbishop and the Convent

Administrator. You can look down on to the tomb from a small window in the art gallery next to the church.

After his canonization, St Francis's body was shown on each anniversary of his death until 1707, when it was restricted to a few special private expositions. In 1752, the cadaver was again paraded to quash rumours that the Jesuits had removed it. The exhibition now happens every 10 to 12 years (the last exposition was in 2005), when the relics are taken to the Sé Cathedral. Feast Day is 3 December.

Sé Cathedral

Across the square sits the Sé Cathedral, dedicated to St Catherine on whose day (25 November) Goa was recaptured by Albuquerque. Certainly the largest church in Old Goa, it could even be the biggest in Asia and was built on the ruins of a mosque by the Dominicans between 1562 and 1623. The building is Tuscan outside and Corinthian inside, with a barrel-vaulted ceiling and east-facing main façade. One of the characteristic twin towers collapsed in 1776 when it was struck by lightning. The remaining tower holds five bells including the Golden Bell (cast in Cuncolim in 1652). The vast interior, divided into the barrel-vaulted nave with clerestory and two side aisles, has a granite baptismal font. On each side of the church are four chapels along the aisles; on the right, these are dedicated to St Anthony, St Bernard, the Cross of Miracles and the Holy Spirit, and on the left, starting at the entrance, to Our Lady of Virtues, St Sebastian, the Blessed Sacrament and Our Lady of Life. The clerestory windows are protected by a shield crowned by a balustrade to keep out the sun. The main altar is superbly gilded and painted, with six further altars in the transept. The marble-top table in front of the main altar is where, since 1955, St Francis Xavier's remains have been held during their exposition. The main *reredos* has four panels illustrating the life of St Catherine. There is also an **art gallery** ① *Mon-Thu, Sat 0900-1230, Sun 0900-1030, closed during services, Rs 5.*

Around the cathedral

Southwest of the cathedral's front door are the ruins of the **Palace of the Inquisition**, where over 16,000 cases were heard between 1561 and 1774. The Inquisition was finally suppressed in 1814. Beneath the hall were dungeons. In Old Goa's heyday this was the town centre.

There are two churches and a museum in the same complex as the Cathedral. The **Church and Convent of St Francis of Assisi** is a broad vault of a church with two octagonal towers. The floor is paved with tombstones and on either side of the baroque high altar are paintings on wood depicting scenes from St Francis' life while the walls above have frescoes with floral designs. The original **Holy Spirit Church** in the Portuguese Gothic (manueline) style was begun by Franciscan friars in 1517; everything except the old doorway was replaced by the larger present structure in the 1660s (itself restored 1762-1765). The convent now houses the **Archaeological Museum and Portrait Gallery** ① *T0832-228 6133, 1000-1230, 1500-1830 (closed Fri), Rs 5,* with sculptures pre-dating the Portuguese, many from the 12th-13th centuries when Goa was ruled by the Kadamba Dynasty. There are 'hero stones' commemorating naval battles, and 'sati stones' marking the practice of widow burning. There is also a rather fine collection of portraits of Portuguese governors upstairs that is revealing both for its charting of the evolution of court dress as well as the physical robustness of the governors inside. Some governors were remarkable for their sickly pallor, others for the sheer brevity of their tenure of office, which must have set the portrait painters something of a challenge. (The ASI booklet on the monuments, *Old Goa*, by S Rajagopalan, is available from the museum, Rs 10.)

To the west is **St Catherine's Chapel**. It was built at the gate of the old city on the orders of Albuquerque as an act of gratitude after the Portuguese defeat of the forces of Bijapur in 1510. The original mud and thatch church was soon replaced by a stone chapel which in 1534 became the cathedral (considerably renovated in 1952), remaining so until Sé Cathedral was built.

On the road towards the Mandovi, northeast from the cathedral compound, lies the **Arch of the Viceroys (Ribeira dos Viceroys)**, commemorating the centenary of Vasco da Gama's discovery of the sea route to India. It was built at the end of the 16th century by his great-grandson, Francisco da Gama, Goa's Viceroy from 1597 to 1600. Its laterite block structure is faced with green granite on the side approached from the river. This was the main gateway to the seat of power: on arrival by ship each new Viceroy would be handed the keys and enter through this ceremonial archway before taking office. The statue of Vasco da Gama above the arch was originally surmounted by a gilded statue of St Catherine, the patron saint of the city. Walking east towards the convent from the arch you pass the **Gate of the Fortress of the Adil Shahs**, probably built by Sabaji, the Maratha ruler of Goa before the Muslim conquest of 1471. The now-ruined palace was home to the Adil Shahi sultans of Bijapur who occupied Goa before the arrival of the Portuguese. It was the Palace of the Viceroys until 1554 after which it served as both the hall of trials for the Inquisition and to house prisoners.

A little further still stands the splendid, domed baroque **Convent and Church of St Cajetan (Caetano)**. Pope Urban III dispatched a band of Italian friars of the Theatine order to spread the Gospel to the Deccani Muslim city of Golconda near Hyderabad but they got a frosty reception so headed back west to settle in Goa. They acquired land around 1661 to build this church, which is shaped like a Greek cross and is partly modelled on St Peter's in Rome. It is the last domed church in Goa.

The crypt below the main altar, where the Italian friars were buried, has some sealed lead caskets that are supposed to contain the embalmed bodies of senior Portuguese officials who never returned home. Next door is the beautiful former convent building which is now a pastoral foundation (closed to the public).

On a hill a good way further east is the modest **Chapel of Our Lady of the Mount**, dating from 1510, which gives you a good idea of how the other churches here must originally have looked. It is a peaceful spot with excellent panoramic views across Old Goa, evocative of the turbulent past when Albuquerque and Adil Shah vied for control of the surrounding area. The altar gilding inside has been beautifully restored. In front of the main altar lies the body of architect Antonio Pereira whose burial slab requests the visitor to say an Ave Maria for his soul.

Holy Hill

Between the domineering central monuments of Old Goa's broad tree-lined centre and Panjim stand the cluster of churches of Holy Hill. The first building you reach (on your left) as you leave the central plaza is the **Church and Convent of St John of God**, built in 1685 and abandoned in 1835. The **Museum of Christian Art** ① *everyday 0930-1700, Rs 5*, is to the right, with 150 items gathered from Goa's churches, convents and Christian homes to give a rich cross section of Indo-Portuguese sacred craft in wood, ivory, silver and gold. There is a little outdoor café too.

Next door sits the **Convent of St Monica** (1607-1627), the first nunnery in India and the largest in Asia. A huge three-storey square building, with the church in the southern part, it was built around a sunken central courtyard containing a formal garden. At one time it was a royal monastery, but in 1964 it became a theological institute, the Mater Dei Institute for Nuns. It was here in 1936 that Bishop Dom Frei Miguel Rangel is believed to have had a vision of the Christ figure on the Miraculous Cross opening his eyes, his stigmata bleeding and his lips quivering as if to speak. The vision was repeated later that year in the presence of the Bishop, the Viceroy Dom Pedro de Silva and a large congregation.

It is well worth the effort of the hike, taking the left fork of the road, to reach the **Royal Chapel of St Anthony** (1543) – dedicated to Portugal's national saint and restored by its government in 1961 – and, opposite, the **Tower of St Augustine**. The Augustinians came to Goa in 1572; the church they immediately began, bar the belfry, now lies in ruins. It once boasted eight chapels, a convent and an excellent library and was enlarged to become one of the finest in the kingdom. It was finally abandoned in 1835 because of religious persecution. The vault collapsed in 1842, burying the image; the façade and main tower followed in 1931 and 1938. Only one of the original four towers survives. The large bell now hangs in Panjim's Church of the Immaculate Conception. The Archaeological Survey of India is spearheading extensive repairs.

Behind is the **Chapel of Our Lady of the Rosary** (1526). Belonging to the earliest period of church building, it is called Manueline after Manuel I, the Portuguese king who oversaw a period of great prosperity that coincided with the country's conquest of Goa. The use of Hindu and Muslim craftsmen in building the chapel led to an architectural style that borrowed from Iberian decoration but also absorbed both local naturalistic motifs and Islamic elements (seen on the marble cenotaph). The church here has a two-storey entrance, a single tower and low flanking turrets. It was from here that Albuquerque directed the battle against the Adil Shahi forces in 1510.

Around Panjim → For listings, see pages 62-67.

Gaspar Dias Fortress was finished around 1606. The Panjim–Ribandar causeway, built in 1634, gave it direct land access to the capital at Old Goa and its significance grew accordingly. The walls, likely laterite blocks 1.5 m thick and 5 m high, made space for 16 cannons. These saw repeated action against the Dutch until the middle of the 17th century, but the fortress' importance waned after the Maratha onslaught and it fell into disrepair under 15 years of occupation by a British garrison in the early 19th century. It was made new but the Portuguese army finally abandoned it in 1870 as a result of further damage sustained during the mutiny against the Prefect of 1835. For a while the military still stationed soldiers here to convalesce but by the 20th century it had crumbled beyond recognition. All that is left is one cannon at the Miramar circle that marks the possible site of the fort. **Miramar Beach** is a bit grubby but it's a pleasant drive with good views over the sea and, if you've got a little time to kill, it offers the best quick escape from the city.

The nearby fort **Cabo Raj Niwas** has fared little better: six cannons and some bits of wall crumbling in the gardens of Raj Bhavan, or the State Governor's House, are all that remain. It is closed to the public but you can get passes for Sunday Mass at 0930 on the gate. The first small **Our Lady of Cabo shrine** was built in 1541. Documents from 1633 refer to both the chapel and a fort with four guns. A British troops garrison stationed here from 1799 during the Napoleonic Wars explains the overgrown graves in the nearby **British Cemetery**. Around 1844, after the religious orders were abolished, the Archbishop of Goa was given the convent, which he converted into an impressive residence. It was the official address of the governor-general of Goa in 1918. Its grand interior was left intact after the Portuguese left in 1961. The viewing platform near the entrance gives superb views over the sweep of the coastline across the Mandovi estuary to Fort Aguada.

Some 5 km north of Panjim, in Bardez, you will find a fascinating museum **Houses of Goa** ① www.archgoa.org, created by architect Gerard da Cunha on a traffic island. It's a beautiful building shaped like a ship that follows traditional Goan architecture and style. Inside is a collection of doors, tiles, altars, lamps and rare postcards. It offers a unique insight into Goa's heritage.

Panjim (Panaji) and Old Goa listings

For hotel and restaurant price codes and other relevant information, see pages 13-15.

⊖ Where to stay

Panjim has a wide choice of accommodation, Old Goa none. There are upmarket options south of Panjim in the beach resorts of Miramar and Dona Paula, but for character it's best to book into one of the guesthouses in the atmospheric Fontainhas district. If you don't want to stay overnight you can pack the best of Panjim and Old Goa into a day. Guesthouses have early checkout to make way for new arrivals coming off the trains and buses and many do not take advance bookings – it's first come first served.

Panjim *p54, map p54*
\$\$\$\$-\$\$\$ Taj Vivanta, www.vivantaby taj.com. The **Taj Vivanta** opened in Panjim in 2009 and is a smart upmarket option centrally located. Common areas and restaurants are beautiful (the restaurants are highly recommended). Rooms are a little on the boutique-side, ie small and with glass-walled bathrooms where you have to shut the blinds each time if you are sharing the room. Overall everything you would expect from the Taj group.
\$\$\$-\$\$ Mandovi, D B Marg, T0832-242 6270, www.hotelmandovigoa.com. Old building with hints of art deco, relaxing but lacks great character. 66 large a/c rooms (river-facing more expensive); rates include breakfast. 1st floor **Riorico** restaurant, popular pastry shop, terrace bar, exchange.

\$\$ Delmon, C de Albuquerque Rd, T0832-222 6846, www.alcongoa.com. 50 clean rooms, TV, desk, some a/c, breakfast included. Modern, comfortable hotel, popular restaurant.
\$ Blessings, MG Rd, behind Bhatkar House, T0832-222 4770, hotelblessings@yahoo.com. 18 ordinary rooms, TV (extra Rs 50), 2 have huge terraces instead of balconies, restaurant, quiet tree-filled backyard.
\$ Hotel Campal, opposite Kala Academy, Campal, T0832-222 4533. Clean rooms with TV and a/c possible, hidden in beautiful location in Campal area, near Kala Academy, Inox cinemas and the river. Being renovated at time of writing. Recommended.
\$ Panjim Residency (GTDC), overlooking the river, T0832-242 4001. Best views from top floor, 40 good-sized rooms with balcony, some a/c (overpriced), good open-air restaurant, often full, can organize tours and boat trips.
\$ Rajdhani, Dr Atmaram Borkar Rd, T0832-222 5362. Modern business hotel with 35 smallish clean rooms with bath, some a/c (Rs 100 extra), pure vegetarian restaurant.

Fontainhas *p56, map p54*
\$\$\$ The Panjim Peoples, opposite Panjim Inn, www.panjiminn.com. The latest heritage project from the Sukhija family, this one is genuinely top end with just 4 rooms, antique 4-poster beds and bathtubs, plus internet access. Changing art exhibitions on the ground floor.
\$\$ Panjim Inn, E212, 31 Janeiro Rd, T0832-222 6523, www.panjiminn.com. Goa's first heritage hotel is idiosyncratic, even in the

context of the historic Fontainhas district. 14 rooms of varying size all fitted with 4-poster beds, a/c for an extra Rs 250.

$$ Panjim Pousada, up the road from Panjim Inn. Slightly cheaper sister hotel to the Panjim Inn with double rooms set around a permanent art gallery in a courtyard. It is an evocative, attractive renovation. Best rooms at the back overlook another courtyard. Recommended.

$$-$ Afonso, near San Sebastian Chapel, Fontainhas, T0832-222 2359. Atmospheric family-run guesthouse, obliging and friendly, 8 clean rooms with bath, shaded roof terrace for breakfast. It's first come first served, though, as the owners don't take advance bookings. Recommended.

$ Comfort Guest House, 31 Janeiro Rd, T0832-222 8145. Good location, some rooms with TV, but often full and you can't book ahead. The cheaper of its 12 basic rooms have shared bath.

$ Pousada Guest House, Luis de Menezes Rd, T0832-561 8308. Pousada's basic rooms are higgledy-piggledy but have a/c, TV and fridge and attached bath. Will take advance bookings.

Around Panjim *p61*
Miramar Beach

$$$ Goa Marriott Resort, Mandovi River, T0832-246 3333, www.marriott.com. 153 large rooms, good facilities, pool, close to public beach, best hotel in area. Weekend buffet lunches popular with Panjim locals.

$$ Swimsea Beach Resort, T0832-246 4481, swimsea@satyam.net.in. 28 a/c rooms with small balconies, pretty underwhelming, sea-facing best, pool, if you want a quality beach experience better to stay elsewhere.

🍴 Restaurants

Panjim *p54, map p54*
$$ Horseshoe, Rua de Ourem, T0832-243 1788. Mon-Sat 1200-1430, 1900-1030. Portuguese/Goan restaurant set in 2 high-ceilinged rooms with exceptionally good

service. Most meals excellent value (Rs 60-80) but daily fish specials are far more costly (from Rs 300). The house pudding, a cashew cake, *Bolo San Rival* (Rs 50), trumps all the great main courses.

$$ Quarterdeck, next to Betim ferry jetty, T0832-243 2905. Goan, Indian, Chinese. Riverside location is the best in Panjim, very pleasant in the evening when brightly lit cruise boats glide gaudily by. Live music.

$$ Venite, 31 Janeiro Rd, T0832-222 5537. Mon-Sat 0800-2200, closes in the afternoon. The most charming of Panjim's eateries has 1st-floor balconies overlooking the Sao Thome street life and good music. Specializing in fish, this place has a great atmosphere.

$$ Viva Panjim, house No 178, signposted from 31 Janeiro Rd, T0832-242 2405. This family-run joint in the atmospheric Fontainhas quarter spills out of the restaurant and out into a courtyard, and dishes up Goan specials like *xacuti* and *cafreal* along with seafood, plus takeaway parcels of Indian, Chinese and continental.

$ Anandashram, opposite Venite 31 Janeiro Rd. Serving up platters of fish and veg *thali*, this is a great place to break *pao* (local bread) with the locals. Recommended.

$ Café Tato, off east side of Church Sq. Closed evenings. Something of a local institution, tiny little **Tato** is packed at lunchtime when office workers descend for its limited range of Goan vegetarian food. Expect tiny platters of chickpea, tomato or mushroom bhaji served with fresh puffed *puris* or soft bread rolls, or vegetarian cutlets and *thalis*. Upstairs is a/c.

$ Kamat, south end of Municipal Gardens. Pure vegetarian canteen, huge servings of *thalis*, excellent paper *dosas* and *puri bhajis*. Very popular large central dining hall.

$ Satkar, 18 June Rd, opposite Bombay Bazaar. **Satkar** serves up fantastic pure veg food that runs the gamut from South Indian *idlis* and *thalis* to north Indian *sabzi* and tandoor dishes, and the best Punjabi samosas in India. Recommended.

Bakeries, cafés and snacks

$$ A Pastelaria, Dr Dada Vaidya Rd. Good choice of cakes, pastries and breads. **Mandovi Hotel** has a branch too (side entrance).

$$-$ Tea Cafe, house No 5/218, 31 Janerio Rd. In the heart of Fontainhas, this is a cosy little café serving up cakes and sandwiches. A nice place to rest before exploring more of Panjim.

🍷 Bars and clubs

Panjim *p54, map p54*
You can't go 20 paces in Panjim without finding a bar: pokey little rooms with a handful of formica tables and chairs and some snacks being fried up in the corner. Many are clustered around Fontainhas. The *feni* (Goa's cashew- or coconut-extracted moonshine) comes delivered in jerry cans, making it cheaper than restaurants. Try **Café Moderna**, near Cine National, food none too good, claustrophobic upstairs dining area, but quality atmosphere.

😎 Entertainment

Panjim *p54, map p54*
Read the 'today's events' columns in the local papers for concerts and performances.
Astronomical Observatory, 7th floor, Junta House, 18 June Rd (entrance in Vivekananda Rd). Open 14 Nov-31 May, 1900-2100, in clear weather. Rooftop 6-inch Newtonian reflector telescope and binoculars. Worth a visit on a moonless night, and for views over Panjim at sunset.
Inox, Campal, near Kala Academy, www.inoxmovies.com. Fantastic state-of-the-art glass-fronted cinema – like going to the movies in California. You can catch the latest Bolly- and Hollywood blockbusters here, and they try to show the Oscar-nominated Best Movies every year.
Kala Academy, D B Marg, Campal, T0832-222 3288. This modern and architecturally impressive centre designed by Charles Correa was set up to preserve

and promote the cultural heritage of Goa. There are exhibition galleries, a library and comfortable indoor and outdoor auditoria. Art exhibitions, theatre and music programmes (from contemporary pop and jazz to Indian classical) are held, mostly during the winter months. There are also music and dance courses.
MV Caravela, Fisheries dept building, D B Marg, Panjim, www.casinocity.com/in/panjim/caravela. India's first floating casino is docked on the Mandovi, 66 m of high-rupee-rolling catamaran casino, all plush wall-to-wall carpets, chandeliers and sari-bedecked croupiers. The boat accommodates 300 people, has a sun deck, swimming pool and restaurant and the Rs 1200 entrance includes short eats and dinner and booze from 1730 till the morning.

🎉 Festivals

Panjim *p54, map p54*
Feb/Mar In addition to the major festivals in Feb, the **Mardi Gras Carnival** (3 days preceding Lent in Feb/Mar) is a Mediterranean-style riot of merrymaking, marked by feasting, colourful processions and floats down streets: it kicks off near the Secretariat at midday. One of the best bits is the red-and-black dance held in the cordoned-off square outside the old world Clube Nacional on the evening of the last day: everyone dresses up (some cross-dressing), almost everyone knows each other, and there's lots of old-fashioned slow-dancing to curiously Country and Western-infused live music. The red and black theme is strictly enforced.
Mar-Apr Shigmotsav is a spring festival held at full moon (celebrated as **Holi** elsewhere in India); colourful float processions through the streets often display mythological scenes accompanied by plenty of music on drums and cymbals.
1st Sun after Easter Feast of Jesus of Nazareth. Procession of All Saints in Goa Velha, on the Mon of Holy Week.

Dec/Jan Fontainhas Festival of Arts.
Timed to coincide with the film festival
(see below), 30 heritage homes open up
as temporary art and artefact galleries in
an event organized by Fundacao Oriente,
Goa Heritage Action Group and the
Entertainment Society of Goa.
International Film Festival of India,
www.iffigoa.org. India's answer to Cannes:
a 10-day film mart packed with screenings
for the industry and general public alike,
with its headquarters based around the Kala
Academy and the Inox building on the banks
of the Mandovi. Held in Goa since 2004.
Food and Culture Festival at Miramar Beach.
8 Dec Feast of Our Lady of the Immaculate
Conception. A big fair is held in the streets
around Church Sq and a firework display is
put on in front of the church each night of
the week before the feast (at 1930). After
morning Mass on the Sun, the Virgin is carried
in a procession through the town centre.
24 Dec Christmas Eve. This is celebrated
with midnight Mass at 140 churches in the
state, but some of the best attended are
the Church of the Immaculate Conception
and Dom Bosco Church in Panjim and the
Basilica of Bom Jesus in Old Goa.

⊙ Shopping

Panjim *p54, map p54*
Books and music
Broadway Books, next to Rock and Raaga
off 18 June Rd, T0832-664 7038. Largest
bookshop in Goa with good range.
Mandovi Hotel (see Where to stay,
page 62). The hotel bookshop has a
small range of books and magazines,
including American news magazines.
Pedro Fernandes & Co, Rua Jose de Costa,
near Head Post Office, T0832-222 6642. If
you have a hankering to pick up a sitar or
learn to play tabla, this small store has a
great selection of musical instruments.

Varsha, near Azad Maidan. Holds a large
stock in tiny premises, and is especially good
for books on Goa. Obscure titles are not
displayed but ask the knowledgeable staff.

Clothes and textiles
Government handicrafts shops are at the
tourist hotels and the Interstate Terminus.
There are other emporia on RS Rd.
Bombay Store, Casa Mendes, SV Rd,
opposite Old Passport Office. A new branch
of the lifestyle retail store has arrived in Goa
close to the main shopping road 18 June Rd,
with good selection of fabrics and clothes, as
well as cards, stationery and homewares.
Fab India, Braganza Bungalow, opposite
Indoor Stadium, Campal, T0832-246 3096.
This is a particularly lovely branch of the
great chain which sells handblock print
clothes, textiles, home furnishings and
furniture. They have an extensive collection.
Government Emporia, RS Rd. Good value
for fixed-rate clothes, fabric and handicrafts.
Khadi Showroom, Municipal (Communidade)
Building, Church Sq, good value for fixed-rate
clothes, fabric and handicrafts. Nehru jackets,
plus perishables such as honey and pickles.
Sacha's Shop, Casa Mendes, next to
Bombay Store, T0832-222 2035. Dubbed
a 'curious little space' by the owner, the
eponymous **Sacha**, it is a collection of
clothes, flea market finds, designer frocks,
organic soaps and textiles.
Velha Goa Galeria, 4/191 Rua De
Ourem, Fontainhas, T0832-242 6628.
Hand-painted ceramics, wall hangings
and tabletops of tiles.
Wendell Rodricks Design Space, 158 near
Luis Gomes Garden, Altinho, T0832-223
8177, www.wendellrodricks.com. Goa's
own fashion designer, brought up in the
small village of Colvale, has a beautiful shop
in the Altinho district of Panjim. Beautiful
fabrics and stylish cuts.

⚙ What to do

Panjim *p54, map p54*
Cruises
Lots of evening cruises go along the Mandovi River, but as all boats seem to sport loud sound systems it's hardly a peaceful cruise.

Music lessons
Manab Das plays regularly at the **Kala Academy** and the **Kerkar** in Calangute (see page 71). He and his wife, Dr Rupasree Das, offer sitar and singing lessons to more long-term visitors. To arrange lessons T0832-242 1086 or email manabrupasreegoa@yahoo.in.

Tour operators
Alpha Holidays, 407-409 Dempo Tower, 4th floor, 16 EDC Patto Plaza, T0832-243 7450, www.alphagoa.com.
Goa Eco Tourism, Rua de Ourem, T0832 2443551. Some interesting tours including the **Jungle Book Tour** staying a night at Bhagwan Mahaveer Sanctuary.
Pepper Tours, 127 Subash Chandra Bose Rd, Jawahar Nagar, Kadavanthara, PO Cochin 682020, T484-405 8886, T(0)9847-322802 (mob), www.peppertours.com.

⊖ Transport

Panjim *p54, map p54*
Air The airport is at Dabolim. 29 km via the Zuari Bridge from Panjim. Pre-paid taxis charge Rs 700 to Panjim.
Airline offices **Air India**, 18 June Rd, T0832-243 1101. **Indian Airlines and Alliance Air**, Dempo House, D B Marg, T0832-223 7821, reservations 1000-1300, 1400-1600, airport T0832-254 0788.**British Airways**, 2 Excelsior Chambers, opposite Mangaldeep, MG Rd, T0832-222 4573. **Jet Airways**, Sesa Ghor, 7-9 Patto Plaza, T0832-243 1472, airport T0832-251 0354. **Qatar Airways**, 001/003 Dempo Trade Center, Patto Plaza, T079 3061 6000. For more information on domestic flights and expected prices see page 8.

Auto-rickshaw Easily available but agree a price beforehand (often Rs 50 minimum); more expensive after dark. Motorcycle taxis and private taxis are a little cheaper.

Bus Local: Crowded Kadamba (KTC) buses and private buses operate from the bus stand in Patto to the east of town, across the Ourem Creek, T0832-243 8035. Booking 0800-1100, 1400-1630. The timetable is not strictly observed; buses leave when full. Frequent service to **Calangute** 35 mins; **Mapusa** 15 mins(try to catch a direct one, you will hear someone calling out what sounds like "durry, durry, durry"!). Via Cortalim (Zuari bridge) to **Margao** 1 hr; **Vasco** 1 hr. To **Old Goa** (every 10 mins) 20 mins, continues to **Ponda** 1 hr. Fares are between Rs 8-20 for these local services.

Long distance: 'Luxury' buses and 'Sleepers' (bunks are shared). Prices double at Diwali, Christmas and New Year, and during the May school holidays. Private operators include **Paulo Travels**, Cardozo Bld, near Kadamba Bus stand, T0832 6637777, www.phmgoa.com, and charge between Rs 450 and 800 for Panjim to **Mumbai**, for example (15 hrs); similar for Bangalore and Pune.

State buses are run by **Kadamba TC, Karnataka RTC, Maharashtra RTC.** Check times and book in advance at Kadamba Bus Stand. Unlicensed operators use poorly maintained, overcrowded buses; check before travelling. Fares are cheaper than with private operators, but it's not so easy to book or as comfortable. Expect to pay Rs 350-600 for Panjim to **Mumbai** (15 hrs), similar pricing for **Bangalore** and **Pune**; between Rs 150-400 for Hampi (10 hrs).

Car hire Hertz, T0832-222 3998; Joey's, Office No 6, Panjim Park, near Ferry Wharf, T0832-222 8989. **Goa Wheels Unlimited**, T0832-222 4304, is close by in Calangute, www.goawheelsunlimited.com or **Wheels Rental**, airport, T0832-251 2138.

Ferry Flat-bottomed ferries charge a nominal fee to take passengers (and usually vehicles) when rivers are not bridged. **Panjim–Betim** (the Nehru bridge over the Mandovi supplements the ferry); **Old Goa–Diwar Island**; **Ribandar–Chorao** for Salim Ali Bird Sanctuary.

Taxi Tourist taxis are white; hire from your hotel or contact **Goa Tourism**, Trionora Apts, T0832-242 4001. Shared-taxis run on certain routes; available near the the ferry wharves, main hotels and market places (up to 5). **Mapusa** from Panjim, around Rs 10 each.

Train Most trains stop at Thivim and Madgaon, some **Konkan Railway** trains stop at **Karmali**, T0832-228 6398, near Old Goa (20 mins by taxi). **Rail Bookings**, Kadamba Bus Station, 1st floor, T0832-243 5054, 0930-1300 and 1430-1700. **South Central Railway** serves the Vasco–Londa/Belgaum line; for details see page 131, and Margao (Madgaon), page 121.

❶ Directory

Panjim *p54, map p54*
Medical services Goa Medical College, Av PC Lopez, west end of town, T0832-222 3026, is very busy; newer College at Bambolim; CMM Poly Clinic, Altinho, T0832-222 5918.

North Goa

While Baga and Calangute, the fishing villages first settled by the 'freaks', now stand as cautionary tales to all that's bad about mass tourism, Anjuna, a place synonymous with psychedelia, drugs and Goa trance parties, has managed to retain a village feel. Despite the existence of its unquestionably shady underbelly, it's a more tranquil place to be now that a 2200 music curfew has put a stop to outdoor parties. The weekly flea market is a brilliant bazar – like Camden or Portobello but with sacred cows, sadhus, fakirs and snake charmers – and makes it onto every holidaymaker's itinerary. But if you stick around you'll find that the little stretch of shoreline from the northern end of Anjuna Beach to the Chapora River is beautifully desolate: rust-coloured rugged cliffs covered with scrub interrupt scrappy bays strewn with laterite boulders. Pretty cliff-backed Vagator stands just south of the romantic ruins of Chapora Fort, with its busy fishing jetty, where trawler landings are met by a welcoming committee of kites, gulls and herons wheeling hungrily on high. Further upstream, around the pretty village of Siolim, young men wade through mangrove swamps to sift the muds for clams, mussels and oysters. Over the Chapora lies Arambol, a warm, hippy backpacker hamlet, and its beach satellites of Mandrem, Asvem and Keri and the wonderful little Catholic enclave clustered around the ancient Tiracol Fort.

Arriving in North Goa

Getting there

The NH17 acts as the main arterial road between all of Goa's coastal belt. From Panjim, the highway crosses the Mandovi Bridge to the area's main hub, Calangute (16 km from Panjim, 10 km from Mapusa). Buses from Mapusa (20 minutes) and Panjim (35 minutes) arrive at Calangute Bus Stand near the market; a few continue to Baga to the north from the crossroads. You can charter tourist minivans from places such as Panjim and Dabolim. The closest stop on the Konkan Railway route between Mumbai and Mangalore is Tivim near Mapusa. On market days there are boats between Baga and Anjuna. There are buses from Mapusa and Panjim to Calangute, Anjuna, Chapora and Arambol.

Getting around

There are 9 km of uninterrupted beach between Fort Aguada and the bridge over Baga river in the north, which takes you to Anjuna. These are split into four beaches, south to north: Sinquerim, Candolim, Calangute and Baga. Each has its own stab at a high street, Calangute's being the most built up. There are taxis, motorcycle taxis, tourist vans and old Ambassador cabs, or cheap but slow public buses. Roads are fairly good for motorbikes and scooters; watch out for speed bumps. Accidents happen with grim regularity, but bikes give you the independence to zip between beaches.

Baga

To Anjuna (2 km)

To Anjuna (500m)

St Ann's

Salt Lake

Salt Pans

Baga River

Baga Bridge

Football Pitch

BAGA

Lady of Candelaria

Natural Health Centre

Tito's Rd

Bike Hire

To Calangute

Arabian Sea

N

200 metres
200 yards

Where to stay
Alidia Beach Cottages 1
Cavala 6
Nani's & Rani's 8
Riverside 3

Restaurants
Baba Au Rhum 2
Britto's 15
Casa Portuguesa 12
Fiesta 1
J&A's Italiano House 6
Lila's Café 9

Bars & clubs
Mambo's 13
Tito's 16

Background

The name Bardez may have come from the term *bara desh* (12 'divisions of land'), which refers to the 12 Brahmin villages that once dominated the region. Another explanation is that it refers to 12 *zagors* celebrated to ward off evil. Or it could be *bahir des*, meaning 'outside land' – ie, the land beyond the Mandovi River. It was occupied by the Portuguese as part of their original conquest, and bears the greatest direct imprint of their Christianizing influence.

Baga to Candolim → *For listings, see pages 79-101.*

The faultless fawn shoreline of Bardez *taluka*, particularly Calangute, until 40 years ago was a string of fishing villages. Now it acts as sandpit to the bulk of Goa's travel trade. Chock full of accommodation, eateries, travel agents, money changers, beggars and under-dressed, over-sunned charter tourists, the roads snarl up with minivans, buses and bikes, and unchecked development has made for a largely concrete conurbation of breezeblock hotels and mini markets. For all that, if you squint hard or come in monsoon you can still see what once made it such a hippy magnet: wonderful coconut-fringed sands backed by plump dunes occasionally broken by rocky headlands and coves. The main reason to head this way is for business, banks, or posh food and nightlife. To get out again, you can paddle in the waters of the Arabian Sea all the way between the forts of Aguada and Vagator.

Baga

Baga is basically Calangute North: there's continuity in congestion, shops, shacks and sun loungers. Here though, there are also paddy marshes, water tanks and salt pans, the beach is still clean, and the river that divides this commercial strip of sand from Anjuna in the north also brings fishermen pulling in their catch at dawn, and casting their nets at dusk. The north bank, or **Baga River**, is all thick woods, mangroves and birdlife; it has quite a different, more villagey feel, with a few classy European restaurants looking out across the river. You can take an hour to wade across the river at low tide, then walk over the crest of the hill and down into Anjuna South, or detour inland to reach the bridge.

Calangute

More than 25 years of package tourism has guaranteed that there is little left to draw you to Calangute apart from ATMs, some decent restaurants and a quirky hexagonal *barbeiria* (barber's shop) at the northern roundabout. In the 1960s, the village was short-hand for the alternative life, but the main feature of the streets today is their messy Indian take on beach commercialism. Shops peddle everything from cheap ethnic tat to extravagant precious gemstones. The shacks on the beach serve good food and cheap beer and most fly the St George's Cross in tribute to Calangute's charter coin. Between the busy beachfront and the grubby main road, coconut trees give shade to village houses, some of which rent out private rooms.

Calangute

To Baga

Casa Goa

COBRAVADDO

Our Lady of Piety

Arabian Sea

To Mapusa (6 km)

Tibetan Market

Football Pitch

St John's

Tibetan Market

Heritage Kathakali Theatre

SBI

BoB

UMTAVADDO

Menezes Supermarket

CALANGUTE

To Panjim

St Anthony's

GAURAVADDO

Kerkar Art Complex

Literati

Day Tripper

To 1 6 9, Acron Arcade, Candolim (1 km), Sinquerim (3 km) & Aguada Fort (4 km)

Saahil 1

Villa Goesa 20

N

200 metres
200 yards

Where to stay 🛏
Coco Banana 4
Kerkar Retreat 3
Martin's Guest Rooms 13
The Park 10
Pousada Tauma 17

Restaurants 🍴
A Reverie 3
Bomras 1
Café Ciocolatti 6
Fisherman's Cove 9
Infanteria 2
Plantain Leaf 7
Souza Lobo 8
Tibetan Kitchen 5

Away from the town centre, the striking gold and white **Church of St Alex** is a good example of rococo decoration in Goa, while the false dome of the central façade is an 18th-century architectural development. The pulpit and the *reredos* are particularly fine. **Kerkar Art Complex** ① *Gaurawaddo, T0832-227 6017, www.subodhkerkar.com*, is a beautiful art space showcasing Subodh Kerkar's paintings and installation work. Inspired by the ocean, nature is both the theme and medium of his work, using shells, light and water to create static waves or, in his recent installations, using fishermen standing on the beach to create the shapes and forms of fishing boats – all captured in stunning black and white photography.

Candolim and Sinquerim beaches

The wide unsheltered stretch of beach here, backed by scrub-covered dunes, offers unusual visual stimulus courtesy of the unlovely rusting wreck of the *Sea Princess* tanker, an eyesore and environmental nightmare (the currents eddying around its bows are playing havoc with coastal sand deposition) which has been resting offshore for years waiting for someone to muster the will to remove it. Nevertheless, the beach still attracts a fair crowd: more staid than Baga and Calangute to the north, chiefly because its restaurants and hotels are pricier and the average holidaymaker more senior. The road from Calangute to Fort Aguada is lined with shiny glass-fronted shops, while the sands at the foot of the Taj complex offers the full gamut of watersports – jet skis, windsurfers, catamaran and dinghies are all for hire – making it a favourite of India's fun-loving domestic tourists.

Fort Aguada

The Portuguese colonizer's strongest coastal fort was built on this northern tip of the Mandovi estuary in 1612 with one goal: to stay the Dutch navy. Two hundred guns were stationed here along with two magazines, four barracks, several residences for officers and two prisons. It was against the Marathas, though, rather than the Dutch, that Aguada saw repeated action – Goans fleeing the onslaught at Bardez took refuge here – and its ramparts proved time and again impregnable. The main fortifications (laterite walls nearly 5 m high and 1.3 m thick) are still intact, and the buildings at sea level now house Goa's Central Jail, whose 142 male and 25 female inmates are incarcerated in what must be one of the world's prettiest lock-ups.

Reis Magos, the Nerul River and Coco Beach

The position of **Reis Magos**, across the Mandovi River from Panjim, made it imperative for Albuquerque to station troops on this shoulder of headland from day one of Portuguese rule – today, come for the views to the capital, and for the crumbling **Royal Fort** whose angular 16th-century architecture is now overrun with jungle. Its canons served as the second line of defence against the Dutch after Aguada. The next door **church** is where the village gets its name – this was where the first Mass on Goan soil was celebrated in 1550, and the Hindu temple was promptly turned over into a church to the three Magi Kings – Gaspar, Melchior and Balthazar – whose stories are told on the inside *reredos*. Fort Aguada and Fort Reis Magos are divided by the Nerul River: stop off at Nerul's **Coco Beach** for lunch and a swim. The temple in the village dates from 1910 and the Church of Our Lady of Remedies from 1569.

The trance dance experience

The 'freaks' (beatniks with super-nomadic genes, giant drug habits and names like Eight Finger Eddie) first shipped into Goa shortly after the Portuguese left. Some brought guitars on which, after soaking up a bit of Hindu spirituality on the way, they were charged with playing devotional songs at beach campfire parties.

By the end of the 1960s, thousands of freaks were swarming into Goa, often spilling down from Kathmandu, and word got back to proper paid-up acid rock musicians about the scene. Some more substantial entertainment was called for.

The first music to run through the speakers was rock and reggae. Led Zeppelin, The Who and George Harrison rocked up and played live, but the freaks' entertainment was mostly recorded: Santana, Rolling Stones and Bob Marley. Kraftwerk and synth had filtered in by the late 1970s but the shift to electronica only really came in the early 1980s when musicians got bored of the lyrics and blanked out all the words on albums of industrial noise, rock and disco, using the fully lo-fi production method of taping between two cassette decks. Depeche Mode and New Order albums were stripped down for their drum and synth layers. Some of the rock faithful were angry with the change in the soundtrack to their lives; at those early 1980s parties, when the psychedelic-meets-machine-drum sound that still defines Goa trance was first being pumped out, legend has it that the decks had to be flanked by bouncers.

The music, developing in tandem to German nosebleed techno and UK acid house, locked into a worldwide tapestry of druggy drumscapes, but the Goan climate created its own sound. As records would warp in India's high temperatures, music had to be put down on DATS rather than vinyl which in turn meant tracks were played out in full, unmixed. A track had to be interesting enough then, self-contained, so it could be played uninterrupted in full; producers had to pay more attention to intros, middles and outros – in short, the music had to have a story. It also meant there was less art to a set by a trance DJ in Goa than DJs in Manchester, Detroit and Paris, who could splice records together to make their own new hybrid sounds.

Many of the original makers of this music had absorbed a fair whack of psychedelia and had added the inevitable layer of sadhu thinking to this – superficially measured in incense, *oms*, dreads and the swirling dayglo mandalas that unmistakeably mark out a Goa trance party. The music reflected this: sitars noodled alongside sequencer music to make the Goan signature sound.

By the 1990s, though, Ecstasy had arrived in Goa. The whole party scene opened right up, peopled by Spiral Tribe crusties as well as middle-class gap year lovelies and global party scenesters who came looking for an alternative to the more mainstream fare in Ibiza. Paul Oakenfold's Perfecto was a key label in fuelling the sound's popularity but there were more: Dragonfly, The Infinity Project, Return to the Source. Today trance is still a thriving part of the Goa circuit and, although much of it is from European or Japanese studios, there's also the odd homegrown label.

Mapusa → *For listings, see pages 79-101.*

Standing in the nape of one of Goa's east–west ridges lies Bardez's administrative headquarters: a buzzy, unruly market town filled with 1960s low-rise buildings set on former marshland on the banks of the Mapusa River; (Maha apsa' means 'great swamps, a reference to Mapusa's watery past). Mapusa town won't find its way onto many tourist postcards, but it's friendly, small and messy, is an important transport hub and has an excellent daily **municipal market**, worth journeying inland for, especially on its busiest day, Friday. Open from early morning Monday to Saturday, it peters out 1200-1500, then gathers steam again till night, and has giant rings of *chourica* sausage, tumbles of spices and rows of squatting fruit and vegetable hawkers.

Walk east for the small 16th-century **St Jerome's Church**, or 'Milagres', Our Lady of Miracles (1594), rebuilt first in 1674 then again in 1839 after a candle sparked a devastating fire. In 1961 the roof was badly damaged when the Portuguese blew up a nearby bridge in their struggle with the liberating Indian army. The church has a scrolled gable, balconied windows in the façade, a belfry at the rear and an interesting slatted wood ceiling. The main altar is to Our Lady, and on either side are St John and St Jerome: the *retables* (shelves behind the altar) were brought from Daugim. The church is sacred to Hindus as well as Catholics, not only because it stands near the site of the Shanteri Temple but also because 'Our Lady of Miracles' was one of seven Hindu sisters converted to Christianity. Her lotus pattern gold necklace (kept under lock and key) may also have been taken from a Hindu deity who preceded her.

The **Maruti Temple** ① *west of the market opposite taxi stand*, was built on the site of a firecracker shop where Rama followers in the 1840s would gather in clandestine worship of first a picture, then a silver image, of monkey god Hanuman after the Portuguese destroyed the local Hindu temples.

Barely 5 km east of Mapusa lies **Moira**, deep in the belly of a rich agricultural district that was once the scene of Portuguese mass baptisms. The town is ancient – some say it was the site of a sixth or seventh century AD Mauryan settlement – and until the arrival of the Portuguese it must have been a Brahmin village. A total of seven important temples were destroyed during the Inquisition and six idols moved to Mulgaon in Bicholim district (immediately east).

Today the village is dominated by the unusual **Church of Our Lady of the Immaculate Conception**. Originally built of mud and thatch in 1619, it was rebuilt during the 19th century with square towers close to the false dome. The balustrades at the top of the first and second floors run the length of the building and the central doorways of the ground and first floors have Islamic-looking trefoil arches that contrast with the Romanesque flanking arches. There is an interesting exterior pulpit. Inside, the image of the crucifixion is unusual in having its feet nailed apart instead of together. A Siva *lingam* recycled here as the base of the font after its temple was razed is now in the Archaeological Museum at Old Goa. Moira's famous long red bananas (grown nearby) are not eaten raw but come cooked with sugar and coconuts as the cavity-speeding sweet *figada*.

Anjuna and around → *For listings, see pages 79-101.*

When the freaks waded across the Baga River after the squares got hip to Calangute, Anjuna was where they washed up. The village still plays host to a large alternative community: some from that first generation of hippies, but the latest influx of spiritual Westerners has brought both an enterprising spirit and often young families, meaning there's fresh pasta, gnocci, marinated tofu or chocolate brownies to be had, cool threads to buy, great, creative childcare, amazing tattoo artists, alternative therapists and world-class yoga teachers. For the beautiful life lived cheap Anjuna is still hard to beat; the countryside here is hilly and lush and jungly, the beaches good for swimming and seldom crowded. A state crackdown has made for a hiatus in the parties for which Anjuna was once synonymous, but as you head south along the shore the beach shack soundtracks get progressively more hardcore, until **Curlies**, where you'll still find arm-pumping techno and trance.

The **Flea Market** ① *Dandovaddo, south Anjuna, Oct-Apr Wed 0800 till sunset, water taxis (from Baga) or shared taxis from anywhere in Goa*, is a brilliant hullabaloo with over 2000 stalls hawking everything from Gujarati wooden printing blocks to Bhutanese silver and even Burberry-check pashminas. The trade is so lucrative by the subcontinent's standards that for six months a year several thousand Rajasthani, Gujaratis, Karnatakans and Tibetans decamp from their home states to tout their wares. The flea had very

Anjuna

To Ozran Beach
To Vagator & Chapora
Oxford Arcade
Bungee Jump
SORANTOVADDO
$ BoB
Orchard Stores
To Ingo's Night Bazar; Brahmani Yoga, Arpora & Mapsa
ANJUNA
MONTEIROVADDO
Artjuna
Arabian Sea
Flea Market
DANDOVADDO
Happy Hours Paragliding
To Baga & Calangute (500m)

N

200 metres
200 yards

Where to stay
Banyan Soul **1**
La Oasis **9**
Laguna Anjuna **3**
Martha's Breakfast Home **5**
Nilaya Hermitage Bhati **4**
Pebbles Guest House **8**
Rene's Guest House **12**
Saiprasad
 Guest House **10**
Tamarind **2**

Yoga Magic Canvas
Ecotel **7**

Restaurants 🍴
Anand **4**
German Bakery **21**
Gunpowder **6**
Joe Bananas **1**
Orange Boom **18**
Villa Blanche **12**
Xavier's **17**

Bars & clubs 🍸
Curlies **3**
Lilliput **7**
Shiva Valley **11**

different origins, and was once an intra-community car boot-style bric-a-brac sale for the freaks. Anjuna's links with trade pre-date the hippies though – the port was an important Arab trading post in the 10th and 12th centuries.

Saturday Night Bazar ⓘ *Arpora Hill, 1630-2400*, is a more sanitized and less headlong version of the flea. There's no shortage of dazzling stall fronts draped with glittering saris and the beautiful Rajasthani fare, but while there are fewer stalls there's more variety here; expats who've crafted everything from organic yoga clothes and designer mosquito nets to handmade leather goods are more likely to pitch up here than at the Wednesday event. But there's no need to shop at all – the live music and huge range of food stalls make the Night Bazaar the weekly social event for tourist and long-stayer alike. You'll find most of North Goa out for the evening, and many businesses shut up shop for the night as a result of the bazar's magnetic appeal. Bring cash and an appetite.

The Anjuna area is also home to two of Goa's best contemporary yoga schools. **Brahmani** ⓘ *www.brahmaniyoga.com*, housed in in the grounds of **Tito's White House**, runs workshops and drop-in classes, from excellent *ashtanga*, Mysore-style, to more free-flowing movement like dance yoga, and *Scaravelli*. Packages with unlimited yoga are offered, but accommodation is not on site or specifically for yoga students. Ten minutes away in the neighbouring village of **Assagao**, the **Purple Valley Yoga Retreat** ⓘ *T0832-226 8364, www.yogagoa.com, offer retreat packages including yoga and meals (see box, page 99)*, runs two-week *ashtanga* retreats with leading teachers like Sharath Rangaswamy, grandson of Sri K Pattabhi Jois, David Swenson and Nancy Gilgoff, two of the first to introduce *ashtanga* to the West in the 1970s. Lessons are held in a lovely *shala* in delightful gardens, food is vegetarian and the atmosphere collegiate.

Vagator

Vagator's beaches are possibly Goa's most dramatic: here, muddied sand bays upset by slabs of gray rock, quite different from the bubblings of porous laterite in Anjuna, fall at the bottom of terraced red cliffs planted with coconut trees that lean out towards the crashing waves, some of their trunks painted bright neon from past parties.

Big Vagator Beach is a long sweep of beach to the right of the main access road, behind which stands the profile of the wide outer rim of the ruined **Chapora Fort** against a stunning backdrop of India's western coastline, stretching beyond Goa's northern borders and into Maharashtra. The factory you can just pick out in the distance marks the border.

To your left, running inland, is **Little Vagator Beach**, its terracing lorded over by **Nine Bar**, a giant venue with an unswerving musical loyalty to trance (see box, page 72). Just out of sight is **Ozran Beach**, christened 'Spaghetti Beach' by English settlers for its Italian community. Though a bit scrappy and dogged by persistent sarong sellers, **Spaghetti** is more sheltered, more scenic and more remote than the other beaches, ending in tumbled rocks and jungle, with excellent swimming spots. To get straight to Spaghetti from Vagator follow the signposts to Leoney Resorts, then when you reach the headland turn off the tarmac road onto one of the gravel tracks following the sign for Shiva Place shack; coming from Anjuna, take the path that starts just inland from Zoori's and thread your way down the gravelly terracing.

Chapora Fort

Looming over the north end of Big Vagator Beach, there's little left of Chapora Fort but crumbling blocks of black rock overgrown with tawny grasses and a general air of tranquil ruination. Built by Adil Shah (hence the name, Shah pura), the remaining ramparts lead out to a jutting promontory that affords spectacular sunset views across the mouth of the Chapora River, where fishing boats edge slowly out of harbour and seabird flocks settle on the sand spits across from Morjim.

Chapora village itself may be too feral for some tastes. At dusk the smoke from domestic fires spreads a haze through the jungle canopy between which Portuguese houses stand worn and derelict. Down by the river's edge men lean to mend their fuzzy nets while village boys saunter out to bat on threshed fields, and Enfields and Hondas hum along the potholed roads bearing long-stayers and Goan village folk home – many of them toting fresh catch from the buzzing fish market (ignore the stern 'No Entry' signs and ride on in) held every sunset at the harbour. Along the village's main street the shady bars are decked with fairy lights and the internationals (who call Chapora both 'home' and, in an affectionate nod to its less savoury side, 'the Bronx') settle down to nurse their drinks.

The flat arc of the estuary here is perfect for cycling: the rim-side road will take you all the way out to the bridge at **Siolim** where you can loop back to take a look at the **Church of St Anthony**. Built in 1606, it replaced an earlier Franciscan church dating from 1568. Both Goa's Hindu and Catholic communities pray to St Anthony, Portugal's patron saint, in the hope of good fishing catches. The high, flat-ceilinged church has a narrow balustraded gallery and Belgian glass chandeliers, with statues of Jesus and St Anthony in the gabled west end.

Splendid Portuguese houses stand scattered about the village's shadows in varying degrees of disrepair; it's worth walking around to take in some of the facades. You can even stay in one which has been refurbished, the lovely Siolim House, see page 83. The ferry that once crossed the Chapora River at the northern end of the village no longer runs (there's a bridge instead) but it's worth heading up this way for the little daily fish market and the handful of food stalls selling fresh grilled catch. The village also has a basic bar, **Mandola**, on the coast road heading back towards Chapora, selling European snacks and cold beer.

Arambol, Keri, Morjim, Asvem and Mandrem → *For listings, see pages 79-101.*

The long bridge that spans the Chapora River joins Bardez to the last – and thus most heavily Hindu – of the new conquests, hilly Pernem *taluka*. This is the gateway to a series of pretty and quiet beaches that hug the coastal road in a nearly unbroken strip up to the Maharashtra border, where a tiny pocket of Catholicism squats in the shadow of the pretty pride of the district, Tiracol Church and Fort. Haphazard and hippy Arambol has a warm community feel and is rightly popular with open-minded travellers of all ages, who are drawn to its vibey scene, its live music, the dolphins that fin along its beaches and its famous saltwater lake. Sunset takes on the magnitude of a ritual in Arambol: people gather to sing, dance, juggle, do *capoeira* or find a silent spot for meditation and contemplation. To the south, Mandrem and Asvem are more chic and less busy, and will suit those less prepared to compromise on their accommodation. With construction of a new airport near Pernem and a large road bridge over the Tiracol to Maharashtra finally open, Northern Goa is becoming more accessible, and there will be increased development no doubt.

Arriving in Arambol, Keri, Morjim, Asvem and Mandrem
All of Pernem *taluka* is within easy reach of the hotels in Panjim or Calangute, but you'd be doing yourself a disservice to visit what are arguably North Goa's loveliest beaches just on a day trip. Better to set up camp in one and make it your base to explore the rest. If you are

crossing the bridge at Siolim on a motorbike turn left off the new main road immediately after the bridge to use the smaller, more scenic coastal roads. There also regular buses to the villages from Mapusa and from Chopdem. Each beach is about 10 minutes apart.

Background

The Bhonsles of Sawantwadi in modern Maharashtra were the last to rule Pernem before being ousted by the Portuguese in 1788, and Maratha influences here remain strong.

Arambol (Harmal)

Arambol, which you reach when the plateau road noses down through paddy fields and cashew trees, is a beautiful long stretch of sand at the bottom of a bumpy dirt track that's fringed with stalls selling brightly coloured, heavily embroidered clothes and pretty *lungis*. This is the creative and holistic hub of Goa – many Western designers, artists, performers, yogis and healers have been inspired to make the area home, and because people have put down roots here, the village is abuzz with industriousness. Flyers advertise *satsang* with smiling Western gurus: there's also *tabla* classes and drumming circles, yoga teacher training, reiki and belly dancing. Arrive at the right time of year and you might catch the **International Juggling Convention** in full swing, or stumble across a phenomenal fire-dancing show by performers who work their magic on the stages of Vegas. Arambol is

Arambol Beach

Where to stay	
Arambol Plaza **7**	
Atman **5**	
Ave Maria **1**	

Famafa Beach Resort **3**
Go-Ym **4**
Ivon's Guesthouse **9**
Luciano **14**
Oceanic **8**
Om Ganesh **2**
Residensea Beach Huts **10**
MATSYA &
Tamarind Cafe **15**
Whispering Lakes **12**

Restaurants
Coco Loco **12**
Double Dutch **1**
Dreamland **3**
Dylans **7**
Eyes of Buddha **5**
Fellini's **2**
Lamuella **10**
Relax Inn **6**
Rice Bowl **8**

Rutik's Coconuts **13**
Sai Deep **14**

Bars & clubs
Arkan **9**
Loekie's Café **4**
Psybar **11**

also synonymous with live music, with everything from Indian classical to open mike, Sufi musicians and psychedelic metal bands playing in rotation at the beach bars. Inevitably, though, Arambol's ever-growing popularity means both long and short-term accommodation get more expensive by the year.

You have to skirt the beach's northern cliff and tiny basalt rocky bays by foot to reach the real lure: a second bay cut off from the roads and a **natural 'sweet water' lake** that collects at the base of a jungle spring. The lagoon collects just metres from the high tide line where the lush forest crawls down to the water's edge. You can walk up the spring's path to reach a belt of natural mineral clay: an idyllic spot for self-service **mud baths**. Further into the jungle is the famous **banyan tree**, its branches straddling 50 m, which has long been a point of Hindu and hippy pilgrimage. Or clamber over the boulders at the north to join the scrappy dirt track over the headland for the half-hour walk it takes to reach the achingly lovely and reliably empty **Keri Beach**.

Keri (Querim) and Tiracol Fort

Goa's northernmost beach is uniquely untouched. The drive towards Keri (Querim) along the banks of the Tiracol River from Pernem passes through some stunning rural areas untouched by any tourist development.

Walk across deep dunes to a casuarina thicket and out onto empty sand that stretches all the way from the mouth of the Tiracol river to the highland that splits it from Arambol. **Querim** gets busy on weekends with Indian tourists and occasionally hosts parties, but remains a lovely spot of sand. You can reach the beach from the north on foot from the Tiracol ferry terminal, or from the south by walking round the headland from Arambol. The Tiracol ferry runs every 30 minutes 0600-2130 taking 15 minutes, depending on the tides. The ferry is still charming, but more redundant now the bridge is open.

Tiracol (Terekhol), at the northernmost tip of Goa, is a tiny enclave of just 350 Catholics on the Maharashtra border just 3.5 km across where *feni* production is the biggest business. Its name probably comes from *tir-khol* ('steep river bank') and it's a jungly little patch of land full of cashew trees, banyans, orange blossoms, black-faced monkeys and squirrels.

The small but strategic **fort** ① *0900-1800, cross Tiracol river by ferry (every 30 mins 0600-2130) and walk the remaining 2 km; ferries take cars and motorbikes*, stands above the village on the north side of the Tiracol River estuary on a rugged promontory with amazing views across the water. Its high battlement walls are clearly visible from the Arambol headland. Built by the Maharaja Khem Sawant Bhonsle in the 17th century, it is protected from attacks from the sea, while the walls on the land side rise from a dry moat. It was captured in 1746 by the Portuguese Viceroy Dom Pedro Miguel de Almeida (Marques de Alorna), who renamed it Holy Trinity and had a chapel built inside (now St Anthony's). You can explore the fort's battlements and tiny circular turrets that scarcely seem fit for slaying the enemy. The views are magnificent. Steps lead down to a terrace on the south side while the north has an open plateau.

St Anthony's Church ① *open on Wed and Sun for Mass at 1730*, inside the tiny fort, was built in the early 1750s soon after the Portuguese takeover. It has a classic Goan façade and is just large enough to cater for the small village. In the small courtyard, paved with laterite blocks, stands a modern statue of Christ. The **Festival of St Anthony** is held here at the beginning of May (usually on the second Tuesday) instead of on the conventional festival day of 13 June.

Morjim (Morji) to Asvem

Morjim, which stands on the opposite side of the estuary from Chapora, has two wide sweeping beaches that both sit at the bottom of separate dead end streets. This inaccessibility means that, development-wise, it has got away relatively unscathed. The southern, protected, turtle beach appears at the end of the narrow track that winds along the north bank of the Chapora rivermouth. Loungers, which are mostly empty, are strewn haphazardly north of the official-looking **Turtle Nesting Control Room**.

The wide shoreline with its gentle incline (the water is hip height for about 100 m) is washed by easy rolling breakers, making it one of North Goa's best swimming beaches. The northern beach, or **Little Morjim**, a left turn off the main coast road is, by comparison, an established tourist hamlet with guesthouses and beach huts.

The road from Morjim cuts inland over the low wooded hills running parallel to the coast. After a few kilometres the road drops down to the coast and runs along the edge of northeast tilting **Asvem Beach**. (Morjim faces Chapora to the south and west.) The northern end of this peaceful palm-fringed beach is divided by a small river. It's a great stretch of beach, which, alas, is gaining in popularity, with increasing development.

Mandrem

Mandrem creek forces the road to feed inland where it passes through a small commercial centre with a few shops and a bank. Mandrem village has the **Shri Bhumika Temple** housing an ancient image. In the **Shri Purchevo Ravalnatha Temple** there is a particularly striking medieval image of the half-eagle, half-human Garuda, who acts as the *vahana* (carrier) of Vishnu.

A little further on, a lane off to the left leads down towards the main beach and a secluded hamlet in a beautifully shaded setting. The **beach** is one of the least developed along this stretch of coast; for the moment it is managing to tread that fine line between having enough facilities for comfort and enough isolation to guarantee idyllic peace. Further north there is a lagoon fringed by palm trees and some simple rooms, virtually all with sea view.

North Goa listings

For hotel and restaurant price codes and other relevant information, see pages 13-15.

Where to stay

For more on places to stay in this area, see www.goatourism.org/accomodation/north.

Calangute *p70, map p70*
$$$$ The Park, Holiday St Calangute, www.theparkhotels.com. Boutique number offering up chic white rooms – 2 suites have sea views but to enjoy the beach at its best head to the bar and restaurant. There is a lovely pool as well and cute shop on site. Best doors ever with fantastic photography from Rohit Chawla adorning them.

$$$$ Pousada Tauma, Porbavaddo Calangute, T0832-227 9061, www.pousada-tauma.com. A shady little complex built of Goa's trademark laterite rock set around a beautiful pool. It's discreet but full of character, with old-fashioned yet understated service. Suites are spacious, but come with shower not bath. Classy without a modern 5-star swagger.
$$$ Kerkar Retreat, Gauravaddo, T0832-227 6017, www.subodhkerkar.com/retreat. Get inspired by staying above this beautiful art gallery (see page 71). Subodh Kerkar is a visionary artist and has created a beautiful oasis in the midst of Calangute. Just 5 doubles with an overflowing library and an array of stunning artwork. A guesthouse

feel that's ideal for families since it also has a kitchen you can use. Somewhat sedate by Calangute's standards – but that's a compliment. Highly recommended.

$$$-$$ Villa Goesa, Cobravaddo, off Baga Rd, T0832-227 7535, www.nivalink.com/vilagoesa. 57 clean rooms, some a/c, some very shaded, excellent restaurant, lovely gardens, pool, quiet, relaxing, very friendly owners, 300-m walk from the beach. Recommended.

$$-$ Coco Banana, 5/139A Umtavaddo, back from Calangute Beach, T0832-227 6478, www.cocobananagoa.com. In a nice neighbourhood in the backlanes of Calangute, this is one of the best local guesthouses and has 6 spotless en suite bungalows set in a leafy garden. All rooms come with nets and fridges, some have TV and a/c, and the place is airy, light and comfortable. The Swiss-German owners are caring and helpful. They also rent out 2 apartments in **Casa Leyla**, and have a whole house, **Soledad**, with all mod cons and maid service.

$ Martin's Guest Rooms, Baga Rd, T0832-227 7306, martins@goatelecom.com. 5 rooms in family house, attractive verandas, use of kitchen but on the busy main road and could do with a lick of paint.

$ Saahil, Cobravaddo, Baga Rd, T0832-227 6647. Lots of big, clean rooms within walking distance of all the action. Good value.

Baga *p70, map p69*

Of the family guesthouses on the northern side of Baga River up towards Arpora, those to the left of the bridge (west or seaward) are quieter. You might be able to get a room in houses/cottages with good weekly or monthly rates. Standards vary so check room and security first. Try Wilson Fernandes at **Nani's & Rani's**.

$$$-$ Cavala, Sauntavaddo, top end of Baga village, T0832-227 6090, www.cavala.com. Sandwiched between Baga Rd and a big field stretching towards the mountains, **Cavala** is traditional but

very well maintained, with friendly and attentive management, and set in lovely gardens. The 30 rooms are big, with giant fridges and huge bathrooms, although only shower. Some have TV. They have regular music nights in their popular restaurant and they also have a new villa for rent in neighbouring Anjuna. Recommended.

$$ Alidia Beach Cottages, behind the Church, Sauntavaddo, T0832-227 9014, alidia@rediffmail.com. Weave around the pot-plant covered yards to reach this charming hotel in a series of 2-storey cottages, run professionally but with the warmth of a guesthouse. Rooms are spotless and old fashioned, with features including handmade fitted wardrobes, and offer lots of privacy around the well-tended garden. One of the best of its kind so book ahead.

$$-$ Riverside, Baga River by the bridge, T0832-227 7337, www.hotelriversidegoa.com. Nice location overlooking the river. Clean modern rooms with good balconies. Some cottages with kitchens available near the pool. Has a tour group feel about the place, but lovely location.

$ Nani's & Rani's, T0832-227 7014, www.naniranigoa.com. 8 spartan rooms (shared or own bath), budget meals served in pleasant garden, bar, email, STD/ISD. One of the few local budget options with a sea view and a relaxing quiet location – attractive main building. Renowned healer Dr Patrick hosts sessions and workshops here on occasion. Short walk across Baga Bridge for nightlife.

Candolim and Sinquerim beaches *p71*

$$$$ Fort Aguada Beach Resort, Sinquerim, T0832-664 5858, www.tajhotels.com. The self-confessed sprawling Taj complex spreads over 36 ha. In descending order of cost, these are 17 hilltop family villas that make up the Aguada Hermitage, 130 rooms with sea views at the Fort Aguada Beach Resort, built in the fort's ruins, and scores of cottages for up to 8 on the beach in the newer and very beautifully kept **Taj Holiday Village**, about 2 km away – there is a shuttle bus between the 2 resorts. Between the 2 hotels there is a recommended spa, 2 freshwater pools, 9 restaurants, plus golf, tennis and a crèche. The **Banyan Tree Thai** restaurant is especially recommended.

$$$$-$$$ Aashyana Lakhanpal, Escrivao Vaddo, Candolim, T0832-248 9225, www.aashyanalakhanpal.com. One of the most stunning places in Goa – delightful gardens with great swathes of green lead right down to the beach. If you don't fancy the beach, there's a lovely pool. And the rooms and villas are beautifully decorated. This is a great place to hide away. Recommended.

$$$$-$$$ Lemon Tree Amarante Beach Resort, Vadi, Candolim, T0832-398 8188 (central reservations T0991-170 1701), www.lemontreehotels.com. Try to get one of the 6 heritage rooms here, housed inside a grand century-old Portuguese mansion but restored now, as the rest of the hotel, in mock 15th-century Portuguese style. The complex has Wi-Fi, a kids' centre, pool, 2 restaurants, a spa and all mod cons.

$$$$-$$$ The Sol, road opposite Bank of India, Nerul (directly inland 2 km from Calangute/Sinquerim), T0832-671 4141, www.thesol.in. Designed by fashion designer Tarun Tahiliani this is a nouveau heritage-style property where they strive to create an atmosphere that honours Goa as it once was. Tucked in lush foliage with views of Sinquerim river, the rooms are big, the beds are 4-postered.

$$$ Marbella Tourist Home, left off the road to Taj Fort Aguada Beach Resort, T0832-247 9551, www.marbellagoa.com. Splendid mock-Portuguese period mansion with 6 lovingly decorated rooms. Its owners have scavenged bona fide antiques and furnishings like mosaic tiles from old villas to create this elegant and unpretentious homestay in a forest at the end of a dirt track. Lovely garden sit-out for meals. All rooms have a/c and cable TV. Recommended.

$ Ludovici Tourist Home, Dando, Sinquerim, T0832-237 9684. Pretty family home set back off the main road with 4 modest en suite doubles, all with fan. It very much feels that you are one of the family. There's a bar and restaurant and a lovely porch with chairs that gives onto a spacious garden. Sedate and modest guesthouse with traditional charm.

Mapusa and inland *p73*

$$$$ Avanilaya, on the island of Corjuem, 9 km east of Mapusa, T0832-2484888, www.avanilaya.com. Just 4 elegant rooms in this stunning secluded house overlooking the Mapusa River, potentially by time of reading there will be more rooms available in neighbouring properties. Not much to do here except laze in bliss with Ayurvedic massages and facials, amazing food and mesmerizing views.

$$$ Presa di Goa, Arais Wado, Nagoa-Saligao, T0832-240 9067, www.presadigoa.com. Dubbed as a country house retreat, **Presa di Goa** is a beautifully decorated place with antique furniture, some with 4-poster beds. There's a relaxed vibe and a lovely swimming pool. And even though it's not close to the sea and there's not much going on around there, it's perfect for getting away from it all.

$$$ Wildernest, www.wildernestgoa.com. Amazing eco resort tucked into the border of Goa with Maharashtra and Karnataka – it's 1½ hrs from Mapusa. This eco-hotel sprung up as a protest – the land was to be sold to a big mining company and in order to save it **Wildernest** was created. So this place is the real deal, they are concerned with the local wildlife and there is a research centre on-site and for guests there are birdwatching tours and waterfall treks. The luxe log cabins hug the valley with amazing views of the ghats and there is an infinity swimming pool hanging just above the horizon. Working closely with 6 local villages from all 3 states, they offer up delicious home-cooked food. This is an alternative view of Goa. Wholeheartedly recommended.

Anjuna and around *p73, map p74*
At the budget end, the best options in Anjuna, Vagator and Chapora tend to be unofficial, privately owned residences.

$$$$ Nilaya Hermitage Bhati, T0832-227 6793, www.nilayahermitage.com. A luxury retreat in topaz on a hilltop in Arpora overlooking Anjuna. Elite accommodation in 10 unique bungalows and 4 tents in lush gardens set around a beautiful plunge pool. Tennis, badminton, gym, yoga, jogging trail, DVD library and excellent restaurant, highly prized music room, but some have found fault with the warmth of service and food.

$$$ Laguna Anjuna, Sorantovaddo, T(0)9822-162111, www.lagunaanjuna.com. Atmospheric cottages spiralling off behind stunning swimming pool and lush gardens, some with amazing domed ceilings and divan daybeds. Beautiful bathrooms and comfy beds. It's good for a romantic getaway. This is a vibey place serving up great food from the popular restaurant by the frangipani-fringed pool. You can come and use the lovely pool for Rs 150.

$$$ La Oasis, Flea Market Rd, T0832-227 3181, www.theverda.com. New kid on the block offering up a 3-storey hotel with all mod cons in the heart of Anjuna. It's all quite typical fare but there is a lovely rooftop pool – you are literally up in the palm leaves.

$$ The Banyan Soul, behind German Bakery, off Flea Market Rd, T(0)9820-707283, sumityardi@thebanyansoul.com. Chic complex of rooms nestled under giant banyan tree. Funky modern rooms with beautiful artistic lighting and all mod cons, sexy showers, TVs and compact verandas. The only drawback is the rooms take up the whole site; there are smart gardens bordering the hotel, but it is a bit boxed in.

$$ The Tamarind, 3 km inland from Anjuna, behind St Michael's Church, Kumar Vaddo, Mapusa Rd, T0832-227 3074, www.the tamarindhotel.com. With a chic facelift and change in management, The Tamarind is offering up stylish accommodation in a quiet part of Anjuna. There is a pretty pool and new restaurant.

$$ Yogamagic Canvas Ecotel, 2 km from Anjuna beach, T0832-652 3796, www.yogamagic.net. With Maharani suites and Rajasthani hunting tents with added bamboo roofs, this is a luxe campsite surrounded by fields of paddy and palms. Beautifully landscaped, there is a naturally filtered pool, immaculate gardens of bougainvillea, lilies and lotus flowers, yoga and holistic therapies, delicious vegetarian South Indian food and everything has been built with a nod towards the environment. The yoga temple is very beautiful.

$$-$ Martha's Breakfast Home, House No 907, Monteiro Vaddo Anjuna, T0832-227 3365, mpd8650@hotmail.com. Set in the gardens of a house that give onto an orchard where pigs roam in the shade. 8 spic-and-span rooms, twin beds, small shower rooms (cold water) with nice little balconies. Better though are the 2 villas with 2 doubles, little lounges with telly, and kitchenettes with gas stove, sink and fridge. Ask for the Sunset Villa, which has incredible views. Basic but perfect.

$ Pebbles, Piqueno Peddem, Flea Market Rd, T(0)880-685 9992, www.anjunapebbles.com. Well located for market and beach – you could almost get away without getting your own transport which is a rarity for Anjuna. Basic rooms but great value, friendly owner. You might want to hide on Wed when the road will be busy outside.

$ Rene's Guest House, Monterio Waddo, opposite Artjuna, T0832-227 3405, renesguesthousegoa@yahoo.co.in. A gem: 14 rooms around a colourful garden run by a friendly family. Best are the 3 self-contained cottages, with 4-poster beds, good kitchens with gas stove, sinks and big fridges; these are meant for long lets (2 are designed for couples, the other sleeps 3). Individual rooms are decent too.

$ Saiprasad, north beach, T(0)9890-394839, saiprasadguesthouse@gmail.com. Uninspiring rooms some with a/c, but great location – right on the beach which is unusual for Anjuna. Pretty little gardens and beachside restaurant.

Vagator p75
$$$ Living Room, T(0)830-881 1640, www.livingroomhotel.in. Brand new shiny hotel in stark contrast to the rest of the Vagator abodes. Definitely a sign of the changing face of Goa, chic rooms with all the mod cons, nice courtyard pool, Arabian-themed restaurant.

$$$ Ozran Heights Beach Resort, Ozran Beach, T0832-227 4985, www.ozran heights.com. "We promise the best view in Goa", proclaims their website and for once they might just be right. This cliffside hangout is a bit pricey, but what a view. High-end cabins nicely decorated, there is also a small pool and on-site restaurant as well as being neighbours to the immensely popular Greek restaurant, **Thalassa**.

$$ Leoney Resort, 10-min walk from beach, T0832-227 3634, www.leoneyresort.com. 13 rooms, 3 cottages, a/c extra Rs 400. Clean, modern, family run, low-key, quiet, pool.

$$-$ Julie Jolly, **Jolly Jolly Lester**, **Jolly Jolly Roma**, T0832-227 3620, www.hotel jollygoa.com. With 3 different properties offering a whole range of a/c and non-a/c rooms with hot showers, TV and a pool.

$ Paradise Huts, Small Vagator, Ozran, T(0)9922-230041. Good selection of huts on the cliff, some with views, shared bathroom.

$ Santonio,Ozran Beach Rd, near Holy Cross Chapel, T09769-913217, www.santonio.in. Cluster of little garden sheds, sweet though with nice bathrooms.

$ Thalassa Huts, T(0)9850-033537, www.thalassagoa.com. Tucked behind popular atmospheric Greek restaurant, great huts with attached bathrooms and a couple have their own rooftop chill-out area. Short walk down the cliff to the beach. Although staying here might seriously affect your waistline. And there are 2 nice boutiques on site too – be warned.

Chapora Fort p75
Chapora Fort and Siolim caters mainly for long-term budget travellers.

$$$$-$$$ Casa Colvale, inland on the Chapora river, T0832-241 6737, www.casacolvale.com. Beautiful chic rooms and stunning river views make this an exceptional find. Perfect for getting away from it without actually having to go too far – that's the gift of inland Goa. There is a lovely pool right on the river as well as another high level infinity pool. There's lots of fresh seafood and plenty of other dishes on offer.

$$$$-$$$ Riverside Shakti, Guddem Village on the Chapora river, www.river sideshaktiretreat.com. Beautiful new villa with inspired design, a spiral staircase takes you up to several bedrooms and a rooftop pyramid fit for yoga or chilling. There are lots of nice outdoor spaces with swing chairs and river views. This is a great space for families or small retreat groups as it sleeps up to 10. Great Goan food is available from the caretaker, and yoga, healing and massage can be arranged. Wholeheartedly recommended.

$$$$-$$$ Siolim House, opposite Vaddy Chapel, Siolim, T0832-227 2138, www.siolimhouse.com. Lovingly restored 300-year-old house. This is a stunning property once owned by the governor of Macau. 4-poster beds, epic bathrooms and fantastic large windows. Restored in 1999, it recently had a further facelift in 2009 and the pool is one of the most beautiful places you could find yourself. Great food, chilled atmosphere. There is a sister property with just 3 rooms away in another beautifully crafted house – **Little Siolim**. And further up on the Arpora Hill there is a new development for rent aimed at yoga groups. Highly recommended.

$ Noble Nest, opposite the Holy Cross Chapel, Chapora, T0832-227 4335. Basic but popular, 21 rooms, 2 with bath but ample facilities for sharing, exchange and internet.

Arambol *p77, map p77*

$$$-$$ Samata Holistic Retreat Centre, Temple Rd, 10 mins from downtown Arambol, www.samatagoa.com. Inspiring new retreat centre in beautiful location just outside of Arambol. Bringing hints of Bali and using reclaimed wood from Indonesia, this exceptional site has accommodation for 40 people with a beautiful pool surrounded by nature and an organic farm. There is also a drop-in space MATSYA and Tamarind Cafe with 2 great restaurants on-site, a beautiful swimming pool and drop-in yoga, dance classes and workshops. It's super family friendly with a kindergarten and swimming lessons. Coming in 2014 there will also be another lovely retreat space with huts in a cashew plantation for those on a tighter budget. Samata keeps on inspiring as its profits also go to the Dunagiri Foundation, which works to preserve Himalayan herbs and Ayurvedic plants.

$$-$ Atman, Palm Grove Girkar waddo, next to Surf Club, T(0)869-888 0135, www.atmangoa.com. A lovely collection of palm-fringed coco huts with good use of sari drapes and chic decor, all surrounding a pretty restaurant. There is also a yoga space and it's all just steps from the beach. Lots of pretty artwork.

$$-$ Residensea Beach Huts, north end of Arambol Beach, close to Arambol Hammocks, T0832-224 2276, www.arambol residensea.com. Pretty location with basic bamboo shacks set back from the beach, all have fans and secure locker facilities. There are some rooms with attached bathroom, but some huts have shared facilities. German Shepherd keeps watch.

$ Arambol Plaza, Beach Rd, T 0832-2242052, www.hotelsarambol.com. Very different to the usual Arambol fare but lacking any design aesthetic, basic modern rooms with swimming pool.

$ Ave Maria, inland, down track opposite police post, Modhlowado, T0832-224 7674, avemaria@satyam.net.in. One of the originals, offering some of the best accommodation. Simple but nevertheless recommended. Very popular but hard to reserve in advance.

$ Famafa Beach Resort, Beach Rd, Khalchawada, T0832-224 2516, famafa_in@ yahoo.com. 25 rooms in an unimaginative development on the right of the stall-studded road down to the beach. No a/c, but many pitch up for the hot showers.

$ Go-Ym Beach Resort, Bag Dando, south end of Arambol beach, T(0)9637-376335, www.go-ym.com. Great little cottages with swathes of coloured fabric and views of the coconut grove. Just moments from the beach, there is also an on-site restaurant.

$ Ivon's Guest House, Girkarwada, near Kundalini Yoga Roof Garden, T(0)9822-127398. Popular rooms looking out on to the coconut grove, from the top floor you can just about see the sea. Basic clean rooms with attached bathrooms.

$ Luciano Guest Rooms, Cliffside, T(0)9822-180215. Family house with toilet and shower. Cliffside rooms get heavily booked up.

$ Oceanic, inland at south end, T0832-224 2296. Secluded guesthouse with simple rooms, all hidden behind wall in mature gardens, popular. Recommended.

$ Om Ganesh, Cliffside on way to Sweet Lake, T0832-224 2957. Lots of rooms clustered on the cliffside – great views and lots of places to hang a hammock. Rooms are basic, but with attached bathroom. Ask at Om Ganesh restaurant on cliff or in town at Om Ganesh General Store. Now have rooms on high street above general store too. Recommended.

$ Whispering Lakes, Girkar Waddo, follow signs to Surf Club and Wooden Heritage, T(0)9823-484333. Simple huts hugging lake, each with it's own cushioned sit-out hanging over the lake. A bit pricey for what you get and noise can carry from the Surf Club, but a very pretty location – catch special sunsets from your lakeside podium.

Keri and Tiracol Fort p78

Keri is pretty out of the way and it helps to have your own transport. The beaches around here are dotted with typical budget beach shacks.

$$$$ Fort Tiracol Heritage Hotel, Tiracol, T0236-622 7631, www.forttiracol.com. In 2003 the owners of **Nilaya** in Arpora, took over Fort Tiracol to create an outpost of isolated, personalized luxury with unbroken views of the Arabian Sea. Just 7 exquisite rooms, all with giant en suite, set in the fort walls that surround the Catholic Church which is still used by the 350 villagers of the wholly Christian Tiracol for their Mass. Goa's most romantic hotel. Prices include breakfast and delicious dinners. Highly recommended.

$ Dream House, Keri, off main road on way to beach, T(0)9604-800553. Large rooms with attached bathroom sandwiched between family house and **Coconut Inn** rooftop restaurant.

$ Raj Star, Keri, near New English High School, T(0)9881-654718, raj-star@hotmail.co.uk. Pretty rooms in attractive guesthouse. Nice communal sitting areas.

Morjim to Asvem p79

This is a beautiful stretch of coastline which is becoming more and more happening and increasingly built up, but there are some special places to stay dotted along the coast.

$$$ Ku, Asvem Beach, www.kugoamorjim.webs.com. In stark contrast to its naff neighbour in Asvem, **Marbela Beach Resort**, Ku is quite possibly one of the most beautiful places you can stay in India. With just two handbuilt Japanese-style wooden bungalows with sliding doors and true rustic elegance you will not want to leave. And sitting on the upper deck looking out at rice fields and palm trees or gazing down at the water feature that runs through Ku like an aorta, is pretty close to Nirvana. A change in management means that now food is Goan thali style rather than Mediterranean.

$$$ Sur La Mer, above Asvem Beach, T(0)9850-056742, www.surlamergoa.com.

Beautiful rooms with 4-poster beds and super-stylish bathrooms around lovely pool. All have good views of the neighbouring fields and the beach; with special mention going to the stunning penthouse with almost 360° views of paradise. The food is also highly praised.

$$$ Yab Yum Eco Resort, Asvem Beach, T0832-651 0392, www.yabyumresorts.com. 10 deluxe 'eco-domes' made of local materials – blue painted lava rocks make up the bases, woven palm leaves and mango wood the roofs, spread across a huge shady expanse of coconut and banana grove tucked behind a row of trees from the sand dunes. The pods come in 2 sizes – family or single – but both have living areas, and en suite bathrooms. It's classy, discreet and bohemian. There are also some cottages on-site. There's a reading room over the sea, a yoga *shala*, swimming pool and a children's teepee crammed with toys. The price includes breakfast and papers. Also now new chic accommodation at their villa, **Artists' House**, which is absolutely stunning.

$$$-$$ Leela Cottages, Asvem Beach, T(0)9823-400055, www.leelacottage.com. Close to the beach, these are posh wooden huts with antique doors from a palace in Andhra Pradesh and decorated with beautiful furniture. Very stylish. Alas their new neighbours are the lovely but noisy clubs of **Soma** and **Bardo** so bear that in mind, perfect if you want to party.

$$$-$$ Yoga Gypsys Asvem, close to Yab Yum, T(0)9326-130115,www.yogagypsys.com. 5 beautifully decorated terracotta bungalows, charming floppy-fringed bamboo huts and tipis in palm grove right on the beach and close to a Hindu temple. Yes certainly as the name suggests you can explore all things yogic here, but it's also simply a relaxed place to stay and meditate on the sound of the waves. You can check the website for forthcoming retreats and workshops. Wholeheartedly recommended.

$$-$ Montego Bay Beach Village, Vithaldas Wado, Morjim, T(0)9822-150847,

www.montegobaygoa.com. Rajasthani-style luxury tents pitched in the shade past beach shrubs at the southern end of the beach, plus log cabins, a/c rooms and a beach villa.
$$-$ Palm Grove, Asvem towards Morjim, T(0)9657-063046, www.palmgroveingoa. com. Quirky place with cottages and huts named 'Happy Hippie' and 'Rosie Slow' there are comfy beds and a sweet beach restaurant.
$$-$ Simply Special, House No 750, 759, Ashwem–Morjim road, T(0)9820-056920, www.simplyspecialinn.com. Great for families as some rooms have little kitchens, but if you don't want to cook there is a lovely rooftop restaurant. They also have some nice art events and fair-trade markets.

Mandrem p79

$$$$ Elsewhere's Beach House, T(0)9326-020701, www.aseascape.com. **Elsewhere** is 4 lovingly restored 19th-century houses, just a sigh from the beach. Some are closer to the sea while others have views of the saltwater creek. Facilities include maid service, day and nightwatchman, but you pay extra for a cook. Minimum rental period 1 week at US$2000-4000. There are also the beautiful **Otter Creek Tents** with 4-poster beds Rajasthani style close to the creek.
$$$ Ashiyana, Mandrem River, opposite **Villa River Cat** by footbridge, www.ashiyana-yoga-goa.com. Revamped in 2013, **Ashiyana** offers up a beautiful place for yoga holidays and detox retreats. Many rooms have river views and are stacked with Rajasthani furniture and heaps of character. It's a peaceful place on large grounds with 2 yoga shalas, spa and natural swimming pool. There are a couple of lovely rooms with domed ceilings as well as the stunning Lake View and Ashiyana Villas. The good onsite restaurant serves nourishing healthy food. Prices are per person and often rooms are shared.

$$$ Beach Street, T(0)9423-882600, www.beachstreet.in. Summer house of the Deshprabhu family built in the early 1920s, this interesting building has had many incarnations including a prawn hatchery and nightclub. Now the family have transformed it into a beautiful resort with a courtyard swimming pool, restaurant and chic beach cabanas. There is also a yoga space here with regular drop-in classes and workshops run by the highly recommended **Himalaya Yoga Valley** team.
$$$-$$ Mandala, next to Ashiyana, access from Asvem–Mandrem road, T(0)9657-898350, www.themandalagoa.com. The highlights at Mandala are the chic 2-storey open-plan chalets – downstairs you will find a swing seat, up the stairs a tented bedroom with 2 loungers on the front deck. Murals by Danish artist Ulrik Schiodt decorate the walls. There are also stylish rooms in the main house and smaller huts and Maharajah tents. The large pretty gardens often host live music and an open-air film festival.
$$-$ O'Saiba, Junasvaddo, T(0)9552-997440//(0)8308 415655, sunnymehara@ yahoo.com. O'Saiba offers a range of coco huts, bungalows and nicely decorated rooms. It also has a good restaurant by the beach.
$$-$ Villa River Cat, Junasvaddo, T0832-224 7928, www.villarivercat.com. 13 rooms in a 3-tiered roundhouse overlooking the river and a wade over deep sand dunes from the beach. The whole place is ringed with a belt of shared balconies and comes with big central courtyards stuffed with swings, sofas, plantation chairs and daybeds. There's a mosaic spiral staircase and a cavalier approach to colour: it's downbeat creative and popular with musicians and actors – in the best possible way. Cat lovers preferred.
$ Oceanside, Junasvaddo, T(0)9421-40483. Great little sunny coloured huts and pretty cottages a short walk from the beach and with an excellent restaurant on site.

🍴 Restaurants

Even Calangute's most ardent detractors will brave a trip for its restaurants, some of which are world class. While costly by Indian standards, a slap-up meal will cost you a fraction of its equivalent at European prices.

Calangute and Candolim *p70, map p70*
$$$ A Reverie, next to **The Park**, Holiday St, T(0)9823-14927, areveriegoa@gmail.com. Award-winning restaurant offering a globally inspired menu in chic surrounds. You can try a Thai vegetable *thali* or opt for Australian John Dory. Although when there is so much local fish available do you need to have Norwegian salmon?
$$$ Bomras, Candolim towards Sinquerim, T(0)9822-106236, bawmra@yahoo.com. Mouth-watering Burmese and Asian fusion food, such as seared rare tuna, mussel curry and Nobu-esque blackened miso cod. Fantastic vegetarian dishes and curries too, washed down with quite possibly the best cocktail in the world spiced with lemongrass and ginger. Chic setting – amidst the bright lights of Candolim, you could almost blink and miss it. Highly recommended.
$$$-$$ Souza Lobo, on the beach. Somewhat of an institution, this place serves up excellent fresh seafood, lobster and sizzlers served on a shaded terrace, well-known restaurant that has managed to retain a good reputation for years.
$$ Café Ciocolatti, main road Candolim, T(0)9326-112006. Fantastic range of all things chocolate. Lovely daytime café. They also do salads to outweigh any potential guilt incurred by eating the orange marmalade brownie.
$$ Fisherman's Cove, main road Candolim, T0832-248 9538. Sometimes you just have to go on the busyness of a place – and this one is always packed to the rafters. They serve up good portions of traditional Goan fare such as *xacuti* and *sorpotel* and other Indian and Euro dishes.

$ Infanteria, Baga Rd, near beach roundabout. 'The breakfast place' to locals, Rs 125 set breakfast, eggs, coffee, juice, toast. Bakery and confectionery. Very atmospheric.
$ Plantain Leaf, near petrol pump, Almita III. T0832-227 6861. Mean *dosas*, jumbo *thalis*, sizzlers and a range of curries; unbeatable for your pukka pure vegetarian Indian.
$ The Tibetan Kitchen, at the bottom of a track leading off Calangute Beach Rd. This airy garden restaurant is part tent, part wicker awning, part open to the skies. Tibet's answer to ravioli – *momos* – are good here, but more adventurous starters such as prawns, mushrooms and tomatoes on wilting lettuce leaves are exceptional.

Baga *p70, map p69*
$$$ Casa Portuguesa, Baga Rd. An institution of a restaurant run by German/ Goan couple with live music in the gloriously overgrown jungle of a garden. Strongly recommended.
$$$ Fiesta, Tito's Lane, T0832-227 9894. Open for dinner Wed-Mon. Stunning restaurant hidden behind the gaudy Tito's Lane. Beautifully decorated intimate restaurant with fabulous Italian-style food as well as great steaks, fish suppers and cocktails. Recommended.
$$$ J&A's Ristorante Italiano House, 560 Baga River, T0832-228 2364, italyingoa. com. Jamshed and Ayesha Madon's beautiful restaurant has earned them an evangelical following. Whether its authentic pastas or wood-fired pizzas, tender steaks or delicious desserts, it's all served passionately. They also have a beautiful homestay – **Capella**.
$$ Britto's Bar and Restaurant, Baga Beach, T0832-227 7331. Cajie Britto's puddings are an institution and his staff (of 50) boast that in high season you'll be pushed to find an inch of table space from the restaurant's inside right out to the seashore. Fantastic range of traditional Goan dishes such as *vindaloo* and *cafreal*. It's a great spot to watch India on the beach. Highly recommended.

$ Baba au Rhum, off the main road between Arpora and Baga. Serving up fantastic cappuccino, breads, croissants and salads in a laid-back vibe. Extraordinarily good desserts, coffee éclair or chocolate and passion fruit pie anyone?

$ Lila's Café, north bank of Baga River, T0832-227 9843, lilacafe@sify.com. Closed in the evenings. Slick German-run restaurant, good selection of European dishes, check blackboard for specials, smoked kingfish. Home-made cheeses and jams. Also serves beers. Shaded terrace overlooking the river.

Mapusa *p73*

$ Ashok, opposite the market's entrance. Serves genuine South Indian breakfasts like *uttapam* and *dosa*.

$ Café on the Corner, in the middle of the market. A good pit-stop for refuelling during the market.

$ Navtara, on Calangute Rd. Excellent range of Goan, South and North Indian fare – great *dosas* and yummy mushroom *xacuti* with *puris* for breakfast.

Anjuna and around *p73, map p74*

$$$ Xavier's, Praias de San Miguel (follow signs from behind small chapel near Flea Market site, bring a torch at night), T0832-227 3402. One of the very first restaurants for foreigners has grown into a smart restaurant with 3 separate kitchens (Indian/Chinese/continental), excellent fresh seafood, tucked away under palm trees.

$$$-$$ Villa Blanche, Badem Church Rd (better known as International Animal Rescue Rd), Assagao, T(0)9822-155099. 10 mins' drive from downtown Anjuna, you will find this beautiful daytime retreat. Some of the firm favourites are German meatballs with potato salad, smoked salmon bagels with capers and home-made ice creams. They serve up an infamous Sunday brunch, which you must book a table in advance for.

$$ Anand, Siolim Rd, Anjuna. Roadside shack which looks like any other, except for the queue of people waiting for a table.

This place has a devoted following from here to Mumbai and serves up the freshest seafood with every type of masala and all the Goan favourites.

$$ Gunpowder, Mapusa road, Assagao, T0832-226 8091, www.gunpowder.in. Inland from Anjuna you will find the delicious **Gunpowder** restaurant, which offers more unusual South Indian food and dishes from Andhra Pradesh. They have an acclaimed sister restaurant in Delhi and they stay open during the monsoon. Another Delhi institution, **People Tree**, is on site selling fair-trade clothes and recycled products.

$$ Joe Bananas, through the Flea Market behind **Curlies**, family-run place serving amazing fish *thalis* – the fish is seasoned to perfection or there is a great array of bhaji.

$$-$ German Bakery, south Anjuna, towards the Flea Market and **Curlies**. A little fiefdom of bohemian perfection: the bakery's sign is hung over a huge garden with an awning of thick tropical trees, where comfortable mattresses pad out the sides of low-slung booths. Huge salads with every healthy thing under the sun (including sprouts and avocado) plus good veggie burgers, Indian food and extreme juices. There is massage available on site and a small health food counter. This, ladies and gentlemen, is the original German Bakery, don't be put off by the copy cats that have taken over every baking tray around India.

$ Orange Boom, south Anjuna, Flea Market Rd. Daytime only. Efficient and spotlessly clean canteen. Food is hyper-hygienic and meticulously made, with a menu offering the usual breakfast fare plus 100 ways with eggs (from poached eggs to French toast), most served with mushrooms and grilled tomatoes. Baked beans can be masala or Heinz (proper ketchup on the tables), also croque madame and sautéed avocado on toast.

Vagator *p75*

$$$ Sakana, past petrol pump on Chapora Rd, T(0)9890-135502. Fantastic Japanese food, **Sakana** is packed out with the

Westerners that call Goa home. They serve delicious tuna *teriyaki*, beef *yakinuki*, sushi and wakame salads. With the potential of green tea or *wasabi* ice cream (made by **Niko's** in Assagao). Remember to book a table in advance.

$$$ Thalassa, on the clifftop overlooking Ozran Beach, T(0)9850-033537. Beautiful restaurant perched on the cliff, amazing sunset views and great Greek food from *dolmades* and *souvlaki* and many varieties of lamb dishes and feta for the vegetarians. Booking essential. Great boutique on site too.

$$$-$$ Sri, close to **Thalassa**, T09822-383795. Having migrated from Anjuna's **Shore Bar** to Vagator, Richard has opened up **Sri** serving up his trademark salad platters and delicious Indian and seafood. There is often live music. Incidentally, the new-look **Shore Bar** is a real disappointment.

$$ The Alcove, on the cliff above Little Vagator. Smartish, ideal position, excellent food, pleasant ambience in the evening, sometimes live music.

$$ Bean Me Up, near the petrol pump, Vagator, T0832-227 3479. Closed all day Sat and daily 1600-1900. You can choose from salad plates and delicious tempeh and tofu platters. There's massage offered on site, a useful noticeboard for mind-body-spirit stuff, kids' area and a few simple, clean rooms for rent. Under new management, so maybe in for a revamp.

$$ Mango Tree, in the village. Wide choice of continental favourites.

Chapora Fort *p75*

$$ Da Felice & Zeon, above **Babba's**. Open 1800-2400. Just a handful of tables dancing with fairy lights and psychedelic art at this rooftop restaurant run by the Italian brothers Felice and Zeon. Felice is an Italian chef in London over monsoon, Zeon makes trance music and trance art. Carbonara, lasagna, prosciutto, *spaghetti alle vongole* all feature, but meat is recommended.

$$ La Befa, Chapora Market road. Some people drive an hour for the roast beef sandwich here. Or there's parma ham or marinated aubergine – all on freshly baked French bread.

$ Jai Ganesh Juice Bar, the hub of Chapora. This is the only place to be seen in Chapora for every juice under the sun.

Arambol *p77, map p77*

There are beach cafés all along the main beach and around the headland to the north. The 2 German bakeries fall short of the lovely restaurant in Anjuna.

$$ Double Dutch, Beach Rd, T0832-652 5973, doubledutchgoa@yahoo.co.uk. Open 0700-2300. Lovely laid-back garden restaurant with sand underfoot and lots of leafy foliage and sculptures created by the owner around. Breakfasts are tip top here with home-made breads (such as carrot or watermelon) seed and also home-made jams – you can also get a full 'English', Goa style. Candlelit in the evening, there are lots of great salads as well as Dutch dishes, Indonesian, Thai, pastas and the steaks come with the best recommendation. There is a lively Sun morning second-hand market. Recommended.

$$ Fellini's, Beach Rd, T0832-229 2278, arambolfellini95@yahoo.com. Thu-Tue 1000-2300, Wed 1800-2300. **Fellini's** is an institution serving up pizzas and calzone to the hungry masses.

$$ Lamuella, Main Rd, T0832-651 4563. Atmospheric restaurant in the heart of Arambol. Home-made mushroom or pak choi raviolis, great fish, tagines, salads and huge breakfast platters. This is a great spot to meet and greet. There's also a great shop specializing in clothes crafted by Westerners in Arambol. If you can't face the night market, see what Westerners get up to creatively here. Recommended.

$$ MATSYA, Temple Rd, www.samatagoa. com. This beautiful restaurant is inspired by the organic garden of **Samata Retreat** (see Where to stay, page 84), the fresh seafood of Goa and fused with delights from Israeli chef Gome. Breakfasts are a lazy affair and dinners draw a crowd of Westerners that call north Goa home – take their word for it, the food is amazing. For lunches, there is another beautiful restaurant on site: **Tamarind Cafe** by the pool offers up healthy vibrant treats and lots of raw food specialities from Japanese chef Kaoru. If you get a chance ask to visit their organic farm. And you can always work off the calories by taking a drop-in yoga or dance class here too. Highly recommended.

$ Dreamland Crepes, main road, near Double Dutch. Blink-and-you'll-miss-it 2-tier coffee house serving up fabulous cappuccinos and healthy juices, as well as a wide range of crêpes and sandwiches. And Wi-Fi.

$ Dylans, coconut grove near El Paso Guesthouse. Coffee houses have sprung up in Arambol to fuel the creative types and designers that make Arambol their home. If you like your coffee strong, this Manali institution delivers, along with hot melty chocolate cookies and soups and sandwiches. Film nights and occasional live music.

$ Eyes Of Buddha, north end of Arambol Beach. Long on Arambol's catering scene, this place has you well looked after with scrupulously clean avocado salads, a wide range of fish and the best Indian food in town, all topped off with a great view of the beach. Highly recommended.

$ Relax Inn, north end of beach. The only beach shack with a good reputation, this is a firm favourite with the expats. Slow service but worth the wait for *spaghetti alle vongole*, grilled kingfish with ratatouille and a range of fresh pasta dishes. Exceptional, although you cannot book and in season it can be tough to get a table.

$ Rice Bowl, next door to Eyes of Buddha. Great views south across Arambol Beach, with a billiard table. Simple restaurant that has been serving reliably good Chinese for years. All the usual chop suey, wontons, noodles and sweet and sours of calamari, pork, beef or fish, plus Japanese dishes such as *gyoza*, *sukiyaki*, tempura and Tibetan *momos*.

$ Rutik's Coconuts, entrance to beach behind Coco Loco. Serving up *thalis* all day, this place is best visited for coconuts. It's a great place to hang-out, see and be seen.

$ Sai Deep, Beach Rd. A family-run *dhaba* offering amazing veg and fish plates at lunchtime, mountainous fruit plates and a good range of Indian and continental food. Great value.

Morjim to Asvem *p79*

Join the masses as they descend on La Plage every Sun. Restaurants in Morjim central cater mainly to Russians.

There are plenty of shacks catering to Asvem and Mandrem beaches. Some have free loungers, others charge up to Rs 100.

$$$ Bardo, Asvem-Morjim Beach. T(0)9890-167531. The Sunday brunch at newly opened **Bardo** has gained a great reputation. It's a pricey affair but has a good range of food and drinks. You can sit inside, but poolside is best. Come sunset time the DJs take over.

$$$ La Plage, Asvem, T(0)9822-121712. Hidden slightly from the beach, you can still feel the breeze in this lovely laid-back restaurant. The food is excellent and changes seasonally; you might discover seared rare tuna with *wasabi* mash, calamari risotto, great steaks or even a giant hamburger. Vegetarians well catered for too, try the sage butter ravioli. Most people daydream about the chocolate *thali* or the *ile flottante*. There is a good selection of wines and cocktails, including a fabulous peppery Bloody Mary with mustard seeds and curry leaf. Also has rooms to let and an excellent shop featuring jewellery from expat designer Simona Bassi. Booking essential.

$$$ Sublime, Morjim Beach, T(0)9822-484051. Exceptional food is guaranteed at this Goa institution. Chris Saleem Agha Bee has opened up the latest incarnation of **Sublime** on Morjim beach and it's a chic spin on the beach shack offering punchy Asiatic beef, delicious rare tuna with

anchovy sauce, the renowned mega organic salad and delicious melt-in-the-mouth pesto and mozzarella parcels, to name but a few. The cocktails go down very easily and it's a laid-back vibe – the perfect combination for balmy Goan nights. Booking essential.
$ Change Your Mind, Asvem Beach. This typical beach shack serves up great Indian food, tasty fried calamari and monumental fruit plates. You can get refreshing lemon and mint juices and strawberry shakes in season.
$ Pink Orange, Asvem Beach. Low-level seating overlooking the beach with chilled trance vibe. Menu serves up a great range of salads, tagines, sweet and savoury crêpes, juices, coffees and great chocolate brownies. Recommended.

Mandrem p79
$$$-$$ Café Nu, Junnaswaddo, Mandrem Beach, T(0)9850-658568. Another helping from Sublime guru Chris Saleem Agha Bee – great food in laid-back locale. Mustard-encrusted fish, the non-yogi burger (Mandrem does cater to a large yogi clientele), the phenomenal mega organic salad for the aforementioned yogis and the legendary chocolate bon-bons. People have been known to cry when there was a problem with the oven and the bon-bons were temporarily unavailable. Good food to linger over. Highly recommended.
$$$-$$ Lazy Dog, Beach St, Mandrem Beach, T(0)94238-82600, www.beachstreet.in. Great food served up at this consciously renovated summer palace. Lazy Dog is a manali institution, so this is their summer residence. There is an eclectic menu with some tasty Korean food and sushi, as well as the fabulous breakfast burrito (you might have worked up an appetite if you go to the great drop-in yoga class on site) and a good range of seafood and Indian dishes.
$$-$ Sunset, next to Beach St. For classic Indian food and tandoori dishes, you cannot do better than Sunset. Their fish and chicken tikkas are fantastic. They also have the usual

selection of European and Chinese food, but all done well.
$ Well Garden Pizzeria, near O'Saiba, off main road. Sweet garden restaurant with great range of pizzas, broccoli and pesto pastas and an almost infamous warm chickoo cake. Service can be a bit hit or miss though.

🎵 Bars and clubs

The new place to be seen is Asvem where there are now 6 clubs in 1 sq km – right on the beach. Elsewhere, perennial favourites are **Cubana** next to the Night Market and **Titos**, in Baga. The newest additions to the scene are **LPK** and **Sinq** in Candolim.

Calangute and Candolim p70, map p70
LPK, inland from Candolim on Nerul river, www.lpkwaterfronts.com. Billing itself as India's first super club and "the world's most unique architectural construction", LPK have a little bit of ego and a little bit of media savvy. It certainly is an unusual place to party – dancing in a massive sculpture overlooking the river and Goa jungle, but what's the music like? They appeal to the masses. They are also offering themselves up as the ultimate wedding venue.

Saligao
Club WestEnd, near Porvorim, 3 km out of Calangute towards Panjim. This club gets away with hosting 3-day parties by being too remote to disturb anyone.

Baga p70, map p69
Many bars here have a happy hour 1700-1930 and show live Premier League football, in a bit of a home-from-home for many visitors. Along the beach, shacks also serve a wide range of drinks and cocktails to sip while watching the sunset.
Cavala, Sauntavaddo, top end of Baga village. A genuine bar, with friendly atmosphere, attentive staff, great cocktails, and occasional live music and 1960s evenings.

Tito's, Tito's Lane, T0832-227 5028, www.titosgoa.com. Tito's is an institution in Goa, and has adapted down the decades to reflect the state's changing tourist reality by going from down-at-heel hippie playground in the 1960s to swish international dance club. Now the focus seems to be more on food – are the dancing days of Goa really over? Further along Tito's Lane towards the beach is the **Tito's** spin-off, **Mambo's**. It's more laid back than the club and free to get in.

Anjuna *p73, map p74*
The days of all-night parties in North Goa are long gone, and politicians imposed a ban on loud music after 2200 for several seasons – they keep changing the rules so sometimes you might be lucky and find yourself dancing until dawn. Indoor venues like **Bardo** in Asvem and **West End** in Saligao stay open later. Wed and Fri tend to be the big nights especially at places like **Curlies** (see below) and Sunday Night at **Soma Project** in Asvem is the place to be seen but there is usually something going on each night over the Christmas and New Year period; just ask around (taxi drivers invariably know where).
Curlies, at the very far south of Anjuna. A kind of unofficial headquarters of the scene, playing techno and ambient music, although **Shiva Valley** next door has taken over in recent years.
Lilliput, a few hundred metres north of Curlies, www.cafelilliput.com. Lots of live music and fire-dancing performances at this beach shack – usually after the flea market on Wed and sometimes on Fri. Also has an a/c internet booth.

Vagator *p75*
Hilltop, Little Vagator Hill, above Vagator. Although it has suffered from the 2200 curfew, **Hilltop** just celebrated it's 30th birthday fully dressed up for the occasion in fluoro! It has been inventive with day parties Sun 1600-2200. They often host concerts too – in 2013, Talvin Singh played here and Prem Joshua plays each season.
Nine Bar, Ozran Beach. A booming mud-packed bar with huge gargoyle adornments and a manic neon man carved out of the fountain. Majestic sunset views.

Arambol *p77, map p77*
Live music and performances are the highlight of being in Arambol. **Ash**, **Surf Club**, **Coco Loco** and **Psybar** offer up both live music and DJ nights. **Arkan Bar** and **Loekie's** have open mic nights. Special mention goes to **Ash**, a stunning performance space with beautiful artwork hosting nights as diverse as mesmerizing bellydancing performances, Siberian shamanic singing or fantastic fire dancing. At dusk there's normally drumming, dancing and high spirits outside **Full Moon** on the beach to celebrate the sun going down on another day.

Morjim to Asvem *p79*
With pricey drinks and sometimes entry fees, the venues in Morjim and Asvem are mostly Russian affairs, but **Soma Project** is a fun and welcoming place. Check www.facebook.com/somaprojectgoa for listings – it has a chic seafront locale and great music know-how as they also run a renowned club in Moscow. Guest DJs from Europe and Russia feature on the playlist, but great coups have been Djuma Sounsystem, Talvin Singh and DJ Cheb i Sabbah – open every night but Sun is the big night out here. You will also find **Bardo**, **Blue Waves** and **Marbella** in this Asvem club zone, all competing for the attention of the beautiful people.

Mandrem *p79*
There are frequent concerts and an open-air cinema festival at **Mandala** in Mandrem and live music and DJs often at **Beach Street**.

☻ Entertainment

Calangute *p70, map p70*
Heritage Kathakali Theatre, Hotel
Sunflower, opposite the football ground,
Calangute Beach Rd, T0832-258 8059. Daily
in season, 1800-2000. The breathtakingly
elaborate mimes of 17th-century Keralan
mime dance drama take over 12 hrs to
perform in the southern state. Here, however,
it comes abbreviated for tourist attention
spans: watch the players apply their make-
up, brief background of the dance, then a
snatch of a classic dance-drama.

✹ Festivals

Calangute *p70, map p70*
Mar Carnival is best celebrated in villages
or in the main district towns but Calangute
has brought the party to the tourists.
May (2nd week) The Youth Fête attracts
Goa's leading musicians and dancers.

Mapusa *p73*
Mon of the 3rd week after Easter Feast
of Our Lady of Miracles The *Nossa Senhora
de Milagres* image is venerated by Christians
as well as Hindus who join together to
celebrate the feast day of the Saibin. Holy oil
is carried from the church to Shanteri temple
and a huge fair and a market are held.

Mandrem *p79*
Jan International Juggling Convention,
Gala performances, juggling workshops,
firedancing, creative movement of a
phenomenally high standard. This is an event
not to be missed – check out www.injuco.org.

◯ Shopping

Do your homework before you buy: prices
in tourist shops are massively inflated, and
goods are often worth less than a 3rd of the
asking price. 92.5 silver should be sold by
weight; check the current value online, but

be ready to pay a little more for elaborate
workmanship. The bigger Kashmiri shops,
particularly, are notorious both for refusing
to sell by weight and for their commission
tactic whereby rickshaw and taxi drivers
get Rs 100 per tourist delivered to shops
plus 10% commission on anything sold.

Calangute *p70, map p70*
Casa Goa, Cobravaddo, Baga Rd, T0832-
228 1048, cezarpinto@hotmail.com. Cezar
Pinto's shop is quite a razzy lifestyle store:
beautifully restored reclining plantation
chairs next to plates brought over by the
Portuguese from Macau plus modern-day
dress from local fashion designer Wendell
Rodricks. Cool modern twists on old Goan
shoes by local Edwin Pinto too.
Literati, off main road, Calangute, parallel
to Holiday St, T0832-227 7740, www.literati-
goa.com. Wonderful bookshop in beautiful
old house – it's like stumbling into
someone's library. The best selection of
books, novels, non-fiction and poetry you'll
find in Goa. There are sometimes readings
here, including an inaugural reading by
William Dalrymple.
PlayClan, Shop No S-3, Ida Maria Resort,
next to HDFC bank, Calangute, T(0)9372-
280862, www.theplayclan.com. Fantastic
shop selling all manner of clothes,
notebooks, lighters and pictures with great
colourful cartoon designs created by a
collective of animators and designers –
giving a more animated view of India's
gods, goddesses, gurus and the faces of
India Purple Jungle in same strip of shops
sells similar kitsch India-centric gifts.

Candolim and Sinquerim beaches *p71*
Supermarkets like Delfinos on Calangute
Beach Rd or Newtons on Fort Aguada Rd
sell staples, plus adaptor plugs, water
heating filaments, quince jam, wine,
cashew *feni* in plastic bottles to take
home, full range of sun lotion factors and
brands, tampons, etc and money change.

For silver, head for either of the Tibetan covered handicraft markets where you can buy by weight.

Fabindia, Sea Shell Arcade, opposite Canara Bank, Candolim. Branch of this great shop selling textiles, homewares and funky traditional Indian *kurtas* and clothes.

Rust, 409A Fort, Aguada Rd, Candolim, T0832-247 9340. Everything from wrought-iron furniture to clothes.

Sangolda, Chogm Rd, opposite Mac de Deus Chapel, Sangolda, T0832-240 9309, sangolda@sancharnet.in. Mon-Sat 1000-1930. Lifestyle gallery and café run by the owners of **Nilaya Hermitage** selling handcrafted metalware, glass, ethnic furniture, bed and table linen, lacquerware, wooden objects.

The Private Collection, 1255 Annavado, Candolim Beach Rd, T0832-248 9033. Ramona Galardi has a good eye and has brought together a great collection of clothes and jewellery from designers based in Goa and also offers some of her own creations. She is also a healer and has a healing space on site.

Mapusa *p73*
Municipal Mapusa Bazaar, on south edge of the fruit and veg market. Fixed-price basic food supplies like rice, spice, lentils and cereals; useful if you're here long term.

Other India Bookstore, 1st floor, St Britto's Apartment, above Mapusa clinic, T0832-226 3306. Unconventional and excellent. Heavily eco-conscious. Has a large catalogue and will post worldwide.

Union Ayurveda, 1st floor, opposite the taxi and bus stand. Great one-stop shop for all things Ayurvedic, herbal and homeopathic – phenomenal range of products to keep you travelling healthy.

Anjuna *p73, map p74*
Artjuna, House No 972, Monteiro Vaddo, T0832-321 8468, www.artjuna.com. Beautiful collection of mainly jewellery and clothes, but with a few nice bits of home decor too.

Stunning collection of gold jewellery, but also cheaper tribal trinkets from Nagaland. Owners Moshe and Anastasia showcase quite a few local designers here as well as offering up their own wares. You will also find art and photography on sale here. Stays open through monsoon. Recommended.

Flea Market, Wed. Attracts hordes of tourists from all over Goa. By mid-morning all approach roads are blocked with taxis, so arrive early.

Orchard Stores, Monteirovaddo. Amazing selection catering for Western cravings. Olive oil, pasta, fresh cheese, frozen meats, etc, as well as a good range of organic products from all over India and fresh produce from Ambrosia farms in Goa. Locally made soaps and organic supplements too.

Oxford Arcade, De Mellovaddo, next to Munche's. Good general store close to beach.

Chapora Fort *p75*
Narayan, Chapora. Book stall, local newspapers.

Arambol *p77, map p77*
Arambol Hammocks, north end of Arambol Beach, near Eyes of Buddha, www.arambol.com. The original and the best place for hammocks and their famous flying chair designs – these are no ordinary hammocks and are extremely comfortable. And now they even have baby hammocks.

Lamuella. Serving up the best of the Western designers who make Arambol their home, as well as imported clothes and bikinis from Thailand and Europe. Stunning jewellery for little magpies too. Highly recommended.

Vishwa Book Shop, T(0)992-146 1107. Excellent bookshop on main road with good holiday reads and for all the yogi types he has a great range of holistic titles.

Morjim to Asvem *p79*
As well as having a great little boutique on site with lovely clothes and jewellery from Simona Bassi, **La Plage** has competition on its hands from a cluster of neighbouring chic

beach shack boutiques including one little black number from Jade Jagger. But special mention goes to **Dust** which sells beautifully designed clothes in raw silk and hand-block prints from JonnyJade (www.jonnyjade.com) and also a handful of one-off pieces crafted by local Westerners.

🕐 What to do

Calangute *p70, map p70*
Body and soul
Cyril Yoga, Naikavaddo, T0832-249 7400, www.cyrilyoga.com. 4 classes daily, 0830, 1000, 1530 and 1630, Rs 300 a class. All abilities. Inner healing yoga meditation, juice bar, yoga camps and good karma-promoting volunteer activities.

River cruises
Floating Palace, book through **Kennedy's Adventure Tours and Travels**, T0832-227 6493, T(0)9823-276520, kennedy@goatelecom.com, opposite **Milky Way** in Cobravaddo. Try a Kerala-style backwater cruise by staying overnight in this 4-cabin bamboo, straw and coir houseboat. You sail from Mandovi in late afternoon, are fed a high tea then a continental dinner as you drift past the Chorao Island bird sanctuary. International standards of safety. Much pricier than a similar boat trip in Kerala.

Tour operators
Day Tripper, Gauravaddo, T0832-227 6726, www.daytrippergoa.com. Offers tours all over Goa, best deals in the region. Also runs trips to spice plantations, or short tours out of state, for birdwatching or empty beaches in Karnataka. Recommended.

Baga *p70, map p69*
Boat trips and wildlife
Mikes Marine, Fortune Travels, Sauntavaddo, by the bus stand at the top end of Baga, T0832-227 9782. Covered boat, dolphin trips, river cruises and birdwatching.

Rahul Alvares, all over Goa, based in Parra, T(0)9881-961071, www.rahulalvares.com. Fancy getting eye-to-eye with a cobra? For an alternative day out in Goa, maybe you want to handle or at least see a wild snake. For the less wild at heart or snakeaphobic, there are also amazing birdwatching trips and jungle camping expeditions. You will be in expert hands with Rahul. He organizes trips all over Goa.

Body and soul
Ayurclinic Goa, Baga Creek, T(0)9822-312021, www.ayurvedagoa.com. Under the watchful eye of fantastic Dr Rohit Borkar, you can get a whole host of treatments, massages and *panchakarma* processes here. Has another branch in Mandrem.
Ayurvedic Natural Health Centre (ANHC), Baga–Calangute road, Villa 2, Beira Mar Complex, www.healthandayurveda.com; also in Saligao. The **ANHC** is not for the faint-hearted; the centre was originally built for the local community that it continues to serve and hasn't made many concessions to Western sensibilities. Those checking into the 2-week *panchakarma* can expect almost every cavity to be flushed. They do offer smaller, less daunting packages, such as 2½-hr rejuvenations (Rs 300), and have a herb garden where you can taste first-hand leaves that tingle your tongue (used to stop stuttering) or others that eliminate your sense of sweet taste.

Diving and snorkelling
Goa Dive Center, Tito's Lane, T0832-215 7094. Goa isn't really on the diving map, chiefly because it has only 2 dive sites, both of which have what's known as variable, ie less than great, visibility. However, this outfit offers inexpensive PADI courses. Options range from the half-day Discover Scuba programme (from aged 10 years, Rs 2700) to the 4-day Open Water Diver programme, Rs 14,500. Snorkelling tours also available.

Candolim and Sinquerim beaches p71
Body and soul
Amrita Kerala Ayurvedic, next to Lawande supermarket, Annavaddo, T0832-312 5668. Open 0730-2000. Set inside an old Goan villa, this massage centre is geared up for the foreign tourist. Westerners are on hand to explain the philosophy behind Indian life science. The centre also runs courses. A basic course takes 7 days. Courses in *panchakarma* last 6 months.

Dolphin watching
John's Boats, T0832-227 7780. Promises 'guaranteed' dolphin watching, morning trips start around 0900, Rs 550 (includes meal and hotel pickup). Also crocodile-spotting river trips with lunch.

Parasailing
Occasionally offered independently on Candolim Beach, Rs 600-850 for a 5-min flight.

Fort Aguada p71
Taj Sports Complex, Fort Aguada Beach Resort. Excellent facilities that are open to non-residents at the **Taj Holiday Village**, and a separate access between Aguada Beach Resort and the Holiday Village. Rs 450 per day for the complex, Rs 350 for the pool. Tennis (Rs 450 per hr); squash and badminton (Rs 150 for 30 mins); mini golf (Rs 200). Yoga classes, scuba diving, sailing/water skiing/windsurfing/rod fishing Rs 450-500 per hr; parasailing/jet ski Rs 900-950 per hr.

Anjuna p73, map p74
Body and soul
Some excellent yoga teachers teach in Goa during the season, many of whom gravitate towards Anjuna: check the noticeboards at the **German Bakery**, **Thalassa** and **Bean Me Up** (see pages 88 and 89). You'll also stumble on practitioners of all sorts of alternative therapies: reiki healers, acupuncturists, chakra and even vortex cleansing.
Brahmani Yoga, at Tito's White House, night market road, Anjuna, www.brahmani yoga.com. Drop-in centre for all things yogic – flex your limbs Mysore style, or try *vinyasa* flow, hatha, *pranayama*. There are also 1-day workshops and regular *bhajans*. They also promote beach cleaning Karma Yoga. Deservedly popular.
Healing Here And Now, The Health Center, St Michael's Vaddo, T0832-227 3487, www.healinghereandnow.com. If you want an 'ultimate cleanse', sign up for a 5-day detox: fasting, detoxifying drinks and twice-daily enemas. Also offers parasite cleansing, kidney cleanse and wheat grass therapy.
Purple Valley Yoga Retreat (see pages 75 and 99). 2-week retreats with celebrities of the *ashtanga vinyasa* yoga circuit. Beautiful backdrop for downward dog poses.
Watsu, Assagao–Mapusa road, T(0)9326-127020, www.watsugoa.com. Utterly amazing treatment. Working one-on-one, you are in a heated pool and the practitioner takes you through a range of movements both above and below the water. Using the art of shiatsu, this is an underwater massage which takes relaxation to a whole new level. The underwater dance makes you feel that you are flying and can give you a total release – a bit like being reborn. Highly recommended.

Bungee jumping
Offered by a Mumbai-based firm with US-trained staff, at Rs 500 a go. Safety is a priority, with harnesses, carabinas and air bags employed. There are pool tables, a bar, an auditorium for slide/film shows and beach volleyball. 1000-1230 and 1730 until late.

Paragliding
Happy Hours Café, south Anjuna Beach. 1230-1400. Rs 500 (children welcome), or at the hill-top between Anjuna/Baga, or Arambol.

Arambol p77, map p77
Boat trips and dolphin watching
21 Coconuts Inn, 2nd restaurant on left after stepping on to the beach. Dolphin-

watching trips or boats to Anjuna, Rs 150 for each.

Body and soul

You can practise every form of yoga here including *Kundalini* – a rarity in India – as well as learn massage of all styles, have your *chakras* balanced, receive Tibetan singing bowl healing, participate in *satsang*, capoeira on the beach at sunset, do firewalking and learn all styles of dance. There is an amazing group of internationally trained therapists here, along with lots of practitioners with zero qualifications, so ask around.

Balanced View, in the rice fields behind Double Dutch, www.balancedview.com. Arambol has become one of the hubs for Balanced View – guidance to living life in clarity and awareness. Has a great following – definitely worth checking out.

Himalaya Iyengar Yoga Centre, follow the many signs, T01892-221312, www.hi yogacentre.com. Established Iyengar centre in town, 5-day courses and teacher training.

Kundalini Yoga Rooftop Garden and Healing Centre, Girka Waddo, near Temple of Dance, www.organickarma.co.uk. One of the few places in India where you can study Kundalini yoga as taught by Yogi Bhajan. Beautiful space for yoga, meditation, in-depth courses, healing sessions, Ayurvedic yoga massage and therapeutic bodywork. Massage trainings also possible. Highly recommended.

T'ai Chi Garden, near Sufi Woodstock, www.pandayoga.net. Panda has been teaching T'ai Chi and chakra healing in Arambol for many years and has a great reputation. Most courses are 2 weeks.

Temple of Dance, off shortcut road towards Ivons and Kundalini Rooftop Garden, Girko Waddo. Beautiful location offering dance classes from Bollywood to Gypsy, Balinese to tribal fusion belly dance, as well as fire dancing, hula hooping and *poi*.

Bronze casting and sculpting

One-off classes and a 3-week course in bronze casting, held every Jan with Lucie from **Double Dutch** (see Restaurants, page 89), a woman of many talents. Ask at **Double Dutch** for details.

Jewellery making and silversmithing

Several places on Arambol high street offer jewellery-making courses; one of the best is with Krishna at **Golden Hand Designs**, on the Kinara junction before Arambol main road.

Paragliding and kitesurfing

Paragliding is synonymous with the hill between Arambol and Keri – ask for Andy at **Arambol Hammocks** on the cliff near Eyes of Buddha for tandem flights and the paragliding lowdown. Check boards in **Double Dutch** or **Lamuella** for kitesurfing lessons.

Tour operators

SS Travels, Main Rd Arambol, near Om Ganesh General Store. Quality service on tours, tickets and money exchange. Also for Western Union. This is the place where all the local ex-pats go. Tried and trusted.

Morjim to Asvem *p79*
Body and soul

Raso Vai, S No 162/2-A, Morjim–Asvem road (towards Mandrem from Morjim), Mardi Wada, Morjim, T(0)9850-973458 and T(0)9623-556828, www.rasovai.com. Runs training courses in their signature treatments (Ayuryogic massage and Ayurbalancing), fusion massages encompassing traditional Ayurvedic techniques and yoga stretches as well as offering more traditional Ayurvedic treatments such as *panchakarma, swedan, pizhichil, shirodhara* and *snehapanam*, from a community oriented centre with meditation. Ayurvedic doctor on site. Highly recommended.

Tour operators

Speedy, near post office, Mazalvaddo, T0832-227 3208. Open 0900-1830. Very helpful for all your onward travel arrangements; also changes money. Very helpful, comprehensive service.

Sun salutations

It's one of those funny ironies that yoga, now at the zenith of its international popularity, is given a resounding thumbs down by your average metropolitan Indian, who's much more likely to pull on lycra and go jogging or pump iron down the gym than pursue the perfect *trikonasana*. They look with curiosity at the swarms of foreign yogis yearning to pick up extreme postures from the various *guru-jis* scattered about the subcontinent. "For them, it's the equivalent of having hoards of middle-class Indians rocking up in Yorkshire to study something we see as outmoded as morris dancing," admits Phil Dane, who runs Yogamagic Canvas Ecotel.

While some Indians look askance at the vast numbers of *firangi* yogis, others are making the most of it. Yoga is a good line of work on the subcontinent. In some places, there are certainly a fair few yoga teachers to choose from.

There is business to be had in selling enlightenment it turns out. At one place you can pay US$2000 for your course – enlightenment guaranteed and a certificate to prove it. Naturally India has its fair share of spiritual wisdom and compassionate gurus, but there is also a percentage of dodgy dealers and predatory gurus. Be aware of the showmen. Some might baulk at seeking out a Western teacher in India, but often Western teachers have a better understanding of the needs of their students. And it's important that we remember, "The guru is a finger pointing to the moon. If you hold on to the finger, you'll never get to the moon."

India remains, nevertheless, one of the best places to study the ancient art, and many people who have embarked on yoga courses purely for its physical benefits also end up reaping some mental and emotional rewards. Yoga done with awareness can give you a taste of the bigger picture. Just keep asking around to find the right teacher. As Viriam Kaur, who runs the Kundalini Yoga Roof Garden, says, "Maybe even more than finding the yoga that you most resonate with, it is essential that you find a teacher that you resonate with. You want a teacher that inspires you. But you also want a teacher that pushes your limits and makes you grow into your potential. The mantra for the Kundalini Yoga teacher as decried by Yogi Bhajan, is 'to poke, provoke, confront and elevate'!"

The large alternative communities settled around Arambol and Anjuna make good starting points if you are looking for some ad hoc teaching, but if you are travelling to India specifically to practice it's worth doing your homework first. Here are some places that are recommended.

Going furthest north first, where there is more yoga than you can shake a yoga mat at, there are two places of special mention: **Samata Holistic Retreat Centre** (www.samatagoa.com), is 10 minutes inland from Arambol proper on a beautiful swathe of land. Bringing hints of Bali and using reclaimed wood from Indonesia, this exceptional place focuses on retreats and has accommodation for 40 people with a beautiful pool surrounded by nature and an organic farm. There is also a drop-in space **MATSYA** and Tamarind Café with two great restaurants, a beautiful swimming pool and drop-in yoga, dance classes and workshops. Samata keeps on inspiring as its profits also go to the **Dunagiri Foundation** (set up by the founder) which works to preserve Himalayan herbs and Ayurvedic plants. Another good option is **Kundalini Yoga Rooftop Garden and Healing Centre** (www.organickarma.co.uk), close to the beach on the way out of Arambol, is one of the few places in India where you can study Kundalini Yoga as taught by Yogi Bhajan. They have beautiful space for yoga, meditation, in-depth courses, therapeutic bodywork, and offer popular courses in Ayurvedic Yoga Massage.

Travelling south to Mandrem, you will find **Ashiyana** (www.ashiyana-yoga-goa. com) which has had a recent revamp and offers yoga holidays and detox retreats. Many rooms have river views and are stacked with Rajasthani furniture and heaps of character. It's a peaceful place on large grounds with two yoga shalas, spa and natural swimming pool. In the very peaceful beach area of Mandrem you will also find **Himalaya Yoga Valley** (www. yogagoaindia.com). They hold great drop-in classes (morning and late afternoon) at an elevated *shala* at **Beach Street** but the main focus here is the exceptional Yoga Teacher Training with talented team headed up by Lalit Kumar. They run regular trainings throughout the season just outside Mandrem and then head to Europe and Thailand for the summer months. If you want to take your practice to the next level, this place is inspirational. On Asvem beach, you have the lovely **Yoga Gypsys** (www.yogagypsys.com), which hosts yoga holidays, trainings and satsangs. There are terracotta bungalows, charming floppy-fringed bamboo huts and tipis in palm grove right on the beach and close to a Hindu temple.

In Anjuna, you will find excellent drop-in classes, workshops and their own brand teacher trainings at **Brahmani** (www. brahmaniyoga.com), there is Mysore-style self practice and excellent *ashtanga*, as well as a smattering of free-flowing movement yoga classes and and *Scaravelli*. Close by is **Yogamagic Canvas Ecotel** (www.yogamagic.net) who host a whole range of yoga classes and holidays in their beautiful yoga temple and you can stay like a Maharani in a suite or Rajasthani hunting tents – this is a very special place. Some 10 minutes away in the neighbouring village of Assagao you find the renowned **Purple Valley Yoga Retreat** (www.yogagoa. com) who host the heavy weights of the yoga world like Sharath Rangaswamy, grandson of Sri K Pattabhi Jois, David Swenson and Nancy Gilgoff. Lessons are held in a lovely *shala* in delightful gardens, food is vegetarian and the atmosphere collegiate. Travel a little further into inland Goa to find **Satsanga Retreat** (www. satsangaretreat.com), a beautiful space with two inspiring *shalas*, a lovely pool and great accommodation. This is often where **Brahmani** host their longer trainings.

Skipping to South Goa, you will find two inspiring centres in Patnem beach. **Harmonic Healing Centre** (www.harmonicingoa.com) have an enviable location high above the north end of the beach with superlative views so that you can perform your *asanas* while looking out to sea. There is drop-in yoga and holistic treats of all varieties. While **Lotus Yoga Retreats** (www.lotus-yoga-retreat.com) focuses on yoga holidays and retreats with guest teachers from Europe, including the fantastic Dynamic Yoga teacher Dina Cohen.

Seek out different schools in the four corners of India in Pune (BKS Iyengar), Mysore (Pattabhi Jois), Neyyar Dam (Sivananda), Anandapur Sahib (Yogi Bhajan – Kundalini Yoga) and Bihar (Paramahamsa Satyananda). There is also the International Yoga Festival in Rishikesh every year in February or March.

Good books include: BKS Iyengar's *Light On Yoga, Asana, Pranayama, Mudra, Bandha* from the Bihar school and anything by Georg Feuerstein.

Surfing
Banana Surf School, at Shanti on the inlet in Asvem beach, www.goasurf.com.

Mandrem p79
Body and soul
Ashiyana (see Where to stay, page 86). Stunning yoga *shalas* in Balinese-style complex. There is drop-in yoga, meditation and dance here as well as courses and retreats and a range of massage and healing options in their new spa.
Himalaya Yoga Valley www.yogagoa india.com. Great drop-in classes (morning and late afternoon) at beautiful elevated *shala* at **Beach St** but the main focus here is exceptional Yoga Teacher Training with talented team headed up by Lalit Kumar. They run regular trainings throughout the season just outside of Mandrem and then head to Europe and Thailand for the summer months. If you want to take your practice to the next level, this place is inspirational. Highly recommended.

⊖ Transport

Baga p70, map p69
Bicycle/scooter hire The only place in Baga to hire bikes is 200 m down a small lane past the Hacienda, on the left. Rs 40 per day, a little extra to keep it overnight. Almost every guesthouse owner or hotelier can rustle up a scooter at short notice – expect to pay Rs 150-350 for 1 day, discounts for longer periods. Those recycled water bottles of lurid orange liquid displayed at the side of the road are not Tizer but petrol often mixed with kerosene and therefore not good for the engine. Better to find a proper petrol station – dotted around in Baga, Vagator and Arambol. Petrol is Rs 55 per litre or 65/70 at the side of the road.

Mapusa p73
Bus To **Calangute** (every 20-30 mins), some continue on to **Aguada** and **Baga**, some go towards **Candolim**; check before

boarding or change at Calangute. Non-stop minibuses to **Panjim**; buy tickets from booth at market entrance. Buses also go to **Vagator** and **Chapora** via **Anjuna** and towns near by. Buses to **Tivim** for Konkan Railway and trains to **Mumbai** (allow 25 mins).

Long-distance buses line up opposite the taxi stand and offer near-identical routes and rates. Expect to pay between Rs 450 and 800 for Panjim to Mumbai for example (15 hrs); similar for Bangalore and Pune; between Rs 350 and 600 for Hampi with private operators like Paolo Travels or Neeta Volvo; you can book through any travel agent.

Car hire Pink Panther, T0832-226 3180.

Motorcycle hire Peter & Friends Classic Adventures, Casa Tres Amigos, Socol Vado 425, Parra, Assagao, 5 km east (off the Anjuna Rd), T0832-225 4467, www. classic-bike-india.com. To really get off the beaten track and see India in the raw, go on an enfield bike tour with **Peter & Friends**. Recommended for reliable bikes and tours of Southern India, Himachal and Nepal. Also has quality rooms and a lush swimming pool at his Casa. Many families rent out motorbikes and scooters – check the lights etc work before you commit.

Taxis Maximum capacity 4 people. Taxi fares have risen in Goa, just like the rest of the world. To **Panjim**, Rs 250; **Calangute/Baga**, Rs 300; **Arambol**, Rs 500. **Autorickshaws** are cheaper. **Motorcycle taxi** to Anjuna or Calangute, also available.

Train Thivim station, on the Konkan Railway, is convenient if you want to head straight to the **northern beaches** (Calangute, Baga, Anjuna and Vagator), avoiding Panjim and Margao. A local bus meets each train and usually runs as far as the Kadamba Bus Stand in Mapusa. From here you either continue on a local bus to the beach or share a tourist taxi (rates above). Enquiries and computerized tickets: T0832-

229 8682. Bookings through a travel agent or if you have an Indian debit card, you can use it online at www.cleartrip.com. Rather than trying to work out Trains at a Glance, Clear Trip offers you an easy way of finding what trains are available, fares and timings. Timings do change, so double check.

To **Ernakulam** (for junction): *Mangalore Exp 12618*, 18 hrs. To **Jaipur** (from Ernakulam): *Exp 12977*, only Mon. To **Mumbai** (**CST**): *Mandovi Exp 10104*, 1038, 10 hrs; *Konkan Kanya Exp 10112*, 1856, 11 hrs. To **Thiruvananthapuram** (**Trivandrum**): *Netravati Exp 16345*, 2202, 19 hrs (via Margao and Canacona for Palolem beach).

Arambol *p77, map p77*
Bus There are regular buses from **Mapusa** and a frequent service from **Chopdem**, 12 km along the main road (1 hr); the attractive coastal detour via **Morjim** being slightly longer. It's a 2-hr walk north through Morjim and Mandrem by the coast. SS Travels and Tara, in the village, exchange cash and TCs, good for train tickets (Rs 100 service charge); also sells bus tickets.

Keri and Tiracol Fort *p78*
Bus Regular buses from **Mapusa** to Keri, then catch ferry to Tiracol Fort.

Mandrem *p79*
Bus Buses towards **Siolem** pass along the main road at about 0930 and 1345. Direct services also to **Mapusa** and **Panjim**.

ⓘ Directory

Calangute *p70, map p70*
Police T0832-227 8284.

Candolim and Sinquerim beaches *p71*
Medical services Health Centre, Main Rd; Bosto Hospital, Panjim Rd.

Mapusa *p73*
Medical services Ambulance: T0832-226 2372. **Vision Hospital**, T0832-225 6788. **Pharmacies** Including Bardez Bazar; Drogaria, near the Swiss Chapel, open 24 hrs; Mapusa Clinic, T0832-226 2350. **Police** T0832-226 2231. **Post** Opposite the police station.

Anjuna *p73, map p74*
Medical services St Michael's Pharmacy, Main Rd, Sorranto, open 24 hrs. **Police** T0832-227 3233.

Arambol *p77, map p77*
Medical services Best to travel to Mandrem (see below) **Police** T0832-229 7614. **Post** The small village post office is at the T-junction, 1.5 km from the beach.

Mandrem *p79*
Medical services Dr Fernandes clinic, T(0)94233-09338. Will also make house calls. Also Goa Clinic 24/7, T(0)98218-67459.

South Goa

The prosperous south is poster-paint green: lush coconut thickets that stretch along the coastline blend with broad swathes of iridescent paddy, broken by the piercingly bright white spears of splendid church steeples. Beneath the coastal coconut fronds sit the pretty villages of fishermen and agriculturalists: Salcete *taluka* is where the Portuguese were most deeply entrenched, and in the district's interior lie the beautiful remnants of centuries-old mansion estates built by the Goan colonial elite. Sprawling drawing rooms and ballrooms are stuffed with chandeliers and antiques and paved with splendid marble, every inch the fairytale doll's house.

Margao and coastal Salcete → *For listings, see pages 111-122.*

A wide belt of golden sand runs the length Salcete's coast in one glorious long lazy sweep, hemmed on the landward side by a ribbon of low-key beach shacks; tucked inland lie Goa's most imposing and deluxe hotels. The thrumming nightlife of North Goa is generally absent here, but some beaches, Cavelossim in particular, have been on the receiving end of a building boom kept afloat by Russian package tourists, while Colva has gone all out and built itself a line of Baywatch-style lifeguard shacks – buxom blonde lifesavers not included. Inland, in various states of decline, lie the stately mansions of Goa's landowning classes: worn-out cases of homes once fit for princes.

Arriving in Margao and coastal Salcete

Getting there and around The Konkan Railway connects Margao directly with Mumbai, Mangalore and Kerala. Madgaon/Margao station is 1.5 km southeast of the bus stands, municipal gardens and market area (where you'll find most of the hotels and restaurants). Rickshaws charge Rs 15 to transfer or walk the 800 m along the railway line. Interstate buses and those running between here and North Goa use the New Kadamba (State) Bus Stand 2 km north of town. City buses take you to the town bus stands for destinations south of Margao. Colva and Benaulim buses leave from the local bus stand east of the gardens. There are plenty of auto-rickshaws and eight-seater taxis for hire. ►► *See Transport, page 120.*

Tourist information Goa Tourism Development Corporation (GTDC) ① *Margao Residency, south of the plaza, T0832-271 5204.* Also has a counter at the railway station, T0832-270 2298.

Margao (Madgaon)

Margao is a fetching, bustling market town which, as the capital of the state's historically richest and most fertile fertile *taluka*, Salcete, is a shop window for fans of grand old Portuguese domestic architecture and churches. Sadly, in their haste to get to the nearby beaches, few tourists take the time to explore this charming, busy provincial town.

The impressive baroque **Church of the Holy Spirit** with its classic Goan façade dominates the Old Market square, the Largo de Igreja. Originally built in 1564, it was sacked by Muslims in 1589 and rebuilt in 1675. A remarkable pulpit on the north wall has carvings of the Apostles. There are also some glass cabinets in the north aisle containing statues of St Anthony and of the Blessed Joseph Vaz. Vaz was a homegrown Catholic missionary who smuggled himself to Sri Lanka dressed as a porter when the Dutch occupation challenged the island's faith. The church's feast day is in June.

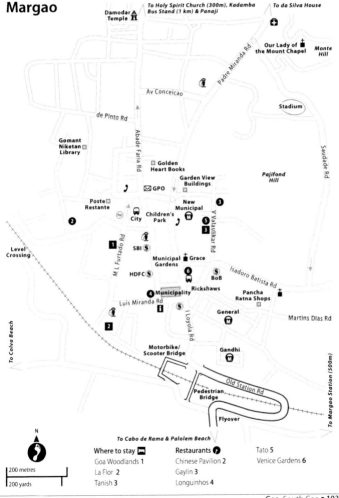

Margao

To Holy Spirit Church (300m), Kadamba Bus Stand (1 km) & Panaji

To da Silva House

Damodar Temple

Our Lady of the Mount Chapel

Monte Hill

Padre Miranda Rd

Av Conceicao

de Pinto Rd

Stadium

Abade Faria Rd

Saudade Rd

Gomant Niketan Library

Golden Heart Books

Garden View Buildings

Pajifond Hill

GPO

Poste Restante

New Municipal

City

Children's Park

V Valaulikar Rd

Level Crossing

M L Furtado Rd

SBI

Municipal Gardens

Grace

HDFC

BoB

Isadoro Batista Rd

Municipality

Rickshaws

Pancha Ratna Shops

Luis Miranda Rd

General

Martins Días Rd

L Loyola Rd

Motorbike/ Scooter Bridge

Gandhi

To Colva Beach

Old Station Rd

Pedestrian Bridge

To Margao Station (500m)

Flyover

N

To Cabo de Rama & Palolem Beach

200 metres
200 yards

Where to stay	Restaurants	
Goa Woodlands 1	Chinese Pavilion 2	Tato 5
La Flor 2	Gaylin 3	Venice Gardens 6
Tanish 3	Longuinhos 4	

The real gem of Margao is the glut of run-down 18th-century houses especially in and around Abade Faria Road, of which **da Silva House** ⓘ *visits arranged via the GTDC*, is a splendid example. Built around 1790 when Inacio da Silva stepped up to become Secretary to the Viceroy, it has a long façade whose roof was once divided into seven separate cropped 'towers', hence its other name, 'Seven Shoulders'; only three of these have survived. The house's grandeur is also evident in its interiors, featuring lavishly carved dark rosewood furniture, gilded mirrors and fine chandeliers. Da Silva's descendants still live in a small wing of the house.

The **municipal market** (Mercado de Afonso de Albuquerque) is a labyrinthine treat of flower garlands, silks and agricultural yield.

Loutolim

By the late 18th century, an educated middle-class elite had emerged in the villages of the Old Conquests. With newly established rights to property, well-to-do Goans began to invest in large homes and very fine living. West of the Zuari River, the villages of Loutolim and Chandor are two of a number that saw the distinct development of estates and houses built on this grand scale. Their houses were stuffed with tokens of their European influence and affluence, mixed with traditions appropriated from their native ancestry, installing personal chapels instead of *devachem kuds*, or Hindu prayer rooms. One beautiful example is the **Figuerda Mansion** (Casa Museu Vicente Joao de Figueiredo) in Loutolim; if you are lucky you will get shown around by the lady of the house who is now in her 80s and has many a story to share about Goa. Ask for directions by the church in Loutolim as there are no signs.

Chandor

Despite being something of a backwater today, the once-grand village of Chandor nonetheless boasts several fine Portuguese mansions. Foremost among them is the enormous **Menezes Braganza family house** ⓘ *13 km east of Margao, both wings usually open 1000-1730 but confirm by telephone; West Wing: T0832-278 4201, 1300-1400 or early evening after 1830; East Wing: T0832-278 4227; a donation of Rs 100 at the end of the tour is greatly appreciated*. Luis de Menezes Braganza was an influential journalist and politician (1878-1938) who not only campaigned for freedom from colonial rule but also became a champion of the less privileged sections of Goan society. The late 16th-century two-storey mansion he inherited (extended in the 18th and 19th centuries), still complete with much of the family furniture and effects, shows the sheer opulence of the life enjoyed by those old Goan families who established great plantation estates. The two wings are occupied separately by members of the Braganza family who have inherited the property.

The **West Wing**, which is better maintained and has finer antiques, is owned by Aida de Menezes Braganza. The guided tour by this elderly member of the family – when she resides here – is fascinating. She has managed to restore the teak ceiling of the 250-year-old library gallery to its original state; the old *mareta* wood floor survived better since this native Goan timber can withstand water. There is much carved and inlaid antique furniture and very fine imported china and porcelain, some specially ordered, and bearing the family crest.

The faded **East Wing**, occupied by Sr Alvaro de Perreira-Braganza, partly mirrors the West Wing. It also has some excellent carved and inlaid furniture and a similar large salon with fine chandeliers. The baroque family chapel at the back now has a prized relic added to its collection, the bejewelled nail of St Francis Xavier, which had, until recently, been kept guarded away from public view.

The guide from the East Wing of the Braganza House can also show you the **Fernandes House** ① *open daily, phone ahead T0832-278 4245, suggested donation Rs 100*, if he's not too busy. It's another example of a once-fine mansion just to the southeast of the village, on the Quepem road. This too has an impressive grand salon occupying the front of the house and a hidden inner courtyard. Recent excavations have unearthed an underground hiding place for when Christian families were under attack from Hindu raiders.

Back in Chandor village itself, the **Church of Our Lady of Bethlehem**, built in 1645, replaced the principal **Sapta Matrika** (Seven Mothers) **temple**, which was demolished in the previous century.

Chandor is closest to Margao but can also easily be visited from Panjim or the beaches in central Goa. It would be an arduous day trip from the northern beaches. Buses from Margao Kadamba Bus Stand (45 minutes) take you within walking distance of the sights but it is worth considering a taxi. Madgaon Railway Station, with connections to Mumbai and the Konkan coastal route as well as direct trains to Hospet, is close by.

Quepem

Heading south from Chandor you can have a tour of the **Palacio do Deao** (Priest's House) ① *T0832-266 4029, www.palaciododeao.com*, opposite Holy Cross Church in Quepem. This house has been lovingly restored by Ruben and Celia Vasco da Gama and has an interesting collection of old Goan stamps, coins and books. Time it so that you can have lunch here on their beautiful veranda – it's a multi-course affair with Indo-Portuguese food. Book in advance.

Colva (Colwa)

Although it's just 6 km from Margao and is the tourist hub of the southern beaches, sleepy Colva is a far cry from its overgrown northern equivalent, Calangute. The village itself is a bit scruffy, but the beach ticks all the right boxes: powdery white sand, gently swaying palms, shallow crystalline waters and lines of local fishermen drawing their nets in hand over fist, dumping pounds of mackerel which are left to dry out in glistening silver heaps.

Margao's parasol-twirling elite, in their search for *mudanca* or a change of air, were the first to succumb to Colva's charms. They would commandeer the homes of local fisher-folk, who had decamped to their shacks for months leading up to the monsoon. The shacks have now traded up for gaudy pink and turquoise guesthouses and the odd chi-chi resort, but Colva's holiday scene remains a mostly domestic affair, beloved of Indian fun-seekers who'll willingly shell out the cash to go parasailing for 90 seconds.

Out on the eastern edge of town, the large **Church of Our Lady of Mercy** (Nossa Senhora das Merces), dating from 1630 and rebuilt in the 18th century, has a relatively simple façade and a single tower on the south side that is so short as to be scarcely noticeable, and the strong horizontal lines normally given to Goan churches by three of four full storeys is broken by a narrow band of shallow semi-circular arches above the second floor. But the church is much less famous for its architecture than for the huge fair it hosts, thanks to its association with the miraculous **Menino Jesus**. Jesuit Father Bento Ferreira found the original image in the river Sena, Mozambique, en route to Goa, and brought it to Colva where he took up his position as rector in 1648. The image's miraculous healing powers secured it special veneration.

The **Fama of Menino Jesus festival** (Monday of 12-18 October) sees thousands of frantic devotees flock to kiss the statue in hope of a miracle. Near the church, specially blessed lengths of string are sold, as well as replicas of limbs, offered to the image in thanks for cures.

Betalbatim to Velsao

A short walk from Colva, **Betalbatim** is named after the main Hindu temple to Betall that stood here before the deity was moved to Queula in Ponda for safety. This is a pleasant stretch with a mix of coconut palms and casuarinas on the low dunes. At low tide, when the firm sand is exposed, you can cycle for miles along the beach in either direction.

The broad, flat open beaches to the north – **Velsao**, **Arossim**, **Utorda** and **Majorda** – are the emptiest: the odd fishing village or deluxe resort shelters under coconut thicket canopy.

Bogmalo is a small, palm-fringed and attractive beach that's exceptionally handy for the airport (only 4 km, and a 10-minute drive away). **Hollant Beach**, 2 km further on, is a small rocky cove that is fringed with coconut palms. From Bogmalo village you can get to **Santra Beach**, where fishermen will ferry you to two small islands for about Rs 350 per boat.

The quiet back lanes snaking between these drowsy villages make perfect bicycle terrain and Velsao boasts some particularly grand examples of old mansions.

Verna

The church at Verna (the 'place of fresh air'), inland from the northern Salcete beaches on the NH17, was initially built on the site of the Mahalsa Temple, which had housed the deity now in Mardol (see page 125) and featured exquisite carvings, but was destroyed and marked by the cross to prevent it being re-used for Hindu worship. As a sanctuary for widows who did not commit *sati*, it was dubbed the Temple of Nuns.

Verna was also picked to house the fifth century BC, 2.5-m-high **Mother Goddess figure** from Curdi in Sanguem, which was under threat of being submerged by the Selaulim Dam project in 1988. Two megalithic sites were found in the area. It is surrounded by seven healing springs. Just north towards Cortalim are the popular medicinal **Kersarval springs**.

Benaulim to Mobor

At Colva Beach's southern end lies tranquil **Benaulim**, which, according to the myth of Parasurama, is 'where the arrow fell' to make Goa. It is now a relaxed village set under palms, where business centres around toddy tapping and fishing. The hub of village activity is Maria Hall crossing, just over 1 km from the beach.

On a hill beyond the village is the diminutive **Church of St John the Baptist**, a fine piece of Goan Christian architecture rebuilt in 1596. Although the gable façade, with twin balustraded towers, is striking, the real treat is inside, in its sumptuous altar *reredos* and wonderful rococo pulpit with its depiction of the Lamb of the Apocalypse from the *Book of Revelation*.

The picturesque lane south from Benaulim runs through small villages and past white-painted churches. Paddy gives way to palm, and tracks empty onto small seaside settlements and deserted beaches. Benaulim has a more alternative vibe to its neighbouring beaches and has the **Goa Chitra Museum** ⓘ *www.goachitra.com*, which is a beautifully created museum giving insight into the day-to-day living of rice farmers, toddy tappers and fishermen of not-so-yesteryear. They are creating another wing, **Goa Chakra**, focusing on transportation. Benaulim beach runs into **Varca**, and then **Fatrade**, before the main road finally hits the shoreline amid a sprouting of resorts and restaurants at **Cavelossim**. Furthest south, **Mobor**, about 6 km from Cavelossim, lies on the narrow peninsula where the river Sal joins the sea. The Sal is a busy fishing route, but doubles as a lovely spot for boat rides.

Betul

Idyllic Betul, which overlooks Mobor from the opposite bank of the Sal in Quepem *taluka*, is an important fishing and coir village shaded by coconut palms and jackfruit, papaya and banana trees. A sand bar traps the estuary into a wide and protected lagoon and the cool breezes from the sea temper even the hottest Goan high noon. Just after the bridge, which crosses the mouth of a small river, a narrow road off to the right by the shops zigzags through the village along the south side of the Sal.

From Cavelossim the shortest route to Betul is by taking the ferry across the Sal (a signposted road leads southeast from a junction just north of Cavelossim) to Assolna; turn left off the ferry, then turn right in the village to join the main road towards Betul. From Margao, the NH17 forks right (6 km) towards Assolna at Chinchinim. After a further 6 km, there is a second turning in Cuncolim for Assolna. Buses from Margao to Betul can be very slow, but there is a fairly regular service stopping in all the settlements along the way (a couple of them continue as far as Cabo de Rama).

Cuncolim

The Jesuits razed Cuncolim's three principal Hindu temples (including the Shantadurga) and built churches and chapels in their stead.

Hindu 'rebels' killed five Jesuits and several converts in reprisal, triggering a manhunt which saw 15 men killed by the captain of Rachol Fort's soldiers. The relics of the Christian

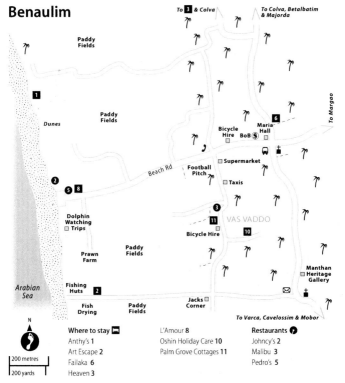

Benaulim

To **3** & Colva
To Colva, Betalbatim & Majorda

Paddy Fields

Dunes

Paddy Fields

To Margao

Bicycle Hire   BoB ⑤
Maria Hall **6**

Beach Rd   Football Pitch   □ Supermarket

□ Taxis

2
5 **8**

3

Dolphin Watching
□ Trips   **11**   VAS VADDO

Bicycle Hire   **10**

Paddy Fields

Prawn Farm

Manthan
□ Heritage Gallery

Fishing Huts   **2**

Arabian Sea

Fish Drying   Paddy Fields

Jacks □ Corner

To Varca, Cavelossim & Mobor

N

200 metres
200 yards

Where to stay ▭		
Anthy's **1**	L'Amour **8**	Restaurants ●
Art Escape **2**	Oshin Holiday Care **10**	Johncy's **2**
Failaka **6**	Palm Grove Cottages **11**	Malibu **3**
Heaven **3**		Pedro's **5**

'martyrs of Cuncolim' now lie in the Sé Cathedral in Old Goa (see page 59). The cathedral's golden bell, Goa's largest, was cast here in 1652.

Cabo de Rama, Palolem and the far south → *For listings, see pages 111-122.*

Palolem is the closest Goa gets to a picture-postcard perfect bay: a beautiful arc of palm-fringed golden sand that's topped and tailed with rocky outcrops. Under the canopy of the dense coconut forests lie numerous restaurants and coco-huts. To the north, a freshwater stream and a short swim or wade will get you to the jungle of the tiny Canacona Island.

Palolem's sheer prettiness has made it popular and perhaps less pretty than it once was, prompting some travellers to drift south to the tranquil beaches of neighbouring Colomb, Patnem and Galgibaga (beautiful Rajbag is ring-fenced by a five-star). Patnem, hemmed in by crags and river at either end, doesn't have the same rash of coconut trees that made Palolem so shadily alluring and has mopped up most of the overspill. Again to the north Agonda is also picking up some of the Palolem overspill, yet it retains its charm as a pretty fishing village strung out along a windswept casuarina-backed bay. There are more dramatic waves here than the calm waters of Palolem and Patnem. The dramatic ruined fort at Cabo de Rama yields some of Goa's most dramatic views from its ramparts and has empty coves tucked about at its shores.

Arriving in Cabo de Rama, Palolem and the far south
Getting there The nearest major transport junction for all these beaches is Canacona, also known as Chaudi, on the NH17 between Panjim and Karwar in Karnataka. Buses from here shuttle fairly continuously down to Palolem, and less frequently to Agonda, while there's a less frequent service from the beaches direct to Margao (37 km) which take about an hour. Canacona station on the Konkan railway is only 2 km from Palolem. Canacona's main square has the bus and autorickshaw stands; rickshaws cost Rs 50-150 to any of these bays.

Getting around The area between the beaches is small and wandering between them becomes a leisure pursuit in itself. The drive to Cabo de Rama, although riddled

Varca to Betul

To Benaulim · To Margao
Varca Beach · Varca · Orlim · To Palolem
Fatrade Beach · Chinchinim · Carmona
Cavelossim
Dona Silvia · Cavelossim Beach · River Sal · Assolna · To NH17
Betty's Place · Fish Port · Velim
Mobor Beach · Betul
Arabian Sea
Tarrie · To Cabo de Rama

N

1 km
1 mile

Where to stay
Bamboo House 1
Taj Exotica 13

Restaurants
River View 4

Bars & clubs
Aqua at Leela Palace Hotel 7

with hairpin bends, is particularly lovely, and going under your own steam means you can hunt out tucked away beaches nearby and stop over at the fishing dock at the estuary north of Agonda. Buses run along this route between the bays roughly hourly.

Cabo de Rama (Cape Rama)

Legend has it that the hero of the Hindu epic *Ramayana* lived in this desolate spot with his wife Sita during their exile from Ayodhya, and the fort predated the arrival of the Portuguese who seized it from its Hindu rulers in 1763. Its western edge, with its sheer drop to the Arabian Sea, gives you a stunning vista onto a secluded stretch of South Goa's coastline.

The main entrance to the **fort** seems far from impregnable, but the outer ramparts are excellently preserved with several cannons still scattered along their length. The gatehouse is only 20 m or so above the sea, and is also the source of the fort's water supply. A huge tank was excavated to a depth of about 10 m, which even today contains water right through the dry season. If a local herdsman is about ask him to direct you to the two springs, one of which gives out water through two spouts at different temperatures.

Agonda

Snake through forests and bright paddy south from Cabo De Rama towards Palolem to uncover artless Agonda, a windswept village backed by mountains of forestry full of acrobatic black-faced monkeys. Local political agitators thwarted plans for a five-star hotel and so have, temporarily at least, arrested the speed of their home's development as a tourist destination. However year on year, more restaurants and coco-huts open up along the length of the beach. There's no house music, little throttling of Enfield engines and you need to be happy to make your own entertainment to stay here for any serious length of time. Less photogenic than Palolem, Agonda Bay has pine-like casuarina trees lining the beach instead of coconuts and palms. The swimming is safe but the sea is livelier than in neighbouring Palolem. The northern end of the beach, close to the school and bus stop, has a small block of shops including the brilliantly chaotic and original **Fatima stores and restaurant** (Fatima Rodrigues, not one to be a jack of all trades, has limited her menu to just spaghetti and *thali*) and **St Annes bookstore**, a video library.

Hourly buses between Betul and Palolem call at Agonda (and Cabo de Rama). It's also easy to visit for the day by taxi, motorbike or bicycle from Palolem Beach. From Palolem/Chaudi Junction, auto-rickshaws charge Rs 120-150; turn off the road by the **Niki** bar and restaurant.

Palolem

For a short spell, when the police cracked down most severely on parties up north, Palolem looked like it might act as the Anjuna overflow. Today, **Neptune's Point** has permission to hold parties every Saturday, but so far, Palolem's villagers are resisting the move to make the beach a mini-party destination and authorities are even stumping up the cash to pay for litter pickers. The demographic here is chiefly late 20s and 30-something couples, travellers and students. The large church and high school of **St Tereza of Jesus** (1962) are on the northern edge of town.

Beaches further south

Over the rocky outcrops to the south you come to the sandy cove of **Colomb**. Wholly uncommercial, its trees are pocked with long-stayers' little picket fences and stabs at growing banana plants, their earthy homesteads cheek by jowl with fishermen's huts. The locals are currently holding firm against a controversial development planned by a Russian group, and for now the only sounds here are the rattle of coconut fronds and bird song. Although just a bay away, you could almost be on a different planet to Palolem.

At the end of the track through Colomb, a collection of huts marks the start of the fine sweep of **Patnem Beach**. The 500 villagers here have both put a limit on the number of shacks and stopped outsiders from trading, and as a result the beach has conserved much of its unhurried charm. The deep sandbanks cushion volleyball players' falls and winds whip through kite flyers' sails: but fishing boats far outnumber sun loungers. A hit with old rockers, Israelis and long-stayers, there is no nightlife, no parties and, no coincidence, a healthy relationship between villagers and tourism. Hindu temples in Patnem have music most Fridays and Saturdays, with tabla, cymbals and harmonica.

Further south, wade across a stream (possible before the monsoon) to reach the dune- and casuarina-fringed **Rajbag Beach**, its southern waters a-bob with fishing boats. Although it's virtually unvisited and has perfect swimming, the luxury five-star that opened here in 2004 provoked a storm of protest; allegations against the hotel have included the limited access to the sea, the failure to meet local employment quotas, and the rebuilding of the ancient Shree Vita Rukmayee Temple, which villagers argue was tantamount to the hotel 'swallowing our God'. The isolated **Kindlebaga Beach** is east of Rajbag, 2 km from Canacona.

Galgibaga

Nip across the Talpona River by the ferry to reach a short strip of land jutting out to sea, where well-built houses lie among lucrative casuarina plantations. Like Morjim, **Galgibaga Beach** is a favourite stopover for Olive Ridley **turtles**, which travel vast distances to lay their eggs here each November. Shacks are mushrooming, to environmentalists' concern.

Partagali and Cotigao Wildlife Sanctuary

At a left turn-off the NH17, 7 km south of Canacona, to Partagali, a massive concrete gateway marks the way to the temple. If you go a little further, you reach a 2-km-long road that leads to the Cotigao Wildlife Sanctuary. Partagali's **Shri Sausthan Gokarn Partagali Jeevotam Math** is a centre for culture and learning on the banks of the river Kushavati. The *math* (religious establishment) was set up in AD 1475 at Margao when the followers, originally Saivites, were converted and became a Vaishnav sect. During the period of Portuguese Christianization (1560-1568), the foundation was moved south to Bhatkal (in northern Karnataka). The sixth Swami returned the *math* to Partagali, and built its Rama, Lakshman, Sita and Hunuman temple. An ancient *Vatavriksha* (banyan tree) 65 m by 75 m, which represents this Vaishnav spiritual movement, is a sacred meditation site known as *Bramhasthan*. The tree and its *Ishwarlinga* (the *lingam* of the Lord, ie Siva) have drawn pilgrims for more than a millennium. The temple, which also has a typical tall Garuda pillar, celebrates its festival in March/April.

Cotigao Wildlife Sanctuary ① *60 km south of Panjim, www.goaforest.com/wildlife mgmt/body_cotigao.htm, year-round 0730-1730 (but may not be worthwhile during the monsoon), Rs 5, 2-wheelers Rs 10, cars Rs 50, camera Rs 25, video Rs 100,* lies in one of the most densely forested areas of the state. The 86-sq-km sanctuary is hilly to the south and east and has the Talpona River flowing through it. There is a nature interpretation centre with a small reference library and map of the park roads at the entrance. The vegetation is mostly moist deciduous with some semi-evergreen and evergreen forest cover. You may be very lucky and spot gazelles, panther, sloth bear, porcupine and hyena, and several reptiles, but only really expect wild boar, the odd deer and gaur and many monkeys. Bird-spotting is more rewarding; rare birds include rufous woodpecker, Malabar crested lark and white-eyed eagle. You need your own vehicle to reach the treetop watchtowers and waterholes that are signposted, 3 km and 7 km off the main metalled road on a variable rough track. There are no guides available, but the forest paths are easy to follow – just make sure you have drinking water and petrol. The chances of seeing much wildlife, apart from monkeys, are slim, since by the opening time of 0730 animal activity has already died down to its daytime minimum.

The first tower by a waterhole is known as **Machan Vhutpal**, 400 m off the road, with great views of the forest canopy. The second tower is sturdier and the best place to spend a night (permission required).

Most visitors come for a day trip, but if you are keen on walking in the forest this is a great place to spend a day or two. You can either stay near the sanctuary office or spend a night in a watchtower deep in the forest. A short way beyond the sanctuary entrance the metalled road passes through a small hamlet where there is a kiosk for the villagers living within the reserve, which sells the usual array of basic provisions. If you are planning to spend a few days in the park it is best to bring your own fresh provisions and then let the staff prepare meals. Rudimentary facilities like snake proof campsites, with canvas tents available from the forest office. You'll also need written permission to stay in the forest rest house or watchtower from the Deputy Conservator of Forests (third floor, Junta House, Panaji), as far in advance of a visit as possible.

The cheapest way to visit the park is to get a group together from Palolem. If you leave the beach just before 0700 you will be at the park gates when they open. Motorbikes are also allowed in the sanctuary.

South Goa listings

For hotel and restaurant price codes and other relevant information, see pages 13-15.

🛏 Where to stay

Margao *p102, map p103*
With Colva and other beaches little over 15 mins away, there is not much point staying in Margao itself.
$$ Goa Woodlands, ML Furtado Rd, opposite City Bus Stand, T0832-271 5522, www.goawoodlandshotel.com. This swish business hotel has 35 clean, spacious and anonymous rooms. Restaurant, bar, good value although reports have been mixed.
$ La Flor, E Carvalho St, T0832-273 1402, www.laflorhotelgoa.com. 35 rooms with bath, some a/c, restaurant, clean, away from bustle of town and very pleasant for the price.
$ Tanish, Reliance Trade Centre, V V Rd, T0832-273 5656. New place with smart, good-value rooms, sharing a business

complex with cybercafés and mobile phone dealers. It's an OK-for-1-night kind of place. Several good restaurants nearby.

Loutolim *p104*
$$$ Casa Susegad, T0832-264 3477, www.casasusegad.com. This gem of a place tucked away in sleepy Loutolim village has just 5 rooms in a converted 300-year-old Portuguese house. There is a beautiful swimming pool, an enormous games room and delicious food cooked up, sometimes even home-smoked mackerel pâté or mango pie from the enormous mango trees dotted around the garden. Norman and Carole have done a remarkable job restoring this place and are very happy to share their little bit of paradise with you.

Chandor *p104*
$$$ The Big House, T0832-264 3477, www.ciarans.com. Ancestral Portuguese/

Goan home of John Coutinho, owner of **Ciaran's Camp** in Palolem (see page 114). 2 bedrooms plus high-beamed ceilings, large sitting room, fully fitted kitchen, hot water, maid service, cable TV, DVD, phone and cooking available. Great for families, couples or groups of friends.

Colva *p105*
Most hotels are 6-8 km from Margao Railway Station. Prices rise on 1 Dec. Discounts are possible for stays of a week or more.
$$ C A Guest House, 470/2 4th Ward), T0832-278 0047. Cool and pleasant 2-bed apartments with balconies and basic kitchen in a huge, pastel-pink house.
$ Sea Pearl, 476/4 South Ward T0832-278 0176. Not particularly well maintained, but the big high-ceilinged rooms upstairs with private bath and balcony offer the best cheap deal in town. Good seafood restaurant downstairs.
$ Tourist Nest, 2 km from the sea, T0832-278 8624, touristnest@indiatimes.com. Crumbling old Portuguese house, 12 rooms in secure new block, fan, Rs 200 with bathroom, 2 small self-contained cottages, good restaurant. Old part of house recommended for long stay (Rs 8000 per month for 2 bedrooms), spacious dining area, large lounge, antique furniture, balcony, bathroom and cooking facilities.

Betalbatim to Velsao *p106*
$$$$ Alila Diwa Goa, Adao Waddo, Majorda, T0832-274 6800, www.aliladiwa goa.com. The latest of the lush hotels to open its doors in the Majorda area, it has already racked up a host of awards. Stunning lobby and beautiful infinity pool – beyond that the rooms are stylish and have lovely balconies. You can even get authentic home cooking; they have enlisted local Goan Edia Cotta to share her family recipes.
$$$$-$$$ Vivenda Dos Palhacos, Costa Vaddo, Majorda, T0832-322 1119, www.vivendagoa.com. One of the most charming places you can lay your hat in

Goa. Stunning renovation of old Portuguese mansion – all rooms are different; Madras has a beautiful outdoor bathroom so you can shower under the stars, The Chummery is a lovely cottage with its own veranda, there is the Darjeeling with a mezzanine floor and you can stay in a huge luxe tent beyond the pretty swimming pool. Dinners are a fantastic communal affair although obviously you can opt out. Run by the hosts with the most Simon and Charlotte Hayward who come from the lineage of Haywards 5000 and their bar is dedicated to the tipple. Wholeheartedly recommended.
$ Baptista, Beach Rd, Thonvaddo, Betalbatim, T0832-288 0048. 2 simple rooms with fan, 2 self-catering flats with gas stove, use of fridge and utensils (Rs 350), good for long stays – discounts, short walk from beach. Friendly family and friendly dog once he gets to know you.
$ Manuelina Tourist House, Thonvaddo, behind Ray's, T0832-880 1154. 5 spacious, clean rooms with bath, TV lounge, some food available, pleasant, secure, quiet with a lovely communal veranda next to the banyan tree.

Benaulim to Mobor *p106,*
maps p107 and p108
Budget hotels and rooms in private houses can be found along Benaulim Beach Rd, in the coconut groves on either side, and along the beach south of Johncy's, but the rock bottom deals are drying up fast. Even simple beach guesthouses don't mind charging Rs 1000 a night for a room with bath.
$$$$ Taj Exotica, Calvaddo, towards Varca, T0832-658 3333, exoticabc.goa@ tajhotels.com. 23 ha of greenery and views of virgin beaches from each of its 138 luxurious rooms. Good restaurants, including Mediterranean, coffee shop, nightclub, excellent pool, golf course, floodlit tennis, kids' activities, jacuzzi, watersports, gym, jogging track, library and bike hire. Spa offers treatments such as Balinese massage, acupuncture and aromatherapy.

$$ Bamboo House Goa, Mobor Beach, Behind Leela Kempinski, T(0)976-664 9369, www.bamboohousegoa.com. This place packs real eco-credentials and works with **Green Goa Works** to reduce their carbon footprint including composting and solar panels. They have also planted 80 varieties of plant around their grounds to prevent soil erosion. Beyond that, it's a pretty little place with 10 bamboo cottages and swanky bathrooms. Recommended.

$$ Palm Grove Cottages, Vas Vaddo, Benaulim, T0832-277 0059, www.palm grovegoa.com. 20 clean, spacious but not stylish rooms. The newer blocks at rear with showers and balconies are better. Pleasant palm-shaded garden, good food, Ayurvedic treatments. Not on the beach but plenty of places to hire a bicycle just outside. Welcoming.

$$-$ Art Escape Vaddi beach, south Benaulim, T(0)989-228 6666, artescape.in. Lovely place to stay with wood and bamboo huts. There is lots of live music including a Qawalli Sufi music festival, art and holistic therapy workshops. It's a great place close to the beach to relax or be inspired.

$$-$ L'Amour, end of Beach Rd, Benaulim, T0832-277 0404, www.lamourbeachresort goa.com. Close to the sea, 20 cottage-style rooms amid pleasant gardens, in a well-established hotel run by same team as **Johncy's** beach shack. Good terrace restaurant, handy for exchange and booking rail and bus tickets.

$ Anthy's, Sernabatim Beach (2-min walk south of **Furtado's**), T(0)9922-854566, www.goaguesthomes.com. A tiny collection of simple white cottages with bed, bathroom, mosquito net and not much more, set behind a popular beach café. Simple but nicely done and on a pleasant bit of beach.

$ Failaka, Adsulim Nagar, near Maria Hall crossing, Benaulim, T0832-277 1270, hotelfailaka@hotmail.com. 16 spotless, comfortable rooms, 4 with TV, quieter at rear, excellent restaurant, friendly family set-up.

$ Heaven, north of Benaulim, Sernabatim Beach, T0832-277 2201, www.heavengoa.in. Absolutely stunning views of palm trees and green foliage, but it's 500 m from the beach. Great-value rooms and deservedly popular – book ahead. Also Ayurvedic massage available on site. Recommended.

$ Oshin Holiday Care, House No 126, Vas Vaddo, Benaulim, T0832-277 0069, www.oshins-guesthouse.com. You'll need a bicycle to get to the beach but the peaceful location overlooking egret and buffalo ponds is well worth it. 14 good large rooms with bath on 3 floors (room 11 is best), breakfast, dinner on request, friendly manager, superb well-kept grounds. Recommended.

Agonda p109

$$$-$$ Dunhill Beach Resort, towards south end of the beach, T(0)832-264 7328, www.dunhillbeachresort.in. Having had a bit of a facelift, **Dunhill** offers up the most stylish accommodation on the beach with 6 chic wooden cabanas and then cheaper, but large and comfortable rooms at the back. There is a good restaurant serving up all of the usual favourites too.

$$$-$ Shanti Village, towards south end of the beach, T(0)9823-962154, www.shantiagonda.com. With lovely views and chic huts, **Shanti** has chic black huts on the beach and an intimate vibe. It's good value and they have another outpost towards the north end of the beach near **Simrose**, where there are some cheaper huts, although still very nice with tribal masks and textiles to decorate.

$$$-$ White Sand, north end of the beach, T(0)9823-548277, www.agondawhite sand.com. **White Sand** has always been a popular choice in Agonda and with a new redesign is offering up stylish great-value accommodation. New cabanas have beautiful outside showers and are nicely decorated inside. The menu has also had a rethink and there are great Euro classics and traditional Goan and Indian fare on offer. They also have **Agonda Villas** – 5 boutique-style Balinese-inspired villas which are more expensive but well worth the money. Recommended.

$$ Blue Lagoon Resort, 4 km north of Agonda at Khola beach, T0832-264 7842, www.bluelagooncola.com. Rajasthani tents set up on this secluded beach north of Agonda – blissful. There are also lovely huts, a restaurant and amazing views. You almost have the beach to yourself for romantic moonlit walks as it is mainly a daytripper beach.

$$-$ Common Home, south end of the beach, T(0)9873-367300. Innovatively designed a/c rooms with Rajasthani wooden doors, and beach huts with sleek slate bathrooms and cow dung walls – all with interesting furniture and draped fabrics. There are also huts available.

$$-$ Simrose, towards north end of the beach, T(0)9420-162474, www.simrose-goa.com. Stylish beach shacks and nice rooms at the back. The pretty restaurant has plenty of little nooks for romantic suppers or shady spots for daytime lounging. Good value. Recommended.

$ Dersy Beach Resort, south end of the beach, T0832-264 7503. 50-year-old family house developed to fit 12 clean rooms with bathrooms. Over the road on the beach are 12 basic bamboo huts with a spotless shared wash block. Good value generally, but in high season the huts are not worth the price.

$ Kaama Kethna, 5 km south of Agonda off Palolem Rd, www.kaamakethna.net, phone reception patchy so email kaamakethna@ymail.com. Beautiful bamboo huts with open-air bathrooms perched in the jungle. Part of an enterprising organic farm there are 5 stylish huts and 2 treehouses and a lot more land to play with for creating new accommodation – really you feel your only neighbour is the jungle itself with just a mosquito net and swaying sari between you and Nature. You will find beautiful land, inspiring people, a yoga platform and a great and nourishing restaurant using the produce from the farm. There is an annual yoga festival, art projects and if you want to get your hands dirty there are opportunities for volunteering. You can walk through the jungle to Agonda beach in 30 mins and to the neighbouring Butterfly beach in 40 mins. Wholeheartedly recommended.

$ Nana's Nook, extreme south end of the the beach, T(0)9421-244672. Simple beach huts dotted around a central café with shared bath. The best huts at the front offer ideal views. Recommended.

Palolem *p109*

Palolem's popularity has soared inordinately and in high season prices go off the scale. Off season, bargain hard and ask around for rooms inside family houses. There is a wide range of accommodation.

$$$-$$ Art Resort, south end of beach in Ourem area, T(0)9665-982344, www.art-resort-goa.com. Colourful seafront cottages with interesting interior design from Riki Hinteregger using khadi natural cotton. Fairly pricey.

$$$-$$ Ciaran's Camp, beach, T0832-264 3477, www.ciarans10.com. Primo glass-fronted wooden huts are spaced wide apart in palm-covered landscaped gardens; many have their own roof terrace with loungers. They have added more rooms so there is more chance of getting a super-stylish hut here. A library, lovely shop, table tennis and great restaurant plus promises of live jazz all make it the leader in Palolem cool.

$$$-$$ Village Guesthouse, beach, off the main road, T0832-264 5767, www.village guesthousegoa.com. Stylish renovation of an old house, which, although only 5 mins' walk from beach feels a million miles away. Beautiful rooms with a/c, TV and chic decor. They pride themselves on sourcing everything locally except the washing machine which came from Korea and the tequila from Mexico! Great views across rice fields from the communal veranda, and a courtyard garden in the back.

$$ Bhakti Kutir, cliffside, south end of the beach, T0832-264 3469, www.bhaktikutir.com. This is a hardy perennial of Palolem offering up eco-friendly chic perched on the hilltop above Palolem beach. A relaxing place with 2-tier huts kitted out with antique furniture, compost toilets and bucket baths. There is a popular super-healthy restaurant on-site offering up a selection of every grain you can think of. Renowned yoga teacher Swami Yogananda is based here and has a dedicated following.

$$-$ Cozy Nook, at northern end, T0832-264 3550. Plastered bamboo huts, fans, nets, shared toilets, in a good location between the sea and river, Ayurvedic centre, art and crafts, friendly. Very popular. Getting a bit pricey.

$$-$ Ordo Sounsar, extreme north end of the beach, over a small bridge, T(0)9822-488769, www.ordosounsar.com. Simple yet stylish beach huts nestling north of the estuary away from the busyness of Palolem Beach. Exceptional location and restaurant serving up traditional Goan dishes. Highly recommended.

$ Chattai, set back from the beach, behind Bhakti Kutir and Neptune's Point, T(0)9822-481360, www.chattai.co.in. Fantastic coco huts, most with loungey roof terraces. Lovely chilled atmosphere. There is another branch in Agonda.

$ Fernandes, next to Banyan Tree, T0832-264 3743. 2 branches of this family-run guesthouse and restaurant on the beach. Lovely wooden cottages with attached bathrooms, good value.

$ Green Inn, on the Agonda road, T(0)9434-053626, www.palolemgreen inn.com. Exceptional location, this 2-storey guesthouse juts out into the vibrant green rice fields offering up almost a 360° view of nature. Nice clean rooms with flatscreen TVs and modern bathrooms, alas no individual balconies, but amazing views from rooftop restaurant.

$ Papillon, south end of beach, T(0)9890-495470, www.papillonpalolem.com. Good-value chic beach huts with laid-back vibe, a cut above the rest.

Beaches further south *p109*
The following places are dotted between Colomb, Patnem and Galjibag. Demand and room rates rocket over Christmas and New Year.

$$$-$$ La Mangrove, Galjibag, T0832 2641243, www.lamangrovegoa.com. Billed as a river lounge, close to the stunning beach of Galjibag you find a unique opportunity to stay in super-chic tipis with kingsize beds, open-air showers and eco toilets. There is a loungey restaurant on site. At the time of writing there were issues with local licenses so fingers crossed that soon gets resolved.

$$ Almond Park, on the road linking Palolem and Patnem, T(0)7875-477788, www.almondpark.com. 5 nice rooms with lovely verandas set amongst, you guessed it, almond trees. Pretty little place and one room has a kitchen. A short walk down to the beach, uphill on the way back!

$$ April 20, next to Home, T(0)9960-916989, vickygoan@gmail.com. Smart 1- and 2-tiered beach bungalows with nice balconies and great views, formerly called **Goyam & Goyam**. It's restaurant is recommended by the local Westerners who make south Goa their home.

$$ Hidden Gourmet, Colomb, T(0)9923-686185, www.gourmetpatnem.com. As the name suggests this place is off the beaten track, or at least through the village and tucked away on the promontory overlooking Patnem beach. Beautifully decorated stone rooms all with a stunning ocean view and 2 mango wood and bamboo huts with stylish open-roofed bathrooms. Recommended.

$$-$ Home Guesthouse, Patnem, T0832-264 3916, www.homeispatnem.com Vibey rooms with nice decor make these a cut above the rest – deservedly popular. Quality linen and fairy lights make for good ambience, although opt for a room set back from the kitchen and very popular restaurant. Staying here could affect your waistline.

$$-$ Papayas, Patnem, T(0)9923-079447, www.papayasgoa.com. Eco-friendly huts running on solar power with beautifully kept gardens. Chilled atmosphere set behind small beachfront restaurant.

$ Bonkers, south end Patnem beach, T(0)9822-664026, rocking.bonkers@gmail. com. Floppy fringed palm huts borrowing their design from neighbours **Lotus Yoga**, laid-back vibe at the quieter end of the beach.

$ Namaste, Patnem, T(0)9850-477189, namaste_patnem@yahoo.in. Variety of wooden huts and bamboo bungalows – good value. Nice vibe and lively restaurant.

$ Solitude Dream Woods, Patnem, T0832-327 7081, solitudedreamwoods@yahoo.com. Included on www.goabeachhuts.com, which gives more listings for the area. Basic plywood structures, but good value and all with attached bathroom. There is a yoga space here and swinging chairs dotted around.

🍴 Restaurants

Margao p102, map p103
$$ Chinese Pavilion, M Menezes Rd (400 m west of Municipal Gardens). Chinese. Smart, a/c, good choice.
$$ Gaylin, 1 V Valaulikar Rd. Chinese. Tasty hot Szechuan, comfortable a/c.
$$ Longuinhos, near the Municipality. Goan, North Indian. Open all day for meals and snacks, bar drinks and baked goodies.
$$ Tato, G-5 Apna Bazaar, Complex, V Valaulikar Rd. Superb vegetarian, a/c upstairs.
$$ Venice Gardens, near Our Lady of Grace Church, opposite Lohia Maidan, T0832-271 0505. Little garden oasis in the middle of Margao offering up the usual fare.

Colva p105
$ Joe Con's, 4th Ward. Excellent fresh fish and Goan dishes, good value.
$ Sagar Kinara, 2 mins back from beach overlooking the main road junction. Rare pure-veg restaurant, offering good-value thalis and biryanis on a breezy terrace.
$ Viva Goa, 200 m south of roundabout at east end of town. Local favourite, serving proper Goan food on red checked tablecloths. Recommended.

Betalbatim to Velsao p106
It's worth coming to Majorda for the food, there are a range of great restaurants.
$$$ Fusion, Majorda Beach Rd, Pacheco Vaddo, T0832-288 1694. Winning a Times Food Award in 2011, this place offers up a lot of meat. Steaks and carpaccio are their specialities, but naturally there are some fish and veg options too. And leave room for their chocolate fondant.
$$$ Martin's Corner, Betalbatim (coming from the south, look for sign on left after village), T0832-648 1518. A huge place in front of an old house, serving great seafood including lobster, tiger prawns and crab. As cricket superstar Sachin Tendulkar has bought a house here, it's become the hangout of choice for holidaying cricket stars and media types.
$$$ Miyabi, Majorda Beach Rd, T(0)9767-704244. Serving up for-real Japanese food – fresh sushi, tasty tempura and all sorts of fish dishes. Beautiful restaurant run by Japanese/Russian couple. Recommended.
$$$ Zeebop, Utorda Beach, follow signs to Kenilworth resort, www.zeebopbythe sea.com. Lovely beachfront restaurant offering up a delicious range of seafood, try the crab papads and great Goan specialities. Recommended.
$$ Roytanzil Garden Pub, set back from the beach at the end of Majorda beach road past **Martin's Corner** (no sea views). Neat grounds, alfresco and small covered area. Seafood and Indian. One of the best restaurants on the south coast.

Benaulim to Mobor p106, maps p107 and p108
Beach shacks all down the coast offer Goan dishes and seafood at reasonable prices.
$$ La Afra, Tamborin, Fatrade. Excellent steaks and fresh fish, sensibly priced. Boatmen ferry holidaymakers to **River Sal**, Betul.
$$ Pedro's, by the car park above the beach, Benaulim. Good seafood and tandoori. Imaginative menu, friendly.

\$\$ River View, Cavelossim. Tranquil, open-air location, overlooking the river. Wide choice, international menu, good ambience despite being surrounded by ugly hotels. Cocktails Rs 100, sizzlers Rs 150-200, tiger prawns Rs 500.
\$ Goan Village, lane opposite Dona Sylvia, Cavelossim. The best in the area for all cuisines.
\$ Johncy's, Benaulim. Varied menu, good seafood, big portions, tandoori recommended (after 1830) but service can be erratic. Pleasant atmosphere though; backgammon, scrabble.
\$ Malibu, Benaulim. Lush garden setting for spicy fish/meat kebabs.

Cabo de Rama *p108*
\$ Pinto's Bar, near the fort entrance. Offers meals and cool drinks on a sandy shaded terrace, may also have rooms available. If there are few visitors about (most likely) order your meal here before exploring the fort to save time waiting later.

Agonda *p109*
Most of the places recommended for accommodation also have good food, especially **White Sand** and **Dunhill**.
\$\$ Blue Planet, Palolem–Agonda road, 5 km before Agonda, T0832-264 7448, www.blueplanet-cafe.com. This Palolem institution has taken a risk and moved into the countryside just outside Agonda – but it's a beautiful risk to take. The drive is great and there's a lovely view from their new abode. On the menu you will find an array of vegetarian and organic healthy treats.
\$\$ Kaama Kethna, Palolem–Agonda road, 5 km before Agonda, www.kaamakethna.net. A little bit further up the track than **Blue Planet**, **Kaama Kethna** offers up simple food using the ingredients from their organic farm as much as possible. Beautiful setting in the jungle. The *thali* is recommended by many.
\$\$ White Sand, north end of beach. Laid-back vibe and traditional Goan and Indian fare, but with some interesting

surprises like sausage and mash and smoked salmon omelettes.
\$ Madhu, north end of beach, T(0)9423-813140, www.madhuhuts.com. Always packed, this beach shack serves up a great range of traditional spicy Goan food as well as a range of Indian, Chinese and continental dishes. Also has nice huts available.

Palolem *p109*
\$\$ Bhakti Kutir (see Where to stay, page 114). Excellent fresh fish dishes, homegrown organic produce and fresh juices. Name any number of obscure nutritious grains and they'll be here.
\$\$ Café Inn, at the beach road junction. Funky courtyard café serving up quality cappuccinos, a huge array of juices, tortilla wraps and unusual pancakes, such as strawberry and meringue.
\$\$ Dropadi Beach Restaurant and Bar. Routinely packed out. Lobster and lasagne and North Indian food are the specials – the ex-pat community do rave about the quality of the fish here.
\$\$ Ordo Sounsar, over bridge at far north end of beach. Simple menu focusing on Goan food – strangely a rarity in these parts. Fantastic stuffed mackerel, calamari masala, Goan-style fishcakes, unique papaya curry, fried plantain chips – exceptional stuff. Highly recommended.
\$\$ Ourem 88, close to Art Resort in Ourem area, T(0)8698-827679. New player on the Palolem scene offering up exceptional food. With Jodi in the kitchen and Brett out front, there is a relaxed vibe and delicious food with specials like sea bass with rucola mash and great steaks on a menu that changes weekly. And leave room for desserts such as espresso brûlée and an awe-inspiring lemon tart. Booking essential. Highly recommended.
\$\$ Tavernakki, south end of the beach, Ourem. T(0)8408-090673. With help from the extremely popular **Thalassa** in northern Goa, **Tavernakki** offers up big portions of steak and lots of feta as well as souvlaki.

$ Banyan Tree, north end of the beach. Sitting in the shade of a lovely banyan tree, the menu here focuses on Thai food and mostly gets it just right – good *pad thai* and green curries. Open mic night on Fri.

$ Shiva Sai, off main road. Great cheap *thalis*.

$ Tibet Bar and Restaurant, Main Rd, T(0)9822-142775. Super-fresh ingredients in these excellent Himalayan dishes. Small restaurant that's worth stepping back from the beach for.

Beaches further south *p109*

Nestled between Palolem and Patnem is Colomb Bay with a few huts, restaurants and the main venue, **Neptune's Point**. Most of the places mentioned for accommodation in Patnem also serve up great food.

$$ Hidden Gourmet, Colomb, T(0)9923-686185, www.gourmetpatnem.com. Passionate about their food, the team here serves up a great range of fish and steaks, crisp salads and delicious desserts – all with a stunning view of Patnem beach.

$$ Home, Patnem. Great range of salads, pastas, and veggie specials like beetroot and vodka risotto – make sure you leave room for their legendary desserts such as chocolate brownie or sharp lemon tart – with a very chilled chic beachfront vibe.

$$ Magic View, Colomb, in front of **Hidden Gourmet**, T(0)9960-917287. Remarkably popular Italian restaurant delivering fantastic pizzas served up on tree trunks, deliciously decadent pastas such as gorgonzola and fish specials. Choose from 2 views, one overlooking the rocks at Colomb and the other gazing over Patnem.

$ Boom Shankar, Colomb, T(0)9822-644035. The latest 'in' venue for sundowners, this place also offers a good range of food and rooms to rent; all have great views over the rocks.

$ Mamoos, set back from beach, T0832-264 4261. **Mamoos** has served up excellent North Indian food at great prices for years.

◯ Bars and clubs

Colva *p105*

Boomerang, on the beach a few shacks north of **Pasta Hut**. Appealing sea-view drinking hole with pool table, sociable circular bar, dancefloor (music veers wildly from cool to cheesy), and daytime massages courtesy of Gupta.

Johnny Cool's, halfway up busy Beach Rd. Scruffy surroundings but popular for chilled beer and late-night drinks.

Splash, on beach, 500 m south of main car park. *The* place for music, dancing and late drinking, open all night, trendy, very busy on Sat (full after 2300 Mon-Fri in season), good cocktails, poor bar snacks. May not appeal to all, especially unaccompanied girls.

Benaulim to Mobor *p106,* *maps p107 and p108*

Aqua, Leela Palace, Mobor. A gaming room and cigar lounge which turns into a late-night disco after 2000.

Palolem *p109*

Cuba Beach Cafe, Palolem road, behind Syndicate Bank, T0832-264 3449. Cool, upbeat bar for a sundowner with regular sunset DJ sessions.

Hare Krishna Hare Ram, Patnem. Latest place for sunsets and dancing run by old schoolmates, local boys done good.

Laguna Vista, Colomb. Come here on Fri nights for French singer Axailles accompanied by Indian classical musicians – great vibe.

Neptune's Point Bar and Restaurant, T(0)9822-584968. Wide dancefloor nestled between the rocks for a mellow daily chill-out from 1700-2200 with a proper party on a weekly basis. This is also the venue for Silent Noise headphone parties (www.silentnoise.com) – an ingenious way to defy the 2200 curfew. Plugged in via wireless 'phones, you can dance your heart out to a choice of 2 DJs and there's no noise pollution. A giant screen plays movies on Wed nights.

✿ Festivals

Chandor p104
6 Jan Three Kings Festival Crowds gather on each year at Epiphany for the Three Kings Festival, which is similarly celebrated at Reis Magos, with a big fair, and at Cansaulim (Quelim) in southern Goa. The 3 villages of Chandor (Cavorim, Guirdolim and Chandor) come together to put on a grand show. Boys chosen from the villages dress up as the 3 kings and appear on horseback carrying gifts of gold, frankincense and myrrh. They process through the village before arriving at the church where a large congregation gathers.

Colva p105
12-18 Oct (Mon that falls between these dates) Fama of Menino Jesus when thousands of pilgrims flock to see the statue in the Church of our Lady of Mercy in the hope of witnessing a miracle.

Benaulim to Mobor p106,
maps p107 and p108
24 Jun Feast of St John the Baptist (Sao Joao) in Bernaulim gives thanks for the arrival of the monsoon. Young men wearing crowns of leaves and fruits tour the area singing for gifts. They jump into wells (which are usually full) to commemorate the movement of St John in his mother's womb when she was visited by Mary, the mother of Jesus.

Palolem p109
Feb Rathasaptami The Shri Malikarjuna Temple 'car' festival attracts large crowds.
Apr Shigmo, also at the Shri Malikarjuna Temple, also very popular.

✪ Shopping

Margao p102, map p103
The Old Market was rehoused in the 'New' (Municipal) Market in town. The covered market (Mon-Sat 0800-1300, 1600-2000) is fun to wander around. It is not at all touristy but holidaymakers come on their shopping

trip to avoid paying inflated prices in the beach resorts. To catch a glimpse of the early morning arrivals at the fish market head south from the Municipal Building.

Books and CDs
Golden Heart, off Abbé Faria Rd, behind the GPO. Closed 1300-1500. Bookshop.
Trevor's, 5 Luis Miranda Rd. Sells CDs.

Clothes
J Vaz, Martires Dias Rd, near Hari Mandir, T0832-272 0086. Good-quality men's tailor.
MS Caro, Caro Corner. An extensive range including 'suiting', and will advise on tailors.

Benaulim to Mobor p106,
maps p107 and p108
Khazana, Taj Exotica, Benaulim. A veritable treasure chest (books, crafts, clothes) culled from across India. Pricey.
Manthan Heritage Gallery, main road. Quality collection of art items.

Palolem p109
Chim, main Palolem Beach road. Good collection of funky Indian-inspired clothes and kurtas, as well as bikinis and accessories.

✪ What to do

Colva p105
Tour operators
Meeting Point, Beach Rd, opposite William Resort, T0832-278 8003. Mon-Sat 0830-1900 (opens later if busy). Very efficient, reliable flight, bus and train booking service.

Betalbatim to Velsao p106
Watersports
Goa Diving, Bogmalo; also at Joet's, and based Chapel Bhat, Chicalim, T0832-255 5117, goadiving@sancharnet.in. PADI certification from Open Water to Assistant Instructor.
Splash Watersports, Bogmalo, T0832-240 9886. Run by Derek, a famous Indian champion windsurfer. Operates from a shack on the beach just below Joet's, providing

parasailing, windsurfing, waterskiing, trips to nearby islands; during the high season only.

Benaulim to Mobor *p106,*
maps p107 and p108
Body and soul
At Taj Exotica, Benaulim, yoga indoors or on the lawn. Also aromatherapy, reflexology.

Dolphin watching
The trips are scenic and chances of seeing dolphin are high, but it gets very hot (take a hat, water and something comfy to sit on). Groups of dolphins here are usually seen swimming near the surface. Most hotels and cafés offer boat trips, including **Café Dominick** in Benaulim (signs on the beach). Expect to pay Rs 250-300 per person.
Betty's Place, in a road opposite the Holiday Inn in Mobor, T0832-287 1456. Offers dolphin viewing (0800-1000, Rs 300), birdwatching (1600, Rs 250) and sunset cruises up the river Sal River (1700, Rs 200). Recommended.

Agonda *p109*
Boat hire and cruises
Monsoon, **Madhu** and Om Sai hotels organize trips to the spice plantations and boat trips to Butterfly and Cola beaches. **Aquamer** rents kayaks.

Palolem *p109*
Boat hire and cruises
You can hire boats to spend a night under the stars on the secluded Butterfly or Honeymoon beaches, and many offer dolphin-watching and fishing trips. You can see the dolphins from dry land around Neptune's Point, or ask for rowing boats instead of motorboats if you want to reduce pollution. Mornings 0830-1230 are best. Arrange through **Palolem Beach Resort**, travel agents or a fisherman. Take sunscreen, shirt, hat and water.
Ciaran's Camp, T0832-264 3477. Runs 2-hr mountain bike tours or charter a yacht overnight through Ciaran's bar.

Body and soul
Harmonic Healing Centre, Patnem, T(0)9822-512814, www.harmonicingoa. com. With an enviable location high above the north end of Patnem beach, you can perform your *asanas* while looking out to sea. You can have massage with just the sky and the cliffs as a backdrop. Drop-in yoga, Bollywood and Indian classical dance classes and a full range of alternative treatments are on offer. The owner Natalie Mathos also runs 2-week non-residential reiki courses and yoga retreats from Nov-Mar.
Lotus Yoga Retreats, south end Patnem beach, T(0)9604-290688, www.lotus-yoga-retreat.com. Offering a range of yoga holidays and retreats with guest teachers from Europe, **Lotus** has an enviable location at the relaxed end of Patnem beach. Beautiful yogashala and stylish accommodation made from local materials.

Language and cooking courses
Sea Shells Guest House, on the main road. Hindi and Indian cookery classes.

Tour operators
Rainbow Travels, T0832-264 3912. Efficient flight and train bookings, exchange, Western Union money transfer, safe deposit lockers (Rs 10 per day), good internet connection.

⊖ Transport

Margao *p102, map p103*
Bus All state-run local and long-distance buses originate from the **Kadamba Bus Stand** 2 km to the north of town, T0832-271 4699. Those from the south also call at the local bus stand west of the municipal gardens, and buses for Colva and Benaulim can be boarded near the Kamat Hotel southeast of the gardens. From the Kadamba stand, city buses and motorcycle taxis (Rs 15) can get you to central Margao.

Frequent services to **Benaulim, Colva** and non-stop to **Panjim** (1 hr, buy tickets from booth at Platform 1. Several a day to Betul, Cabo da Rama, Canacona and Palolem. Daily to Gokarna (1500), but trains are much quicker.

Private buses (eg Paulo Travels, Cardozo Building opposite bus stand, T0832-243 8531), to Bengaluru (Bangalore) (15 hrs); Mangalore (8-10 hrs); Mumbai (Dadar/CST) (16 hrs); Pune (13 hrs).

Car hire Sai Service, T0832-241 7063. Rs 1000-2000 per day with driver.

Rickshaw Most trips in town should cost Rs 30-40; main bus stand to railway Rs 50. The prepaid rickshaw booth outside the station main entrance has high rates but probably better than bartering on the street. Motorcycle taxi drivers hang around quoting cheaper (but still overpriced) fares. Avoid tourist taxis: they can be 5 times the price.

Train Enquiries, T0832-271 2790. The new station on the broad-gauge network is 1 km southwest of central Margao. The reservation office on the 1st floor, T0832-271 2940, is usually quick and efficient, with short queues. Mon-Sat 0800-1400, 1415-2000, Sun 0800-1400. Tickets for Mumbai, Delhi and Hospet (for Hampi) should be booked well ahead.

Konkan Kanya Express (night train) and Mandovi Express (day train) from Mumbai also stop at Thivim (for northern beaches; take the local bus into Mapusa and from there catch another bus or take a taxi) and Karmali (for Panjim and Dabolim airport) before terminating at Margao. Both are very slow and take nearly 12 hrs. From Mumbai (CST): Konkan Kanya Exp 10111, 1800 (arrives 0550).

To Delhi (Nizamuddin), fastest train is Kurj Nzm Exp 02449, 30 hrs (only Thu), for daily service Mangala Ldweep Exp 12617, 33 hrs. Going south to Ernakulam (Jn): Mangala Lakshaweep Exp 12618, 16 hrs. Hospet (for Hampi): VSG Howrah Express 18048, 0750, Tue, Thu, Fri, Sun, 7 hrs. Thiruvananthapuram (Trivandrum):

Rajdhani Exp 12432, 135, Mon, Wed, Thu, 18 hrs (via Mangalore, 5 hrs, and Ernakulam, 13 hrs). Netravati Exp 16345, 23150, 18 hrs (via Canacona for Palolem beach).

The broad-gauge line between Vasco da Gama and Londa in Karnataka runs through Margao and Dudhsagar Falls and connects stations on the line with Belgaum. There are services to Bengaluru (Bangalore) Vasco Chennai Exp 17312, 1520, Thu.

Colva p105
Air From the airport, taxis charge about Rs 800. If arriving by train at Margao, 6 km away, opt for a bus or auto-rickshaw for transfer. Buses pull in at the main crossroads and then proceed down to the beach about 1 km away. Auto-rickshaws claim to have a Rs 30 'minimum charge' around Colva itself.

Scooter hire is available on every street corner, for Rs 200-250 a day; motorbikes for Rs 300 per day, less for long-term rental, more for Enfields. Bicycles are hard to come by – ask at your hotel.

Bus/taxi Bus tours to Anjuna, every Wed for the Flea Market, tickets through travel agents, depart 0930, return 1730, Rs 200; to Margao half-hourly, take 30 mins (last bus 1915, last return, 2000). Also to Margao, motorcycle taxi, Rs 80 (bargain hard); auto-rickshaw, Rs 100-120.

Betalbatim to Velsao p106
Bus Buses from Margao (12 km). The Margao–Vasco bus service passes through the centre of Cansaulim.

Taxi To/from airport, 20 mins (Rs 400); Margao 15 mins (Rs 200). From Nanu Resort, Panjim Rs 700, Anjuna Rs 750, or Rs 1000 for 8 hrs, 80 km.

Train Cansaulim station on the Vasco–Margao line is handy for Velsao and Arossim beaches, and Majorda station for Utorda and Majorda beaches. Auto-rickshaws meet trains.

From Cansaulim and Majorda there are 3 trains a day to **Vasco** via **Dabolim** for the airport. Westbound trains head to **Kulem** (for Dudhsagar Falls) via **Margao**.

Benaulim to Mobor *p106,*
maps p107 and p108
Bus Buses from all directions arrive at Maria Hall crossing, Benaulim. Taxis and autos from the beach esplanade near Pedro's and at Maria Hall crossing. Anjuna Wed Flea Market bus 0930, return 1530, Rs 200; you can take it one-way, but still have to buy a return ticket.

From Margao to **Cavelossim**, the bus is slow (18 km); auto-rickshaws transfer from bus stand to resorts.

Bicycle/scooter hire Cycle hire from Rocks, outside Dona Sylvia in Cavelossim, cycles Rs 10 per hr, Rs 150 a day; scooters Rs 300 a day without petrol, Rs 500 with 7 litres of fuel. In Benaulim, bikes and scooters for hire, Rs 150 and Rs 300 per day.

Agonda *p109*
Bus/rickshaw First direct bus for **Margao** leaves between 0600-0630, last at 1000, takes about 1 hr. Alternatively, arrange a lift to the main road and flag down the next bus (last bus for Margao passes by at around 2000, but it is advisable to complete your journey before dark).

Car/scooter hire Madhu and White Sands in Agonda hire out scooters, motorbikes and cars.

Palolem *p109*
Bus Many daily direct buses run between **Margao** and **Canacona** (40 km via Cuncolim), Rs 20, on their way to **Karwar**. From Canacona, taxis and auto-rickshaws charge Rs 50-80 to Palolem beach only 2 km away. From Palolem, direct buses for Margao leave at around 0615, 0730, 0930, 1415, 1515, 1630 and take 1 hr. At other times of the day take a taxi or rickshaw to the main

road, and flag down the next private bus. Frequent private services run to Palolem and Margao as well as south into **Karnataka**.

Train From Canacona Junction station, 2 km away from Palolem beach. The booking office opens 1 hr before trains depart. Inside the station there is a phone booth and a small chai stall. A few auto-rickshaws and taxis meet all trains. If none is available walk down the approach road and turn left under the railway bridge. At the next corner, known locally as Chaurasta, you will find an auto-rickshaw to take you to Palolem beach (Rs 50) or **Agonda Beach**; expect to pay double for a taxi.

To **Ernakulam Junction**, *Netravati Exp 16345*, 2325, 15 hrs, and on to **Thiruvananthapuram** (20 hrs); **Mumbai** (quicker to get train from Madgaon otherwise you go into more obscure station not Mumbai CST).

Beaches further south *p109*
Bus/taxi For **Canacona**, buses run to Palolem and Margao and also to Karnataka. You can hire a bicycle for Rs 4 per hr or Rs 35 per day. Direct buses for Margao leave at around 0615, 0730, 0930, 1415, 1515, 1630 and take an hour. Alternatively, take a taxi or rickshaw to the main road and flag down the next private bus. Palolem is 3 km from Canacona Junction train station, which is now on the Konkan line.

⊙ Directory

Margao *p102, map p103*
Medical services Ambulance T102; Hospicio, T0832-270 5664; Holy Spirit Pharmacy, 24 hrs. **Police** T0832-272 2175; emergency T100. **Post** North of children's park.

Benaulim *p106, map p107*
Medical services Late-night pharmacy near the main crossroads.

Ponda and interior Sanguem

There is enough spirituality and architecture in the neighbouring districts of Ponda and Salcete to reverse even the most cynical notions of Goa as a state rich in beach but weak on culture. Once you've had your fill of basking on the sand you'll find that delving into this geographically small area will open a window on a whole new, and richly rewarding, Goa.

Just over the water lies Salcete and the villages of Goa's most sophisticated and urbane elite, steeped in the very staunchest Catholicism. Here you can see the most eloquent symbols of the graceful living enjoyed by this aristocracy in the shape of palatial private homes, the fruits of their collusion with the colonizers in faith. Ironically, one of the finest – Braganza House in Chandor – is also the ancestral home of one of the state's most vaunted freedom fighters, Luis de Menezes-Braganza.

Ponda and around → *For listings, see pages 129-131.*

Ponda, once a centre of culture, music, drama and poetry, is Goa's smallest *taluka*. It is also the richest in Goan Hindu religious architecture. A stone's throw from the Portuguese capital of Old Goa and within 5 km of the district's traffic-snarled and fume-filled town centre are some of Goa's most important temples including the Shri Shantadurga at Queula and the Nagesh Temple near Bandora. Ponda is also a pastoral haven full of spice gardens and wonderfully scenic views from low hills over sweeping rivers. The Bondla Sanctuary in the east of the *taluka*, though small and underwhelming in terms of wildlife, is a vestige of the forest-rich environment that once cloaked the entire foothills of the Western Ghats.

Arriving in Ponda
Getting there and around Ponda town is an important transport intersection where the main road from Margao via Borlim meets the east–west National Highway, NH4A. Buses to Panjim and Bondla via Tisk run along the NH4A, which passes through the centre of town. The temples are spread out so it's best to have your own transport: take a bike or charter an auto-rickshaw or taxi; you'll find these around the bus stand. ▸▸ *See Transport, page 131.*

Background
The Zuari River represented the stormy boundary between the Christianized Old Conquests and the Hindu east for two centuries. St Francis Xavier found a dissolute band of European degenerates in the first settlers when he arrived in the headquarters of Luso-India and recommended the formation of an Inquisition. Founded in 1560 to redress the failings within their own community, the Portuguese panel's remit quickly broadened as they found

that their earliest Goan converts were also clinging clandestinely to their former faith. So the inquisitors set about weeding out these 'furtive Hindus', too, seeking to impose a Catholic orthodoxy and holding great show trials every few years with the public executions of infidels. Outside those dates set aside for putting people to death, intimidation was slightly more subtle: shrines were desecrated, temple tanks polluted and landowners threatened with confiscation of their holdings to encourage defection. Those unwilling to switch religion instead had to look for places to flee, carrying their idols in their hands.

When the conquistadors (or *descubridores*) took to sacking shrines and desecrating temples, building churches in their place, the keepers of the Hindu faith fled for the broad river banks and the Cumbarjua creek to its west, to build new homes for their gods.

Ponda

Ponda wasn't always the poster-boy for Goa's Hindu identity that it is today. The **Safa Mosque** (Shahouri Masjid), the largest of 26 mosques in Goa, was built by Ibrahim 'Ali' Adil Shah in 1560. It has a simple rectangular chamber on a low plinth, with a pointed pitched roof, very much in the local architectural style, but the arches are distinctly Bijapuri. Because it was built of laterite the lower tier has been quite badly eroded. On the south side is a tank with *meherab* designs for ritual cleansing. The gardens and fountains were destroyed under the Portuguese, today the mosque's backdrop is set off by low rising forest-covered hills.

Khandepar

Meanwhile, for a picture of Goa's Buddhist history, travel 4 km east from Ponda on the NH4A to Khandepar to visit Goa's best-preserved cave site. Believed to be Buddhist, it dates from the 10th or 11th century. The first three of the four laterite caves have an outer and an inner cell, possibly used as monks' living quarters. Much more refined than others discovered in Goa, they show clear evidence of schist frames for doors to the inner cells, sockets on which wooden doors would have been hung, pegs carved out of the walls for hanging clothing, and niches for storage and for placing lamps. The site is hidden on the edge of a wooded area near a tributary of the Mandovi: turn left off the main road from Ponda, look for the green and red archaeological survey sign, just before the bridge over the river. Turn right after the football pitch then walk down the track off to the right by the electric substation.

Farmagudi

On the left as you approach Farmagudi from Ponda is a **Ganesh temple** built by Goa's first chief minister, Shri D Bandodkar, back in the 1960s. It is an amalgam of ancient and modern styles. Opposite is a statue of Sivaji commemorating the Maratha leader's association with **Ponda's Fort**. The fort was built by the Adil Shahis of Bijapur and destroyed by the Portuguese in 1549. It lay in ruins for over a century before Sivaji conquered the town in 1675 and rebuilt it. The Portuguese viceroy attempted to re-take it in October 1683 but quickly withdrew, afraid to take on the Maratha King Sambhaji, who suddenly appeared with his vast army.

Velinga

Lakshmi-Narasimha Temple ① *just north of Farmagudi at Velinga, from the north take a right immediately after crossing a small river bridge*, is Goa's only temple to Vishnu's fourth avatar. The small half-man, half-lion image at this 18th-century temple was whisked away from the torches of Captain Diogo Rodrigues in 1567 Salcete. Its tower and dome over the sanctuary are markedly Islamic. Inside there are well-carved wooden pillars in the *mandapa* and elaborate silverwork on the screen and shrine.

Priol

Shri Mangesh Temple ① *Priol, northwest of Ponda on a wooded hill, on the NH4A leading to Old Goa*, is an 18th-century temple to Siva's incarnation as the benevolent Mangesh is one of the most important temples in Goa. Its Mangesh *lingam* originally belonged to an ancient temple in Kushatali (Cortalim) across the river. The complex is typical of Goan Hindu temple architecture and the surrounding estate provides a beautiful setting. Note the attractive tank on the left as you approach, which is one of the oldest parts of the site. The complex, with its *agrashalas* (pilgrims' hostel), administrative offices and other rooms set aside for religious ceremonies, is a good representative of Goan Hindu temple worship: the temple is supported by a large community who serve its various functions. February 25 is **Jatra**.

Mardol

Two kilometres on from Shri Mangesh, the early 16th-century **Mahalsa Narayani Temple** is dedicated to Mahalsa, a Goan form of Vishnu's consort Lakshmi or, according to some, the god himself in female form *Mohini* (from the story of the battle between the *devas* and *asuras*). The deity was rescued from what was once a fabulous temple in Verna at around the same time as the Mangesh Sivalinga was brought to Priol. The entrance to the temple complex is through the arch under the *nagarkhana* (drum room). There is a seven-storeyed *deepstambha* and a tall brass Garuda pillar which rests on the back of a turtle, acting as an impressive second lamp tower. The half-human half-eagle *Garuda*, Vishnu's vehicle, sits on top. A stone 'cosmic pillar' with rings, next to it, signifies the axis along which the temple is aligned. The new *mandapa* (columned assembly hall) is made of concrete, but is hidden somewhat under the red tiling, finely carved columns and a series of brightly painted carvings of the 10 *avatars*, or incarnations, of Vishnu. The unusual dome above the sanctuary is particularly elegant. A decorative arched gate at the back leads to the peace and cool of the palm-fringed temple tank. A palanquin procession with the deity marks the February **Mardol Jatra**, **Mahasivaratri** is observed in February/March and **Kojagiri Purnima** celebrated at the August/September full moon.

Bandora

A narrow winding lane dips down to this tiny hamlet and its **temple** ① *head 4 km west from Ponda towards Farmagudi on the NH4A, looking for a fork signposted to Bandora*, to Siva as Nagesh (God of Serpents). The temple's origin is put at 1413 by an inscribed tablet here, though the temple was refurbished in the 18th century. The temple tank, which is well stocked with carp, is enclosed by a white-outlined laterite block wall and surrounded by shady palms. The five-storey lamp tower near the temple has brightly coloured deities painted in niches just above the base, the main *mandapa* (assembly hall) has interesting painted woodcarvings illustrating stories from the epics *Ramayana* and *Mahabharata* below the ceiling line, as well as the *Ashtadikpalas*, the eight Directional Guardians (Indra, Agni, Yama, Nirritti, Varuna, Vayu, Kubera and Ishana). The principal deity has the usual *Nandi* and in addition there are shrines to Ganesh and Lakshmi-Narayan and subsidiary shrines with *lingams*, in the courtyard. The **Nagesh Jatra**, normally in November, is celebrated at full moon to commemorate Siva's victory.

In a valley south of the Nagesh Temple lies the **Mahalakshmi Temple**, thought to be the original form of the deity of the Shakti cult. Mahalakshmi was worshipped by the

Silaharas (chieftains of the Rashtrakutas, AD 750-1030) and the early Kadamba kings. The sanctuary has an octagonal tower and dome, while the side entrances have shallow domes. The stone slab with the Marathi inscription dating from 1413 on the front of the Nagesh Temple refers to a temple to Mahalakshmi at Bandora. The *sabhamandap* has an impressive gallery of 18 wooden images of Vishnu. Mahalakshmi is special in that she wears a *lingam* in her headdress and is believed to be a peaceful, 'Satvik', form of Devi; the first temple the Portuguese allowed at Panjim is also dedicated to her.

Queula (Kavale)

Just 3 km southwest from Ponda's Central Bus Stand is one of the largest and most famous of Goa's temples; dedicated to Shantadurga (1738), the wife of Siva as the Goddess of Peace. She earns the Shanti (Sanskrit for peace) prefix here because, at the request of Brahma, she mediated in a great quarrel between her husband and Vishnu, and restored peace in the universe. In the sanctuary here she stands symbolically between the two bickering gods. The temple, which stands in a forest clearing, was built by Shahu, the grandson of the mighty Maratha ruler Sivaji, but the deity was taken from Quelossim well before then, back in the 16th century. It is neoclassical in design: the two-storey octagonal drum, topped by a dome with a lantern, is a classic example of the strong impact church architecture made on Goan temple design. The interior of polished marble is lit by several chandeliers. Steps lead up to the temple complex which has a large tank cut into the hillside and a spacious courtyard surrounded by the usual pilgrim hostels and administration offices.

Shri Sausthan Goud Padacharya Kavale Math, named after the historic seer and exponent of the Advaita system of Vedanta, was founded between Cortalim and Quelossim. This Hindu seminary was destroyed during the Inquisition in the 1560s and was temporarily transferred to Golvan and Chinar outside Goa. After 77 years, in the early 17th century, the Math regrouped here in Queula, the village where the Shantadurga deity (which had also originated in Quelossim) had been reinstalled. There is a temple to Vittala at the Math. The foundation has another Math at Sanquelim.

North of Ponda → *For listings, see pages 129-131.*

Spice Hills

There are a number of spice plantations in the foothills around northeast Ponda that have thrown open their gates to offer in-depth tours that detail medicinal and food uses of plants during a walk through these cultivated forests. These are surprisingly informative and fun. Of these, Savoi Spice Plantation is probably the most popular and the guide is excellent. Taxis from the coastal resorts cost around Rs 700 return from Candolim, but it's better value to ask a travel agent as many offer competitive rates including entrance fees.

Savoi Spice Plantation ① *6 km from Savoi, T0832-234 0272, www.savoiplantation.com, 1030-1730, tour Rs 350, 1 hr, awkward to reach by public transport, ask buses from Ponda or Banastari heading for Volvoi for the plantation*, now over 200 years old, covers 40 ha around a large irrigation tank. Half the area is wetland and the other half on a hillside, making it possible for a large variety of plants and trees to grow. The plantation was founded by Mr Shetye and is now in the hands of the fourth generation of his family, who regularly donate funds to local community projects such as the school and temple. All plants are grown according to traditional Goan methods of organic farming. The tour includes drinks and snacks on arrival, and concludes with the chance to buy packets of spices (good gifts to take home) and a tot of *feni* to 'give strength' for the return journey to your resort. You will even be offered several cheap, natural alternatives to Viagra, whether you need them or not.

Pascoal Spice Plantation ① *signposted 1.5 km off the NH4A, near Khandepar between Ponda and Tisk, T0832-234 4268, 0800-1800, tours Rs 300*, is pleasantly located by a river and grows a wide variety of spices and exotic fruit. A guided tour takes you through a beautiful and fascinating setting. Spices can be bought directly from the plantation.

Sahakari Spice Farm ① *on the Ponda–Khandepar road, Curti, T0832-231 1394*, is also open to the public. The spice tour includes an authentic banana-leaf lunch.

Tropical Spice Plantation ① *Keri, clearly signposted off the NH4A (just south of the Sri Mangesh Temple), T0832-234 0625, tours Rs 300, boats for hire Rs 100*, is a very pleasant plantation situated in a picturesque valley. Guides are well informed and staff are friendly. It specializes in medicinal uses for the spices, the majority of which seem to be good for the skin. At the end of the tour an areca nut picker will demonstrate the art of harvesting by shinning up a tall palm with his feet tied together in a circle of rope. The demonstration ends with the equally impressive art of descent, a rapid slide down the trunk like a fireman. After the tour a delicious lunch is served in the shade overlooking a lake where there are a couple of boats for hire. Visitors arriving in the early morning will find the boats an excellent opportunity for viewing the varied birdlife around the lake.

Bondla Wildlife Sanctuary

① *20 km northeast of Ponda, mid-Sep to mid-Jun, Fri-Wed 0930-1730. Rs 5, camera Rs 25, video Rs 100, 2-wheelers Rs 10, cars Rs 50. Buses from Ponda via Tisk and Usgaon stop near the sanctuary from where you can get taxis and motorcycle taxis. KTC buses sometimes run weekends from Panjim. During the season the Forest Department minibus runs twice daily (except Thu) between Bondla and Tisk: from Bondla, 0815, 1745; from Tisk, 1100 (Sun 1030) and 1900. Check at the tourist office. If you are on a motorbike make sure you fill up with petrol; the nearest pumps are at Ponda and Tisk. Bondla is well signposted from the NH4A east of Ponda (5 km beyond Usgaon, a fork to the right leads to the park up a winding steep road).*

Bondla is the most popular of Goa's three sanctuaries because it is relatively easily accessible. The 8-sq-km sanctuary is situated in the foothills of the Western Ghats; sambar, wild boar, gaur (Indian bison) and monkeys live alongside a few migratory elephants that wander in from Karnataka during the summer. The mini-zoo here guarantees sightings of 'Goa's wildlife in natural surroundings', although whether the porcupine and African lion are examples of indigenous species is another matter. Thankfully, the number of animals in the zoo has decreased in recent years and those that remain seem to have adequate space compared to other zoos in India. The small **Nature Education Centre** has the facility to show wildlife videos, but is rarely used. Five-minute elephant rides are available 1100-1200 and 1600-1700. A deer safari (minimum eight people), 1600-1730, costs Rs 10. The park also has an attractive picnic area in a botanical garden setting and a 2.4-km nature trail with waterholes, lake and treetop observation tower.

Central and southern interior → *For listings, see pages 129-131.*

Sanguem, Goa's largest *taluka*, covers the state's eastern hill borderland with the South Indian state of Karnataka. The still-forested hills, populated until recently by tribal peoples practising shifting cultivation, rise to Goa's highest points. Just on the Goan side of the border with Karnataka are the Dudhsagar Falls, some of India's highest waterfalls, where the river, which ultimately flows into the Mandovi, cascades dramatically down the hillside.

Both the Bhagwan Mahaveer Sanctuary and the beautiful, small Tambdi Surla Temple can be reached in a day from the coast (about two hours from Panaji).

Arriving in central and southern interior

Getting there Buses running along the NH4A between Panjim, Ponda or Margao and Belgaum or Bengaluru (Bangalore) in Karnataka stop at Molem, in the north of the *taluka*. Much of the southeastern part of Sanguem remains inaccessible. Trains towards Karnataka stop at Kulem (Colem) and Dudhsagar stations. Jeeps wait at Kulem to transfer tourists to the waterfalls. If you are travelling to Tambdi Surla or the falls from north or central Goa, then the best and most direct route is the NH4A via Ponda. By going to or from the southern beaches of Salcete or Canacona you can travel through an interesting cluster of villages, only really accessible if you have your own transport, to see the sites of rock-cut caves and prehistoric cave art. ▶▶ *See Transport, page 131.*

Getting around There is no direct public transport between Molem and the sites, but the town is the start of hikes and treks in December and January.

Bhagwan Mahaveer Sanctuary

ⓘ *29 km east of Pondon on NH4A, T0832-260 0231, or contact Forest Dept in Canacona, T0832-296 5601. Open 0700-1730 except public holidays. Rs 5, 2-wheelers Rs 10, cars Rs 250. Or check Goa Tourism (www.goa-tourism.com). Entrance to Molem National Park, within the sanctuary, 100 m east of the Tourist Complex, is clearly signed but the 14 km of tracks in the park are not mapped. Tickets at the Nature Interpretation Centre, 100 m from the police check post in Molem.*
Goa's largest wildlife sanctuary holds 240 sq km of lush moist deciduous to evergreen forest types and a herd of gaur (*bos gaurus*, aka Indian bison). The **Molem National Park**, in the central section of the sanctuary, occupies about half the area with the **Dudhsagar Falls** located in its southeast corner; the remote **Tambdi Surla Temple** is hidden in the dense forest at the northern end of the sanctuary. Forest department jeeps are available for viewing within the sanctuary; contact the Range Forest Officer (Wildlife), Molem. Motorbikes, but not scooters, can manage the rough track outside the monsoon period. In theory it is possible to reach Devil's Canyon and Dudhsagar Falls via the road next to the Nature Interpretation Centre, although the road is very rough and it may require a guide. Make sure you have a full tank of petrol if attempting a long journey into the forest. You can stay overnight.

Sambar, barking deer, monkeys and rich birdlife are occasionally joined by elephants that wander in from neighbouring Karnataka during the summer months, but these are rarely spotted. Birds include the striking golden oriole, emerald dove, paradise flycatcher, malabar hornbill and trogon and crested serpent eagle.

Dudhsagar Falls

ⓘ *There are train day trips organized though Goa Tourism (www.goa-tourism.com) on Wed and Sun. It's a spectacular journey worth taking in its own right, as the railway tracks climb right across the cascades, but trains no longer stop at the falls themselves; to get to the pools at the bottom you can take a road from Kulem, where jeep owners offer 'safaris' through the jungle to the base of the falls. If taking the train simply for the view, it's best to travel through to Belgaum in Karnataka, from where there are good bus and train services back to Goa.*
The Dudhsagar Falls on the border between Goa and Karnataka are the highest in India and measure a total drop of about 600 m. The name, meaning 'the sea of milk', is derived from the white foam that the force of the water creates as it drops in stages, forming

pools along the way. They are best seen just after the monsoon, between October and December, but right up to April there is enough water to make a visit worthwhile. You need to be fit and athletic to visit the falls.

A rough, steep path takes you down to a viewing area which allows you a better appreciation of the falls' grandeur, and to a beautifully fresh pool which is lovely for a swim (take your costume and towel). There are further pools below but you need to be sure-footed. The final section of the journey is a scramble on foot across stream beds with boulders; it is a difficult task for anyone but the most athletic. For the really fit and adventurous the arduous climb up to the head of the falls with a guide, is well worth the effort. Allow three hours, plus some time to rest at the top.

You can take the train to Kulem, which is about 17 km from the falls, and then pick up a jeep or motorbike to take you to the falls; but it's a rough ride. By road, motorbikes, but not scooters, can get to the start of the trail to the falls from Molem crossroads by taking the road south towards Kulem. There are at least two river crossings, so is not recommended after a long period of heavy rain. The ride through the forest is very attractive and the reward at the end spectacular, even in the dry season. A swim in the pool at the falls is particularly refreshing after a hot and dusty ride. Guides are available but the track is easy to follow even without one. ►► *See also Transport, page 131.*

Tambdi Surla

ⓘ *A taxi from Panjim takes about 2½ hrs for the 69-km journey. There is no public transport to Tambdi Surla but it is possible to hike from Molem. From the crossroads at Molem on the NH4A, the road north goes through dense forest to Tambdi Surla. 4 km from the crossroads you reach a fork. Take the right fork and after a further 3 km take a right turn at Barabhumi village (there is a sign). The temple is a further 8 km, just after Shanti Nature Resort. Make sure you have enough petrol before leaving Molem. It is also possible to reach the site along minor roads from Valpoi. The entrance to the temple is a short walk from the car park.*

This Mahadeva (Siva) Temple is a beautifully preserved miniature example of early Hindu temple architecture from the Kadamba-Yadava period. Tucked into the forested foothills, the place is often deserted, although the compound is well maintained by the Archaeology Department. The temple is the only major remaining example of pre-Portuguese Hindu architecture in Goa; it may well have been saved from destruction by its very remoteness.

Ponda and interior Sanguem listings

For hotel and restaurant price codes and other relevant information, see pages 13-15.

🍽 Where to stay

Ponda *p123*
Ponda is within easy reach of any of Goa's beach resorts and Panjim.
$$-$ Menino, 100 m east of bus stand junction, 1st floor, T0832-664 1585. 20 rooms, some a/c, pleasant, comfortable, good restaurant serves generous main courses, impressive modern hotel, good value.

$ President, 1 km east of bus stand, supermarket complex, T0832-231 2287. 11 rooms, basic but clean and reasonable.

Farmagudi *p124*
$$-$ Atish, just below Ganesh Temple on NH4A, T0832-233 5124. 40 comfortable rooms, some a/c, restaurant, large pool in open surrounds, gym, modern hotel, many pilgrim groups, friendly staff.
$ Farmagudi Residency (GTDC), attractively located though too close to NH4A, T0832-233 5122. 39 clean

rooms, some a/c, dorm (Rs 150), adequate restaurant (eat at Atish, above).

Spice Hills *p126*
$$ Savoi Farmhouse, Savoi Plantation, T0832-234 0243, www.savoiplantations.com. An idyllic traditional Goan-style farmhouse built from mud with 2 adjoining en suite double rooms each with private veranda. Electricity and hot water; rates are for full board and include plantation tour. A night in the forest is memorable, highly recommended. Ideally, stay 2 nights exploring deep into the forested hills, good for birdwatching.

Bondla Wildlife Sanctuary *p127*
$ Eco-Cottages, reserve ahead at Deputy Conservator of Forests, Wildlife Division, 4th floor, Junta House, 18 June Rd, Panjim, T0832-222 9701 (although beds are often available to anyone turning up). 8 basic rooms with attached bath, newer ones better. Also 1 km inside park entrance (which may be better for seeing wildlife at night) are 2 dorms of 12 beds each.

Bhagwan Mahaveer Sanctuary *p128*
Goa Eco Tourism offer the **Jungle Book Tour** where you can stay in tents or cottages inside the sanctuary (www.goaecotourism. com); take provisions. GTDC accommodation is at the Tourist Complex in Molem, east along the NH4A from the Molem National Park entrance.
$ Molem Forest Resthouse. Book via the Conservator's Office, 3rd floor, Junta House, 18 June Rd, Panjim, T0832-222 4747.
$ Tourist Resort (GTDC), 300 m east of police check post, about 500 m from the temple, Molem, T0832-260 0238. 3 simple but well-maintained, clean rooms, some a/c, dorm, check-out 1200, giving time for a morning visit to Tambdi Surla, restaurant has limited menu serving north Indian food and beer.

Tambdi Surla *p129*
$$ Shanti Nature Resort, 500 m from temple, T0832-261 0012. Emphasis on rest, Ayurvedic treatment and meditation, 9 large mud huts with palm-thatched roofs, electricity and running water in natural forest setting. Restaurant, spice garden visits, birdwatching, hikes, trips to Dudhsagar, etc, arranged (2 nights, US$120). Highly recommended for location and eco-friendly approach.

🍽 Restaurants

Ponda *p123*
$ Amigos, 2 km east of centre on Belgaum Rd.
$ Spoon Age, Upper Bazaar, T0832-231 6191. Garden restaurant serving Goan meals for locals, friendly set up. Occasional live music at weekends.

Spice Hills *p126*
Tropical Spice Plantation offers tasty lunches.
$$ Glade Bar and Restaurant, Pascoal Spice Plantation. 1130-1800. Good but pricey.

Bondla Wildlife Sanctuary *p127*
$ The Den Bar and Restaurant, near the entrance. Serves chicken, vegetables or fish with rice. A small cafeteria, inside the park near the mini-zoo, sells snacks and cold drinks.

🎯 What to do

Bhagwan Mahaveer Sanctuary *p128*
Hiking
Popular hiking routes lead to **Dudhsagar** (17 km), the sanctuary and **Atoll Gad** (12 km), **Matkonda Hill** (10 km) and **Tambdi Surla** (12 km). Contact the Hiking Association, 6 Anand Niwas, Swami Vivekananda Rd, Panjim.

⊖ Transport

Ponda *p123*
Bus Buses to **Panjim** and **Bondla** via Tisk (enquiries, T0832-231 1050), but it is best to have your own transport.

Bhagwan Mahaveer Sanctuary *p128*
If coming from the south, travel via Sanguem. The road from Sanvordem to the NH17 passes through mining country and is therefore badly pot-holed and has heavy lorry traffic. From Kulem, jeeps do the rough trip to **Dudhsagar** (Rs 300 per head, Rs 1800 per jeep). The journey is also possible by motorbike (Rs 600 per person). This is a very tough and tiring journey at the best of times. From Molem, a road to the south off the NH4A leads through the forested hills of Sanguem *taluka* to **Kulem** and **Calem** railway stations and then south to **Sanguem**. From there, a minor road northwest goes to **Sanvordem** and then turns west to **Chandor**.

Bus Buses between **Panjim**, **Ponda** or **Margao**, and **Belgaum/Bengaluru** (**Bangalore**), stop at Molem for visiting the Bhagwan Mahaveer Sanctuary and Dudhsagar Falls.

Train From the southern beaches, you can get the *Vasco-Colem Passenger* from Vasco at 0710, or more conveniently Margao (Madgaon) at 0800, arriving at **Kulem** (**Colem**) at 0930. Return trains at 1640, arriving **Margao** at 1810; leave plenty of time to enjoy the falls. Jeep hire is available from Kulem Station.

⊕ Directory

Ponda *p123*
Useful contacts Deputy Conservator of Forests (North) T0832-231 2095. **Community Health Centre**, T0832-231 2115.

Contents

Footnotes

Index

Titles available in the Footprint *Focus* range

Latin America	UK RRP	US RRP
Bahia & Salvador	£7.99	$11.95
Brazilian Amazon	£7.99	$11.95
Brazilian Pantanal	£6.99	$9.95
Buenos Aires & Pampas	£7.99	$11.95
Cartagena & Caribbean Coast	£7.99	$11.95
Costa Rica	£8.99	$12.95
Cuzco, La Paz & Lake Titicaca	£8.99	$12.95
El Salvador	£5.99	$8.95
Guadalajara & Pacific Coast	£6.99	$9.95
Guatemala	£8.99	$12.95
Guyana, Guyane & Suriname	£5.99	$8.95
Havana	£6.99	$9.95
Honduras	£7.99	$11.95
Nicaragua	£7.99	$11.95
Northeast Argentina & Uruguay	£8.99	$12.95
Paraguay	£5.99	$8.95
Quito & Galápagos Islands	£7.99	$11.95
Recife & Northeast Brazil	£7.99	$11.95
Rio de Janeiro	£8.99	$12.95
São Paulo	£5.99	$8.95
Uruguay	£6.99	$9.95
Venezuela	£8.99	$12.95
Yucatán Peninsula	£6.99	$9.95

Asia	UK RRP	US RRP
Angkor Wat	£5.99	$8.95
Bali & Lombok	£8.99	$12.95
Chennai & Tamil Nadu	£8.99	$12.95
Chiang Mai & Northern Thailand	£7.99	$11.95
Goa	£6.99	$9.95
Gulf of Thailand	£8.99	$12.95
Hanoi & Northern Vietnam	£8.99	$12.95
Ho Chi Minh City & Mekong Delta	£7.99	$11.95
Java	£7.99	$11.95
Kerala	£7.99	$11.95
Kolkata & West Bengal	£5.99	$8.95
Mumbai & Gujarat	£8.99	$12.95

Africa & Middle East	UK RRP	US RRP
Beirut	£6.99	$9.95
Cairo & Nile Delta	£8.99	$12.95
Damascus	£5.99	$8.95
Durban & KwaZulu Natal	£8.99	$12.95
Fès & Northern Morocco	£8.99	$12.95
Jerusalem	£8.99	$12.95
Johannesburg & Kruger National Park	£7.99	$11.95
Kenya's Beaches	£8.99	$12.95
Kilimanjaro & Northern Tanzania	£8.99	$12.95
Luxor to Aswan	£8.99	$12.95
Nairobi & Rift Valley	£7.99	$11.95
Red Sea & Sinai	£7.99	$11.95
Zanzibar & Pemba	£7.99	$11.95

Europe	UK RRP	US RRP
Bilbao & Basque Region	£6.99	$9.95
Brittany West Coast	£7.99	$11.95
Cádiz & Costa de la Luz	£6.99	$9.95
Granada & Sierra Nevada	£6.99	$9.95
Languedoc: Carcassonne to Montpellier	£7.99	$11.95
Málaga	£5.99	$8.95
Marseille & Western Provence	£7.99	$11.95
Orkney & Shetland Islands	£5.99	$8.95
Santander & Picos de Europa	£7.99	$11.95
Sardinia: Alghero & the North	£7.99	$11.95
Sardinia: Cagliari & the South	£7.99	$11.95
Seville	£5.99	$8.95
Sicily: Palermo & the Northwest	£7.99	$11.95
Sicily: Catania & the Southeast	£7.99	$11.95
Siena & Southern Tuscany	£7.99	$11.95
Sorrento, Capri & Amalfi Coast	£6.99	$9.95
Skye & Outer Hebrides	£6.99	$9.95
Verona & Lake Garda	£7.99	$11.95

North America	UK RRP	US RRP
Vancouver & Rockies	£8.99	$12.95

Australasia	UK RRP	US RRP
Brisbane & Queensland	£8.99	$12.95
Perth	£7.99	$11.95

For the latest books, e-books and a wealth of travel information, visit us at:
www.footprinttravelguides.com.

 footprinttravelguides.com

 Join us on facebook for the latest travel news, product releases, offers and amazing competitions:
www.facebook.com/footprintbooks.